IMAGES
of America

EAGLE POINT

On the Cover: Standing in front of Zera Dahack's cabin are, in no particular order, Zera, Ernie, Eli, and Everett Dahack.

IMAGES
of America

EAGLE POINT

Margaret LaPlante

ARCADIA
PUBLISHING

ISBN 978-0-7385-9310-4

Published by Arcadia Publishing
Charleston, South Carolina

Printed in the United States of America

Library of Congress Control Number: 2011938367

For all general information, please contact Arcadia Publishing:
Telephone 843-853-2070
Fax 843-853-0044
E-mail sales@arcadiapublishing.com
For customer service and orders:
Toll-Free 1-888-313-2665

Visit us on the Internet at www.arcadiapublishing.com

CONTENTS

ACKNOWLEDGMENTS

The historical photographs in this book are courtesy of the City of Eagle Point and private collections.

INTRODUCTION

Long before the first pioneers settled in Eagle Point, local Indians of the Takelma tribe called this part of Southern Oregon home. The tribe was divided into the Upland Takelmas and Lowland Takelmas. From time to time, a fur trapper or explorer would pass through the area, but for the most part the Indians lived undisturbed. One group of fur trappers found the Takelmas to be rather troublesome, referring to them as "rogues," and soon the entire valley was known as "Rogue Valley."

The Takelmas felled sugar pine trees and used the wood for their "Pitt homes." They dug 18 to 24 inches into the ground along the perimeters of the house, erected posts in the corners, and then used the planks of the sugar pine for the siding. The roofs were made from sugar pine or other natural resources.

The Takelma women wore knee-length deerskin shirts adorned with a fringe that was made of white grass. The men wore deerskin shirts and leggings tied with a belt. They made robes, blankets, and hats from both deerskin and bearskin and lined their moccasins with grass or fur. During the cold months, they wore sleeves made from fox skin. The Indians embellished their garments with abalone, shells, white grass braids, and buckskin tassels. The Takelmas wove baskets from tree roots, vines, and other natural resources. The baskets were used for food gathering, food preparation, and serving. They also wove baskets to carry their infants.

The diet of the Takelma Indians consisted of sugar pine nuts, bark from sugar pine trees, wild berries, seeds from trees, and edible wild plants. The Indians would shell acorns, mash them using a mortar and pestle, then place the mashed acorns on clean sand and pour hot water over them to leach them. This process was repeated, then the mixture was placed in a tightly woven basket filled with water and heated over hot stones to boil it. The Indians would dig a pit in the ground and place Camas bulbs and alder bark into the pit. They would roast the bulbs for a day or two, and then mash them into cakes to store for the colder months. The river and creeks had an abundant supply of salmon and trout, and the men found plenty of hunting opportunities for deer and elk. Trading with other tribes allowed them to obtain unique items that were not available to them locally.

The Takelma Indians lived a peaceful life that was largely undisturbed, but the California Gold Rush and the Donation Land Claim Act eventually brought thousands of pioneers across the plains.

The decision to begin a new life in Oregon was not taken lightly, and preparing for the journey could take a year. Heading out west either by sailing around Cape Horn or crossing the plains meant leaving families behind, knowing they would probably never see them again. Sometimes, two or three generations of families traveled together. Those traveling overland left from jump-off points in Missouri. Towns at the jump-off points were well equipped to provide any last-minute supplies. The covered wagons were 10 feet long and four feet wide. Therefore, the pioneers could only take the bare necessities. Examples of supplies were 50 pounds of dried fruit, 50 pounds of beans, 100 pounds of flour, and 75 pounds of rice. Once everyone was ready, the wagons would leave, and it was not unusual to have 40 or 50 wagons begin the journey together. It was important that the pioneers left the jump-off points in the early spring to ensure they would arrive in Oregon prior to the winter storms.

It was a 2,000-mile walk through rain, heat, wind, and dust. The journey took five to six months. On a good day, the pioneers could cover up to 15 miles. Water along the way was a mixed blessing—it quenched thirst, but it was also the cause of numerous deaths due to cholera. Accidents and diseases were the cause of many deaths along the Oregon Trail. Families would have to bury their loved one in a shallow grave and then continue on their journey.

Food could be scarce along the way. Sometimes there was good hunting and fishing, but other times the pioneers had to rely on what they had brought. Coffee was an important part of each meal as it helped to mask the taste of the water, which was sometimes muddy and polluted. Using their Dutch ovens, the women made biscuits, corn bread, muffins, and bread. They also used their Dutch ovens to cook bacon, beans, fresh meat, and fish. Some pioneers travelled with chickens in cages that hung from the back of their wagon so that they could enjoy fresh eggs. Others brought cows so that they would have milk and butter. The pioneers discovered that by strapping the butter churn to the side of the wagon, they could have butter by the end of the day, since the rough terrain did the churning for them. If they were successful in hunting, they would hang the meat from the wagon to cure it.

The pioneers encountered many Indians on their journey. Most of the Indians were friendly and helpful. It wasn't until later, when thousands of people had crossed the plains, that tensions ran high because the Indians' natural resources were diminishing. The Indians and pioneers found ways to communicate, generally through simple sign language. Many Indians used their river skills and, for a fee, would help the pioneers cross the rivers.

Gold was discovered 15 miles from Eagle Point in Jacksonville during the winter of 1851 and 1852, prompting hundreds of people to come to the area. Some pioneers settled along Little Butte Creek in what would become known as the town of Eagle Point. Soon, a trading post was established, and over time, a town began to take shape. It wasn't long before the small town of Eagle Point became well-known for its excellent farms, ranches, and orchards.

One

In the Beginning

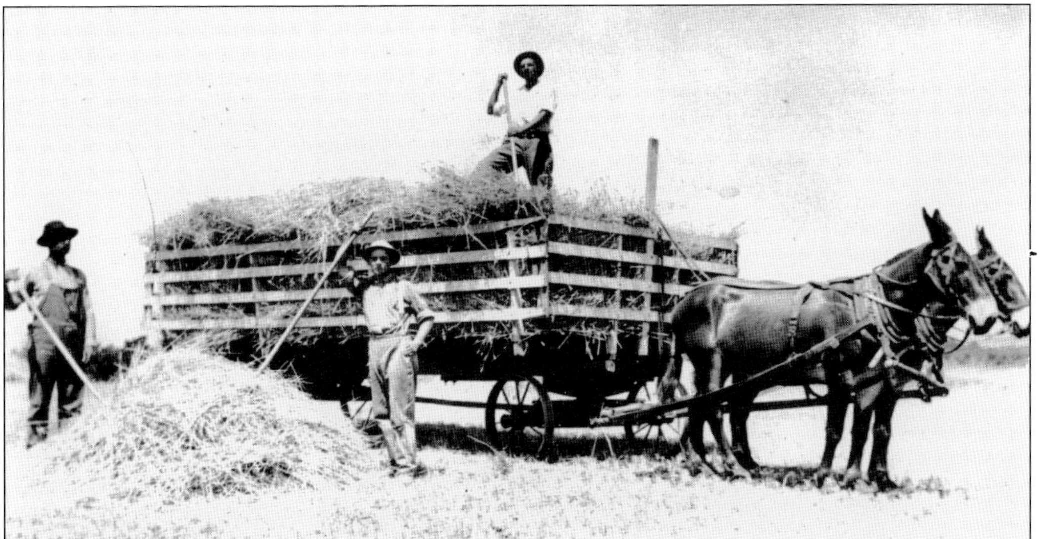

As soon as the pioneers reached Oregon, they had to quickly build their shelter and get their crops planted before winter set in.

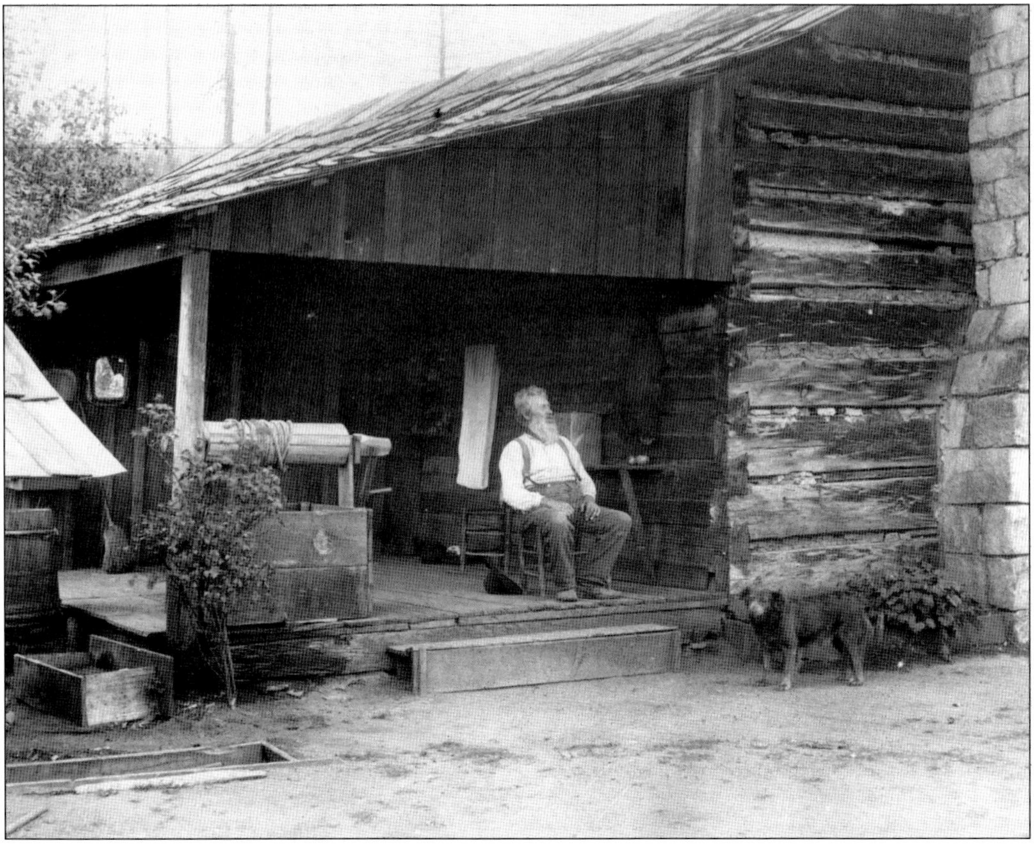

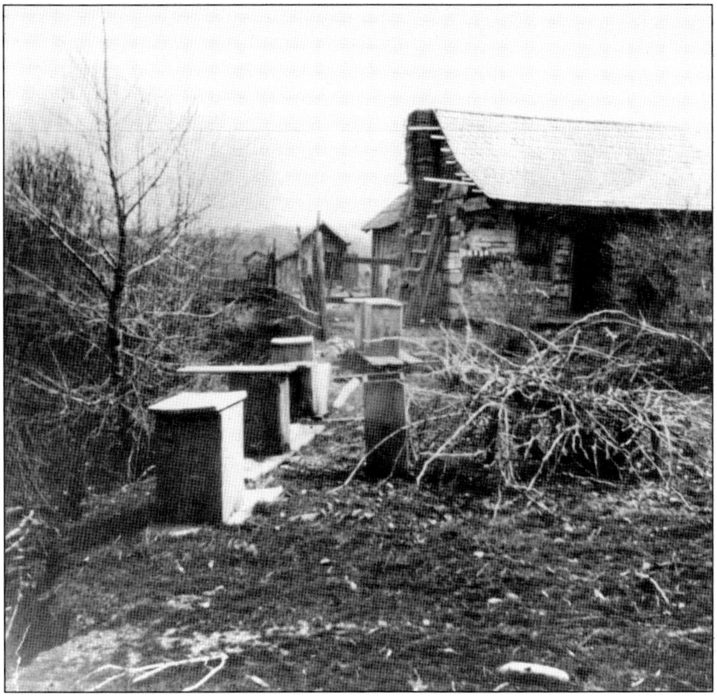

Tobias Linksweiler, known as Charlie by the locals, built this cabin in the mid-1850s. He lived in the cabin for 50 years. On the left is how the cabin appeared in 1907.

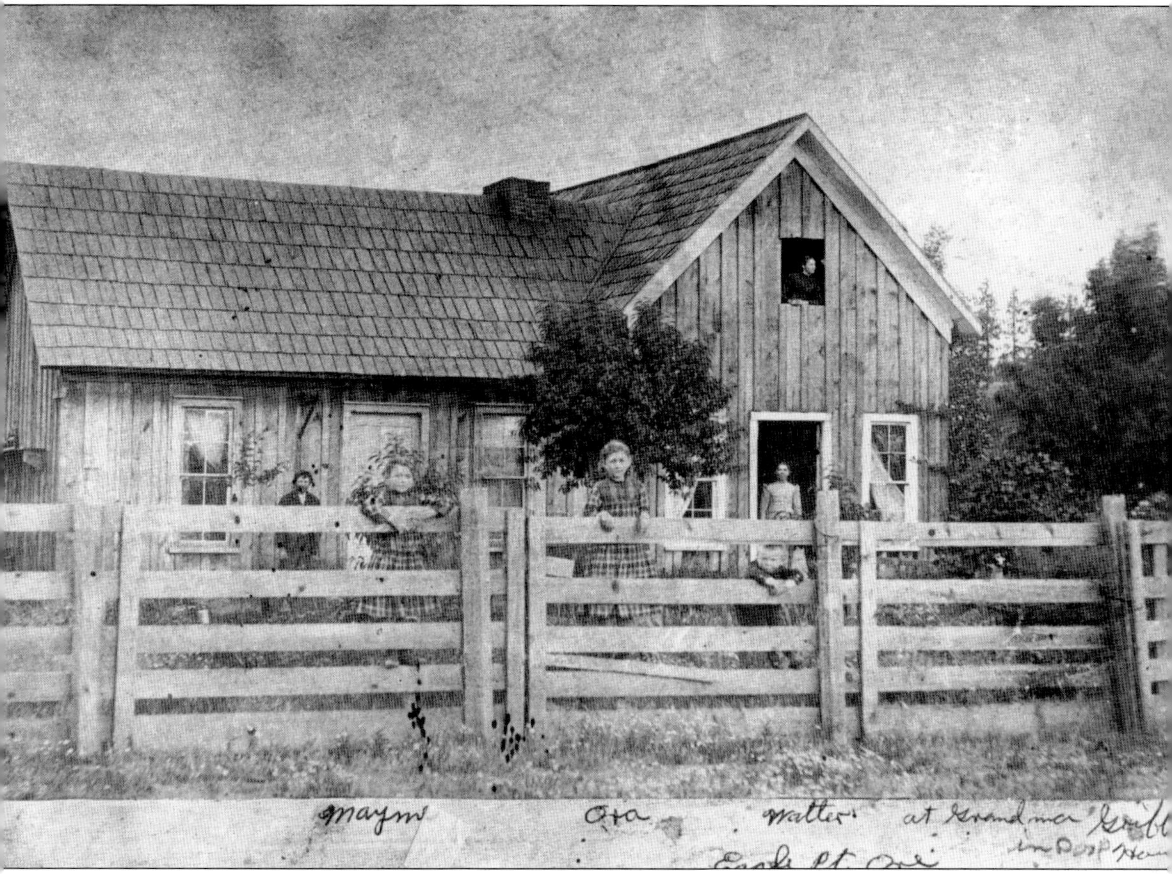

Charlie and Amanda Griffith were married in Jacksonville in 1858. They settled first in Jacksonville and then later in the Applegate Valley. In the mid-1870s, they moved to Eagle Point. In 1889, Charlie built this large house on 160 acres of land just outside of Eagle Point.

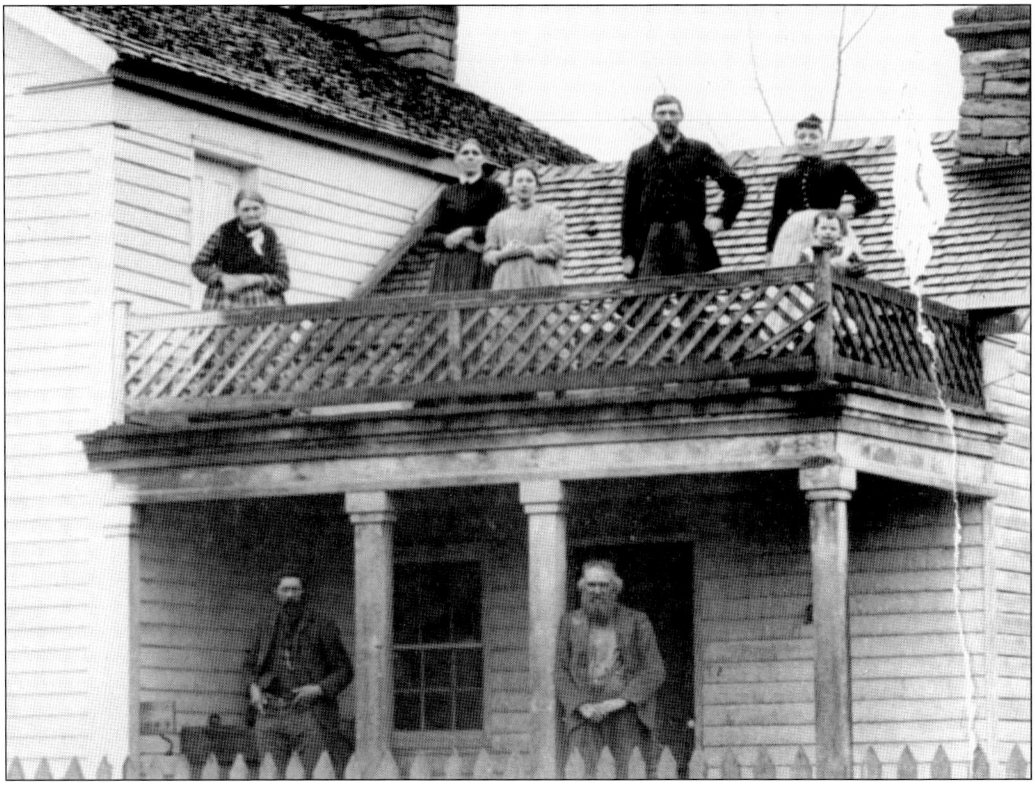

In 1837, John Mathews married Elizabeth Wooley. They lived in Iowa prior to coming overland in 1853. They settled near Little Butte Creek. John and Elizabeth had 14 children. John and his sons ran the ranch and raised horses. John was well-known throughout the valley for his superior ranching. The family is pictured here in front of their home.

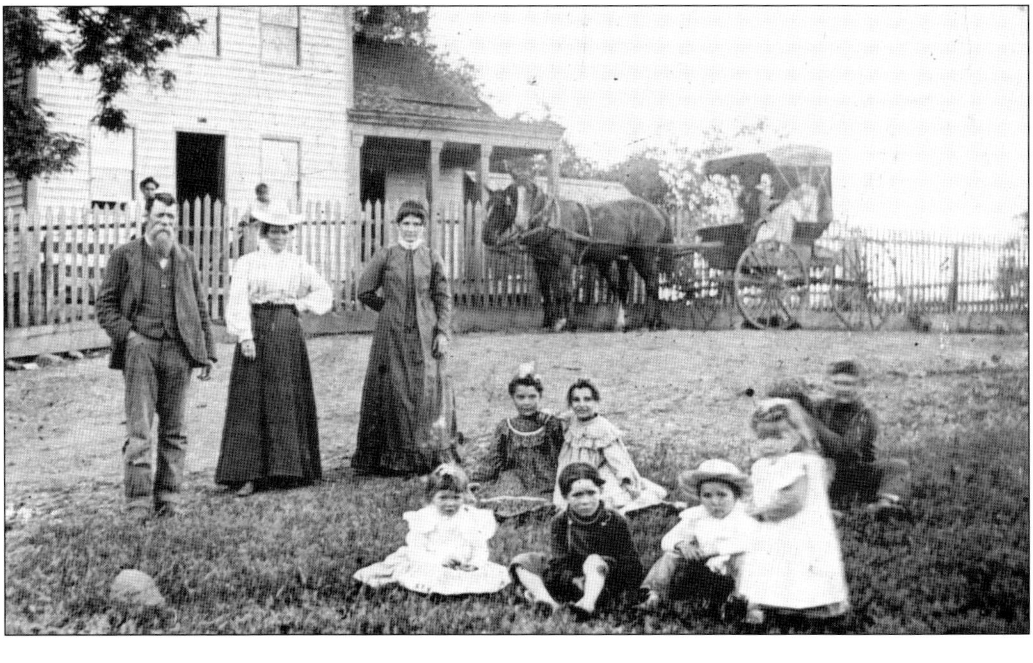

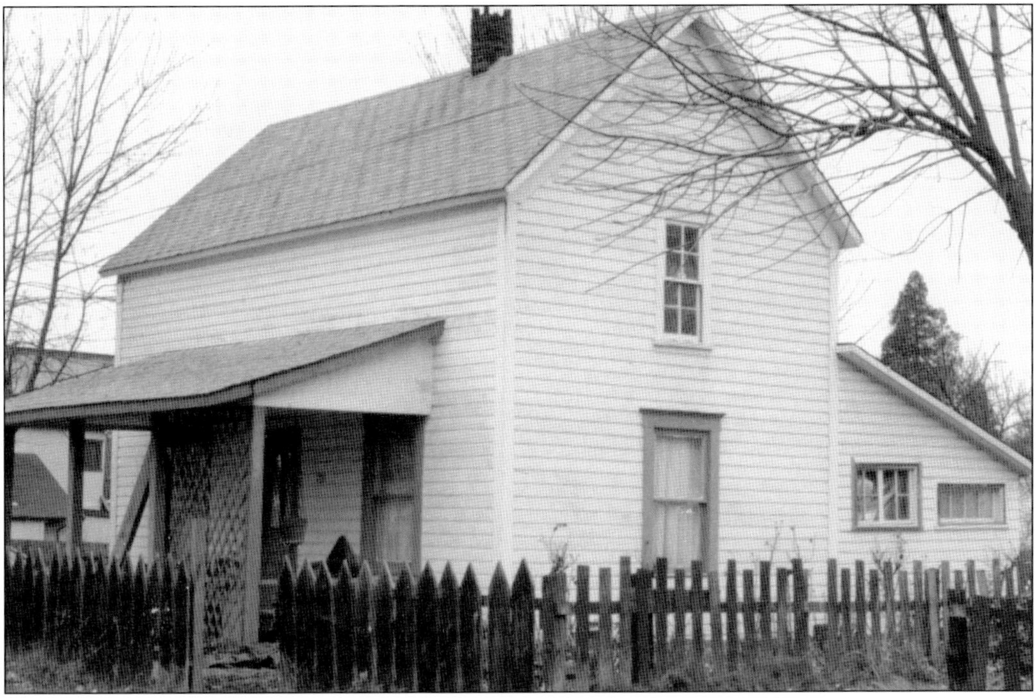

John and Nancy Watkins raised their children in this house on North Shasta Avenue. For many years, John owned a confectionery and lunch restaurant in Eagle Point. He purchased the Eagle Hotel from Art Poole and then added a pool hall and billiard parlor inside of it. He and Nancy operated the hotel for four years before selling the business to Elmer Scudder. The Radar family is pictured below enjoying a nice afternoon at their ranch just outside of Eagle Point.

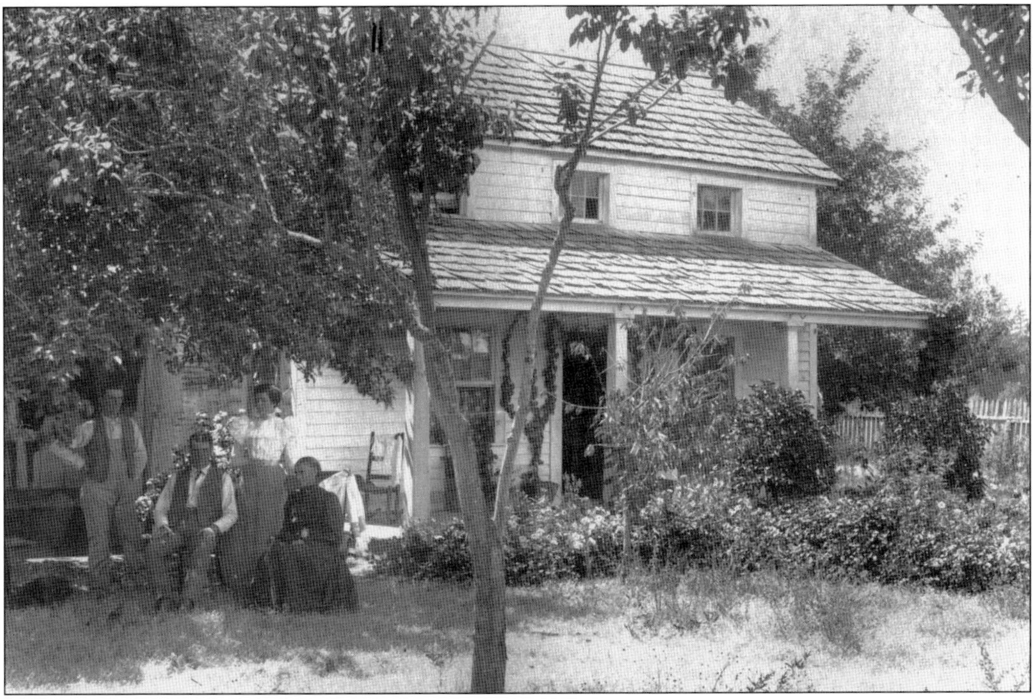

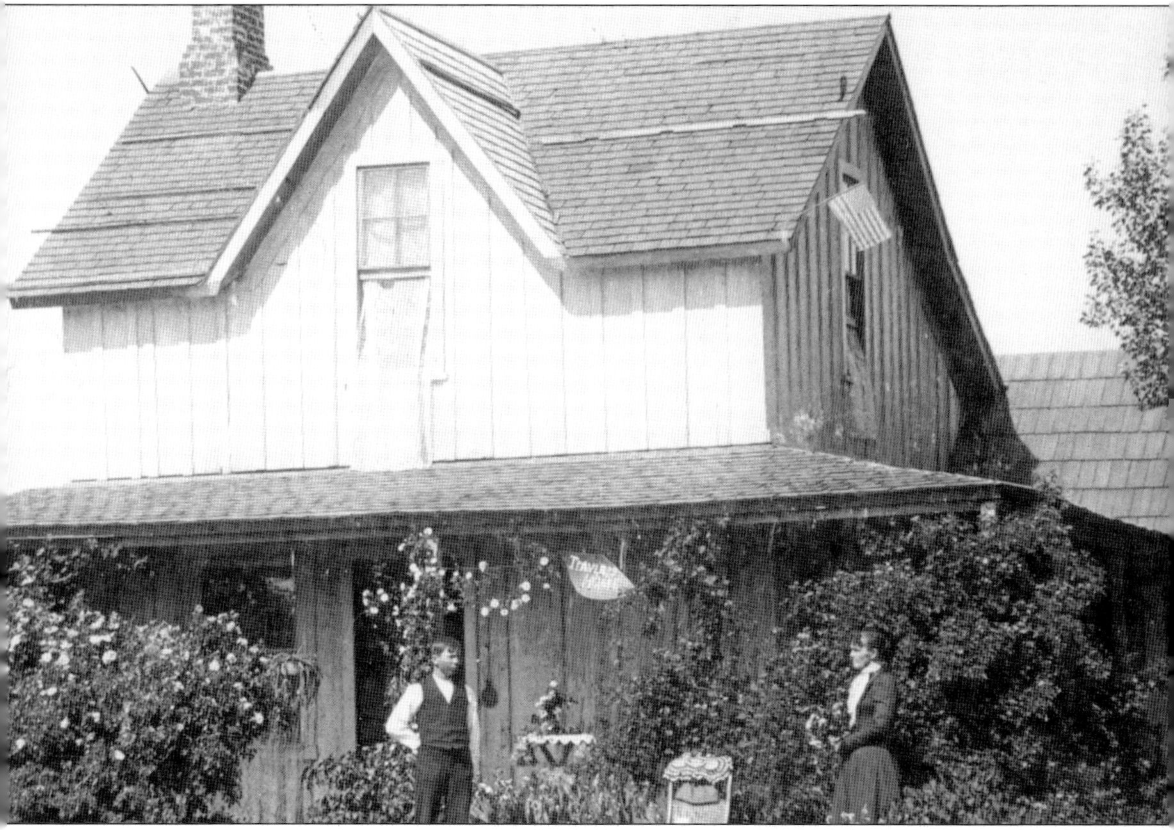

Marvin Wood was born in New York in 1836. During the Civil War, he served as a corporal in Company F of the Michigan Infantry. In 1869, Marvin and his brother sailed around Cape Horn and settled just outside of Eagle Point, where they built a small cabin. In short order, Marvin's brother died and their cabin burned to the ground. Marvin built a new cabin, which would be home to his wife, Susan, and their three children, Mayme, Ora, and Walter.

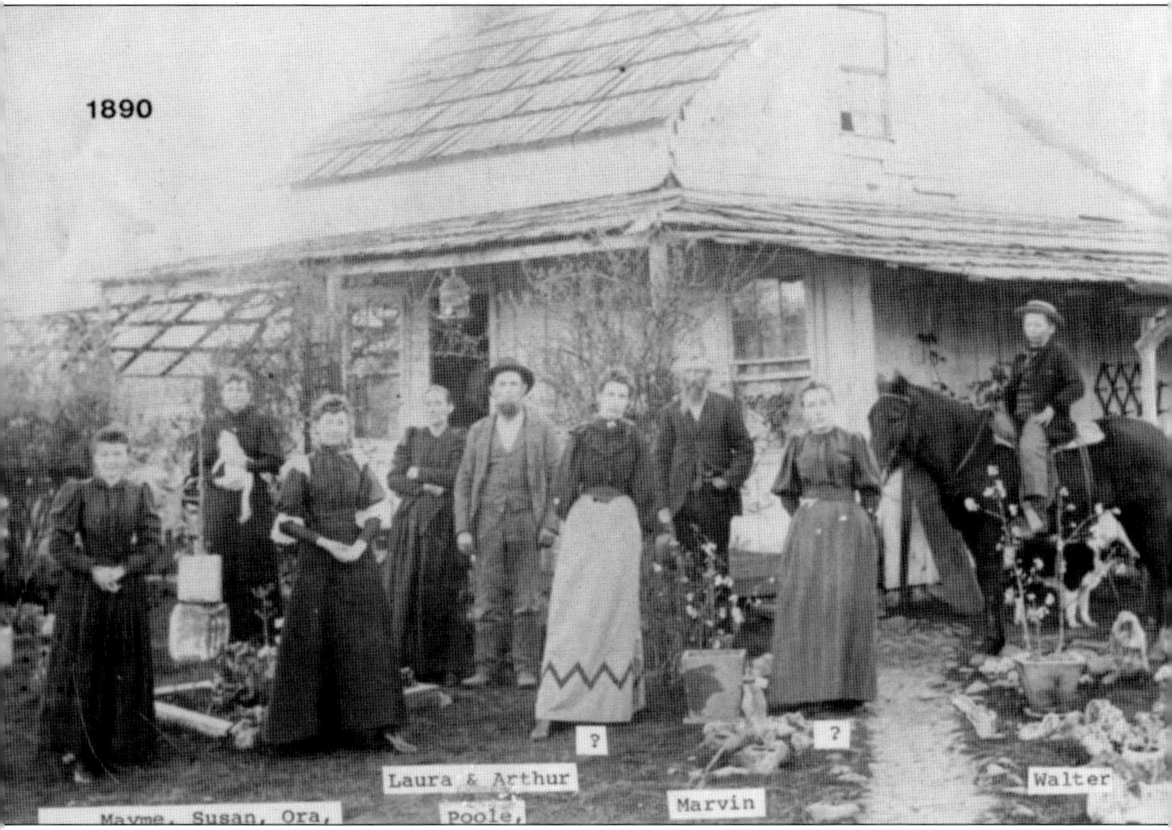

Walter Wood married his cousin Charlotta (Lottie) and they had two sons, Earl (born in 1905) and Harold (born in 1907). The couple divorced in 1925. During Prohibition, Walter was known to keep a still or two, yet every time the sheriff came out to investigate, nothing could be found. The locals remember Walter as quite a character. He would wander into Eagle Point ready to debate anyone on any subject, and he had a reputation for not keeping his opinions to himself. Back at home, he wiled away many afternoons on his front porch. No matter what the weather was, Walter could be found on that porch. As the years passed, Walter's beard seemed to take over his entire face, and he soon became known as "Old Whiskers." Old Whiskers passed away on September 9, 1974, leaving the family home to his housekeeper. It has since changed hands but is taken care of by members of the community.

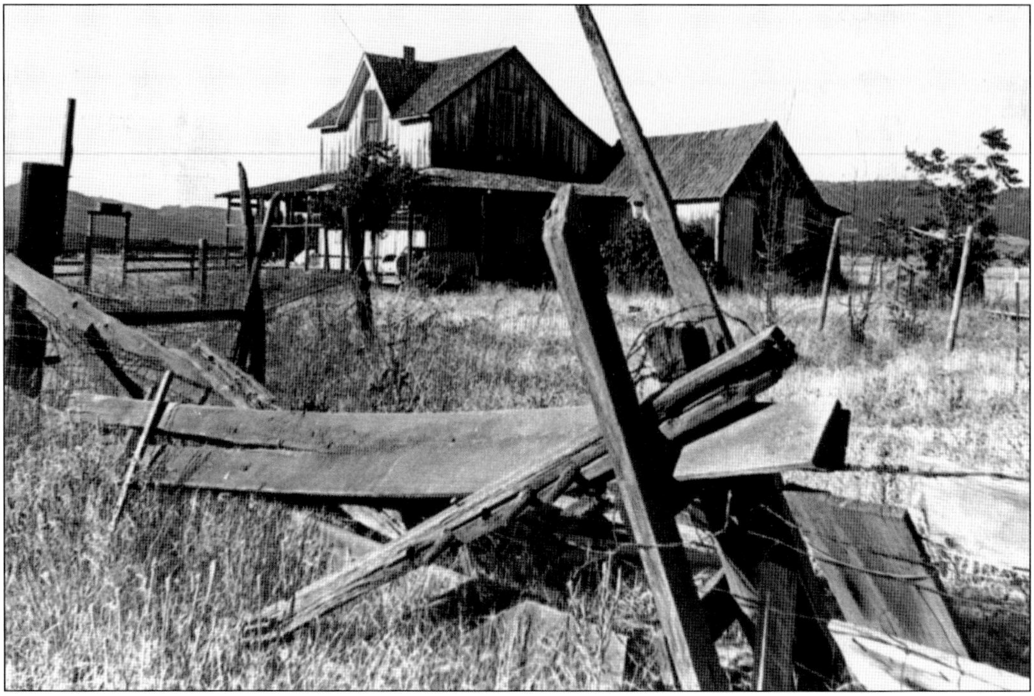

Walter operated the family ranch and was very successful at growing wheat. At one time, he had 300 heads of cattle, plus horses, goats, and chickens. In 1947, he was told that the state was planning on building a highway and that his family home stood directly in its path. Walter fought back, and in the end, the state agreed to relocate the house to the other side of the new highway. The Wood House, pictured below, is seen with Mount McLoughlin in the background. The Wood House is said to be the most painted, drawn, and photographed house in Southern Oregon. It is a popular stop for people traveling to Crater Lake.

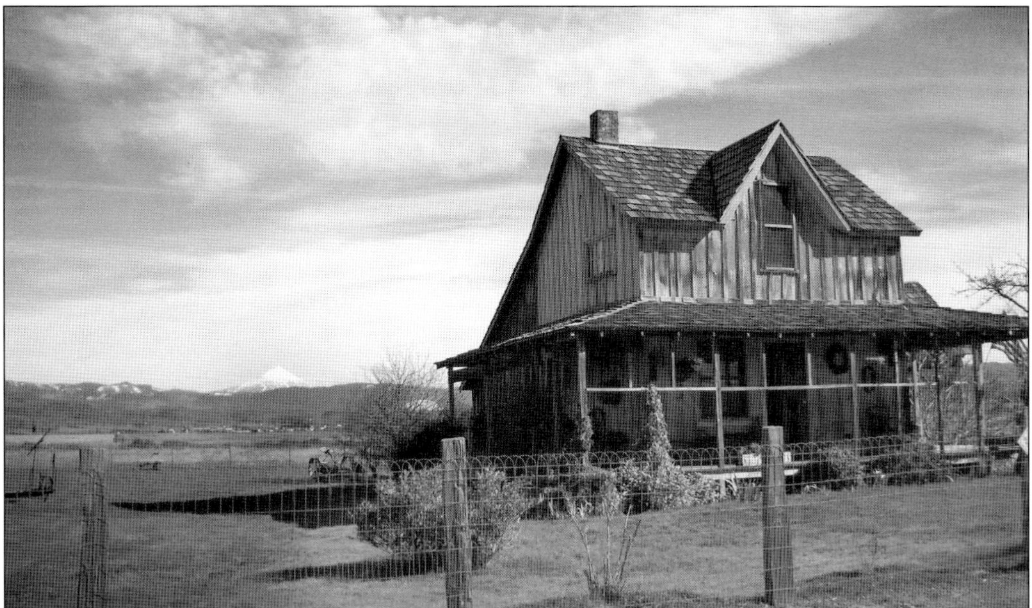

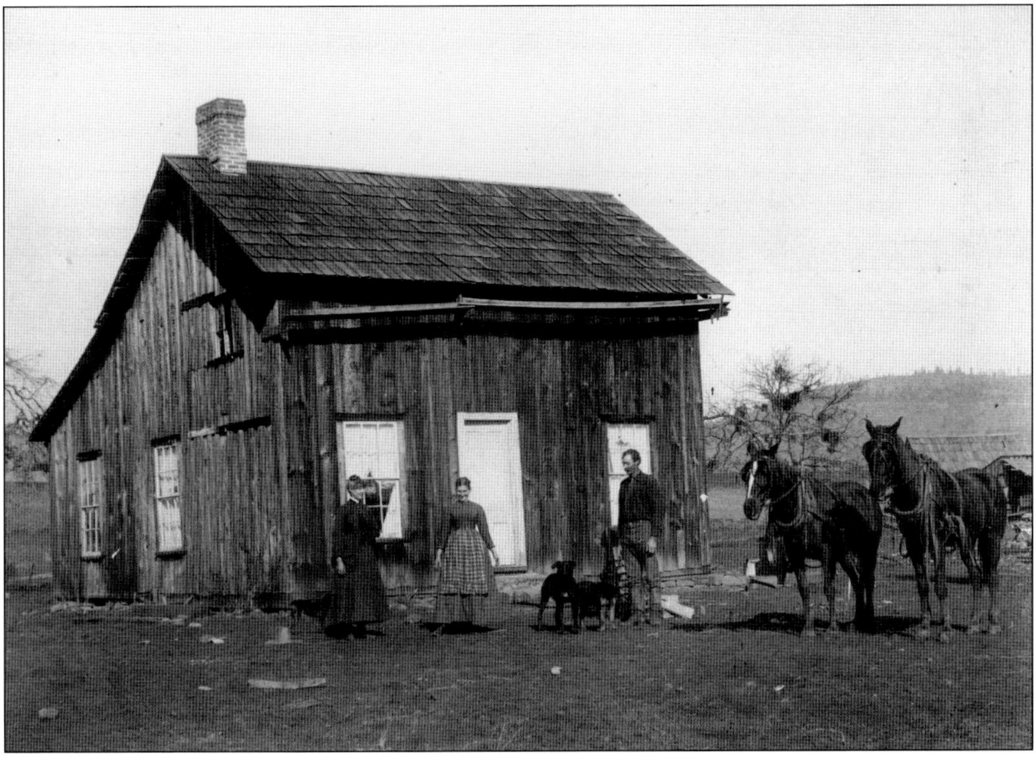

Peter Britt was born in Switzerland and immigrated to America with his father and brother. They settled in Illinois, but it wasn't long before Peter heard the West calling him. He arrived in Jacksonville with $5 to his name. He tried his hand at mining, but soon discovered that hauling freight was more lucrative. Peter was a gifted artist and a skilled photographer. Over time, he became a very successful agriculturist in Jacksonville. He grew some of the first grapes in the valley under the name Valley View Winery. He invested in real estate and mining operations and became a great entrepreneur. As his interests in agriculture grew, Peter purchased land in Eagle Point and built a second home, pictured here.

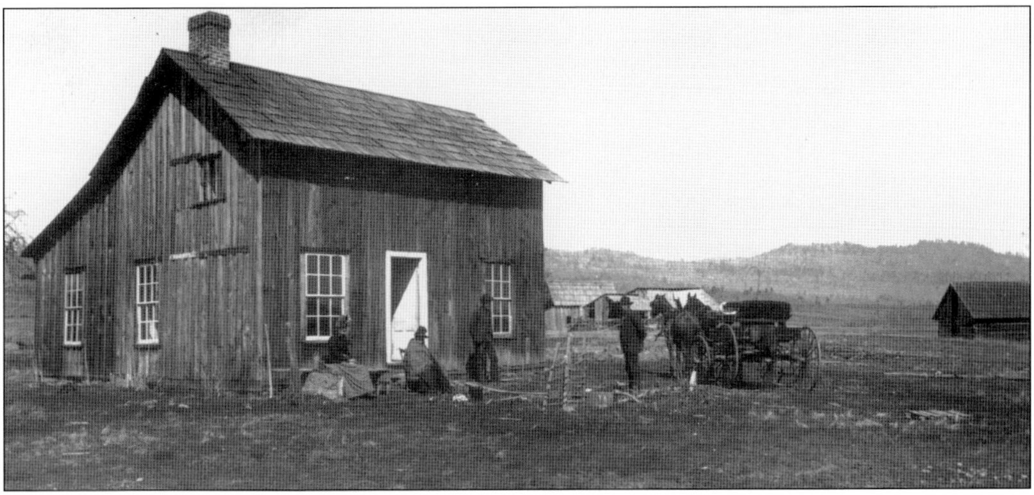

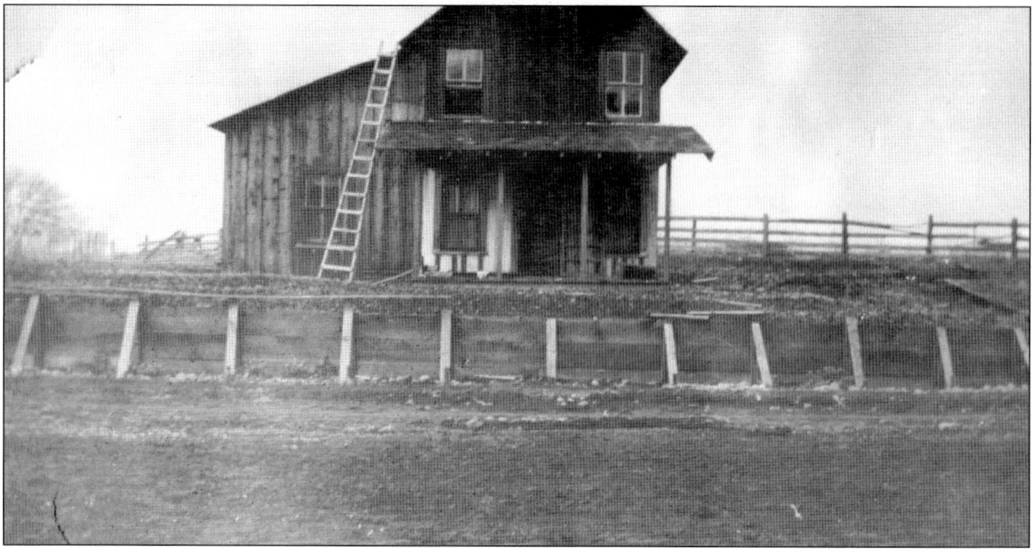

Once the pioneers were established in their new communities, they sometimes built onto their cabins. Other times, they built a new home, which provided plenty of space for the family.

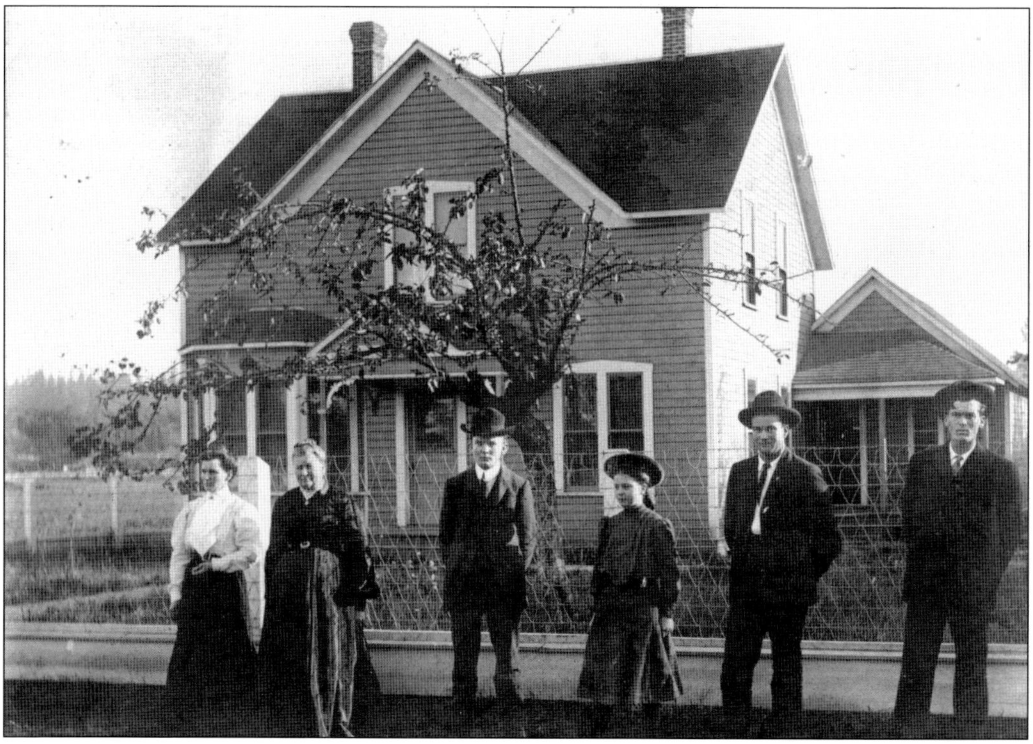

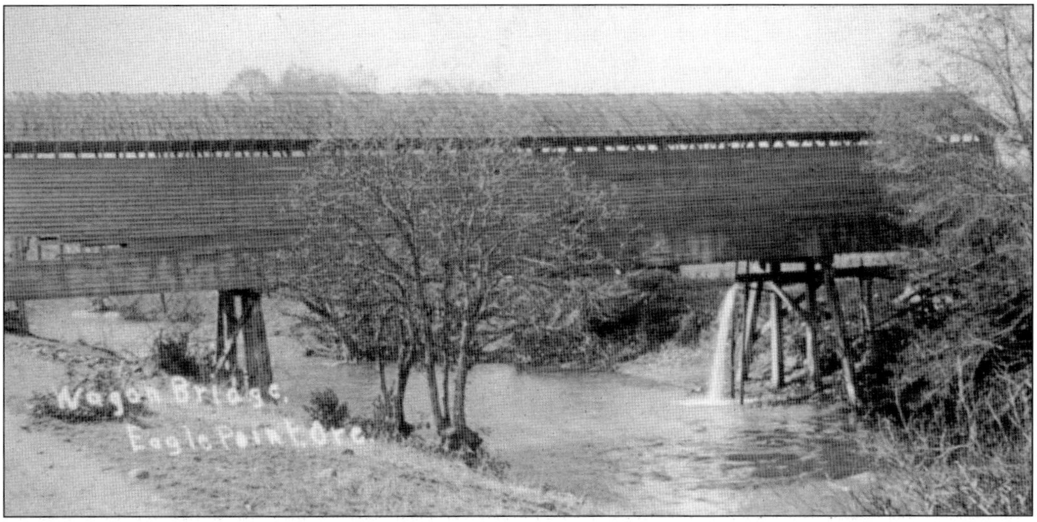

In the beginning, the settlers had to ford the swift waters of Little Butte Creek. They soon discovered that the best place to cross the river was on Frederick Westgate's property due to the smooth river bottom. In 1860, James Fryer built the first bridge across the creek and named it the Westgate Bridge. It was an impressive sight at 80 feet long and 16 feet wide. The bridge was destroyed during the flood of 1861, but was quickly rebuilt. In 1887, the bridge came crashing down under the weight of a large load of cattle and sheep. Describing the scene in his journal, James Fryer wrote, "The bridge fell down with cattle and sheep. Killed five sheep and crippled seven cows. Worked on bridge all day."

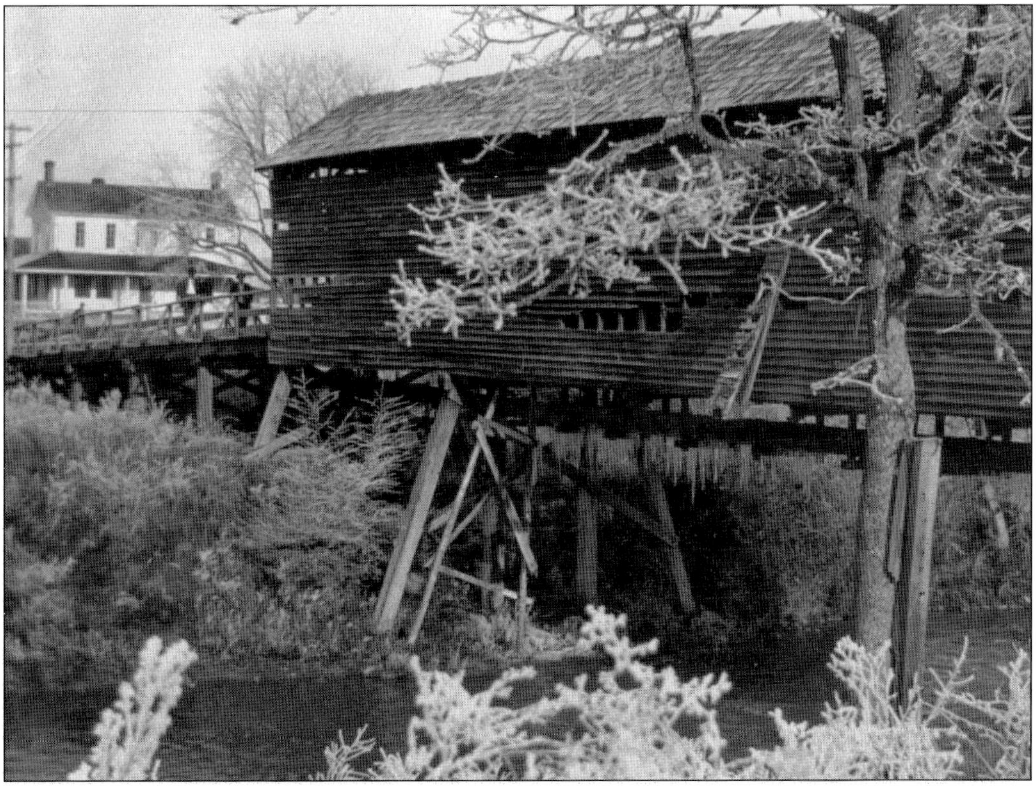

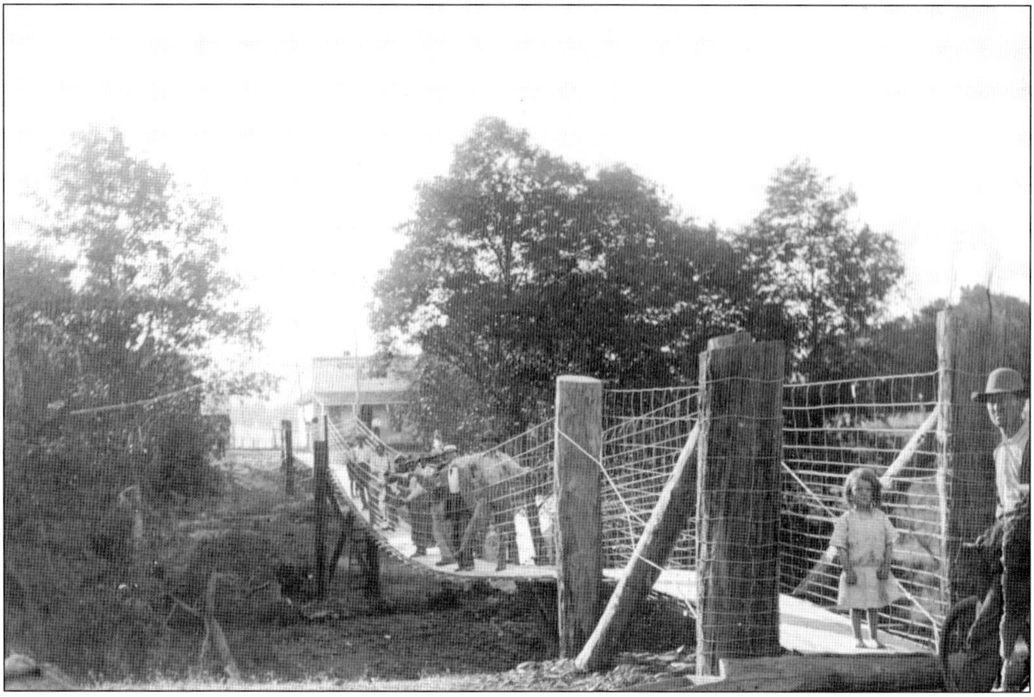

In 1884, A.J. Daley built a wire suspension footbridge over Little Butte Creek. This allowed those living on one side of the creek to get to the business core on the other side of the creek. The bridge lasted for 10 years before Mother Nature came calling. In true community spirit, the citizens came together and built a new footbridge.

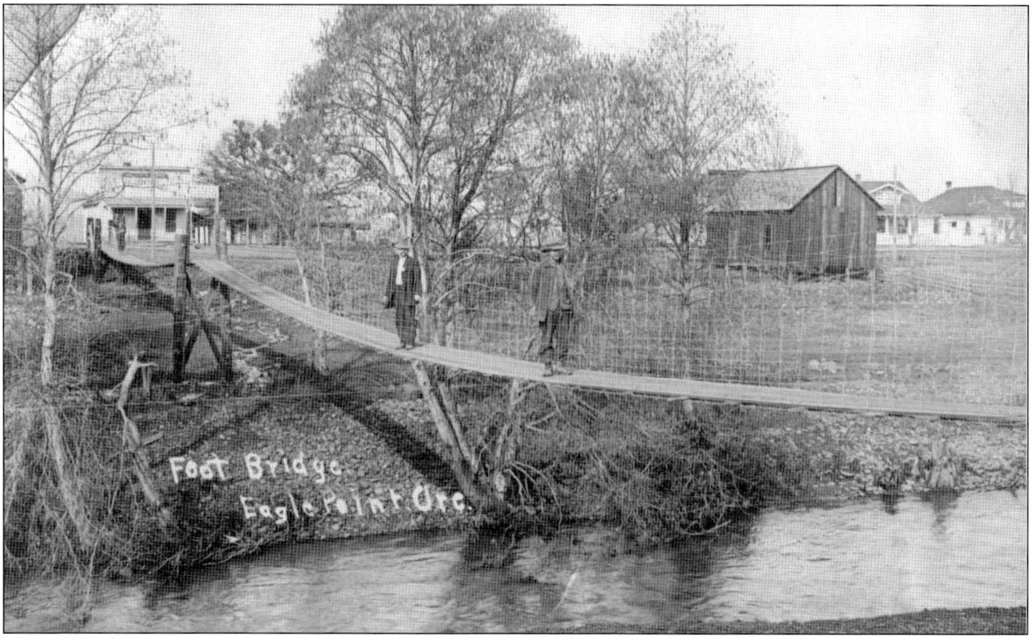

Two

THE PEOPLE OF EAGLE POINT

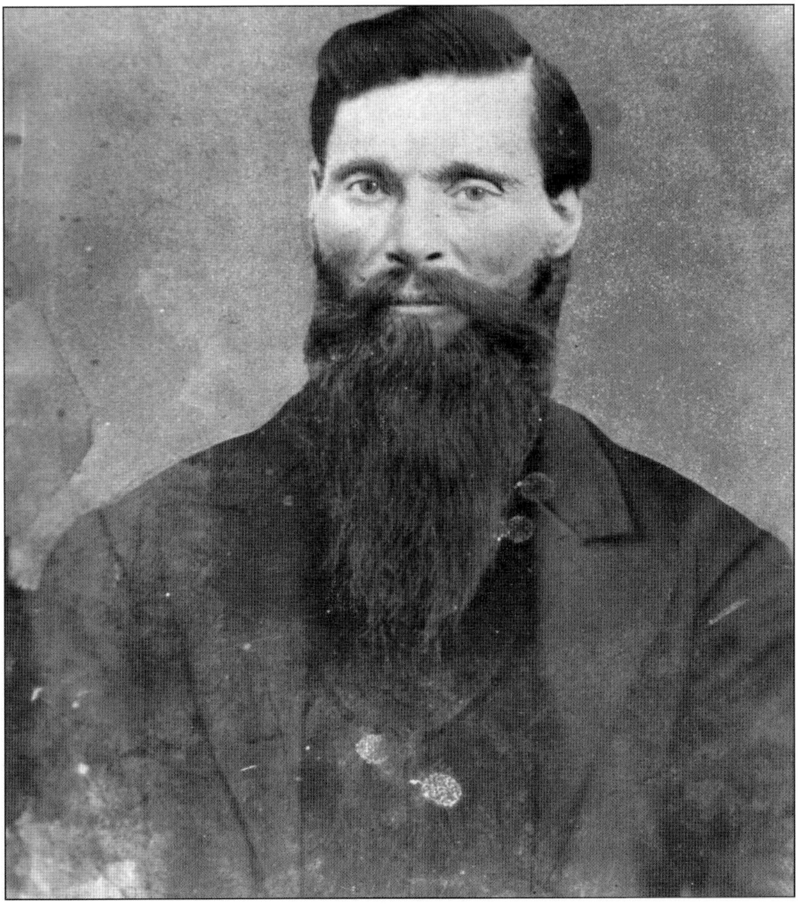

William Mathews is credited with naming the town Eagle Point after watching majestic eagles soaring overhead and nesting high up on a butte.

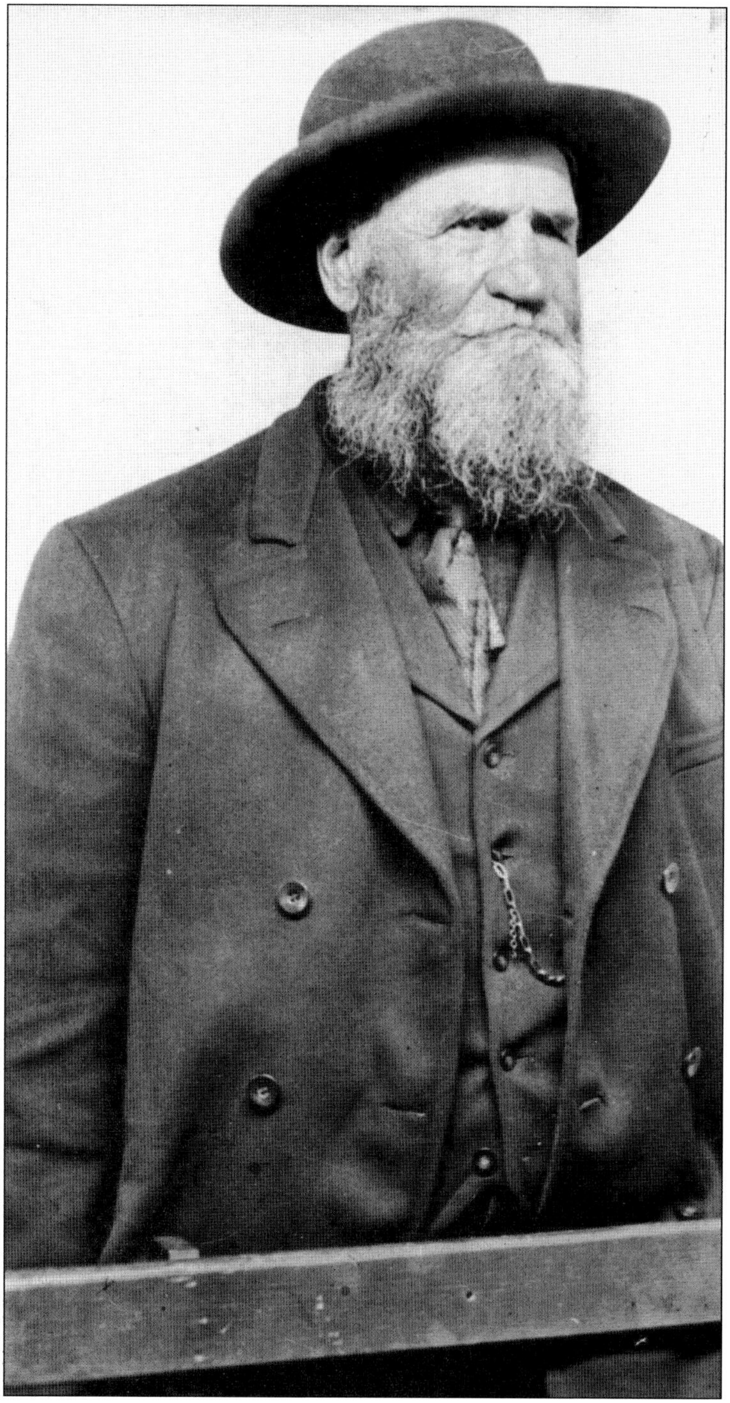

John McDaniel and his sons, Larkin, Lewis, and John Jr., operated a sawmill on Little Butte Creek as early as 1855. They had a hard time keeping up with the demand for lumber when the nearby town of Jacksonville experienced a population boom. John later leased the mill to Jacob Hoffman, who turned it into a flour mill. John took the flour mill back after the lease was up. John operated the flour mill until 1871, when he became ill. He died from typhoid fever the following year.

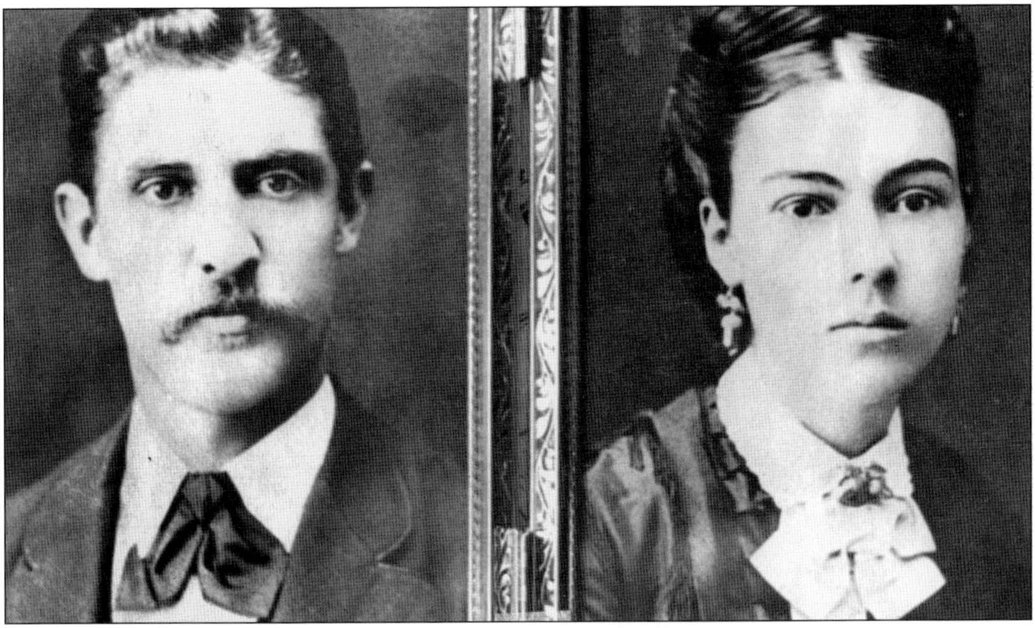

Hugo and Elizabeth Von der Hellen were married in India in 1874. Hugo was of German descent and was living in India while working for the German consulate. Elizabeth was in India with her father, who was a sea captain. The Von der Hellens had seven children, all of whom helped run the family farm in Eagle Point. Hugo also served as an Oregon senator for 12 years. Their sons William and George operated a hardware and pharmacy store in downtown Eagle Point.

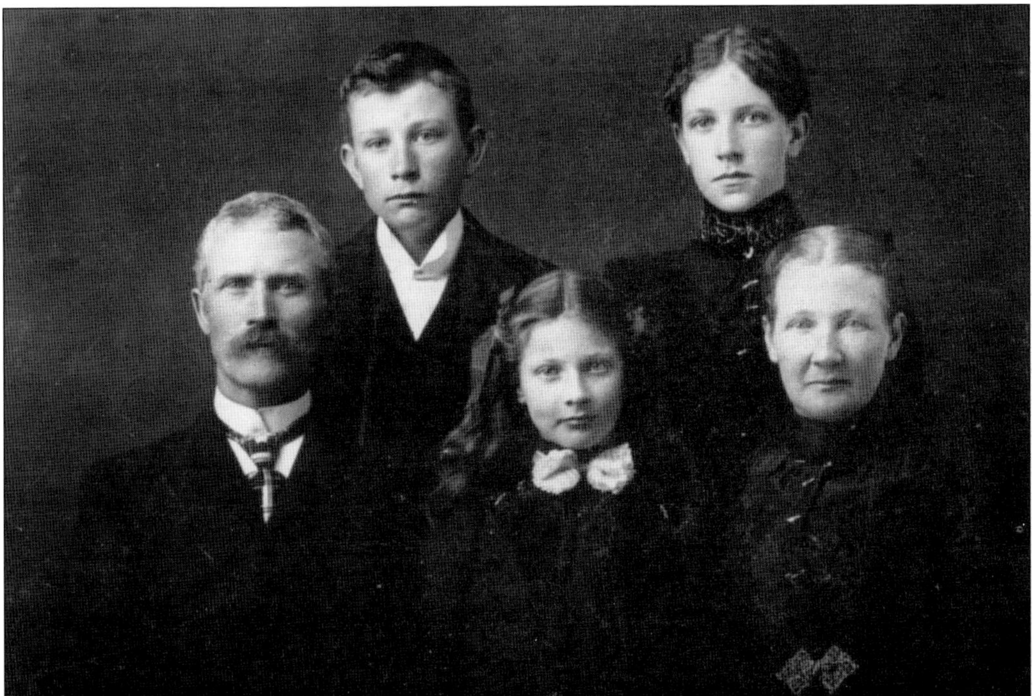

The Riley family made their home in Eagle Point. Pictured here are Thomas Joshua, Thomas Martin, Josephine Isabel, Myrtle, and Sarah Grace.

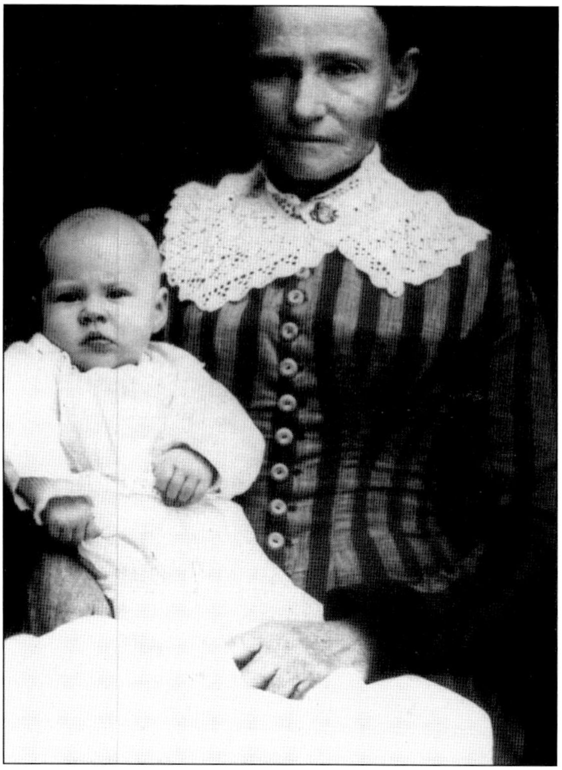

Elizabeth Simon is pictured here with one of her 13 children. The Simons, like many pioneer families, lost several children during infancy and early childhood. Diseases, such as diphtheria and small pox, and accidents were the causes of many deaths.

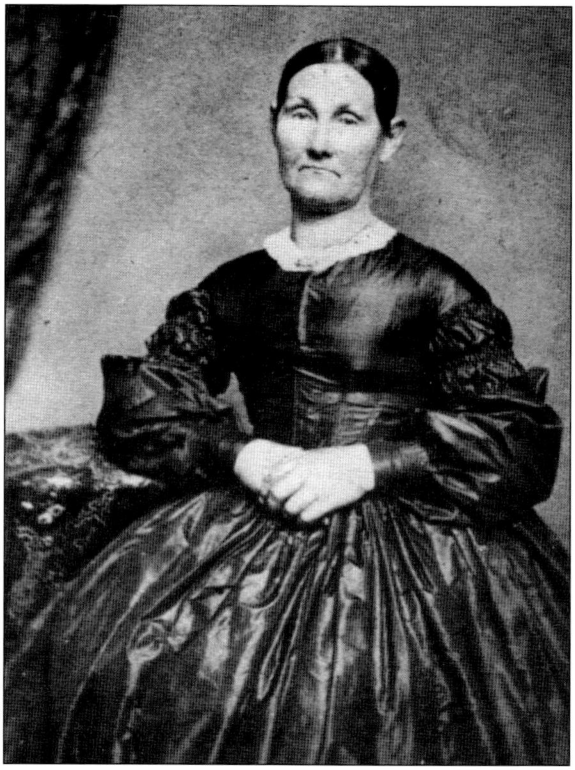

John Daley's wife, Livone, is pictured here in a formal photography studio. During the pioneer era, having a photograph taken was expensive and not readily available. It could take the camera lenses up to five minutes to close, so the person had to sit very still while waiting for the process to be complete.

The Cingcade children are shown sitting for a formal portrait. For a period of time, their father operated a dance hall in Eagle Point.

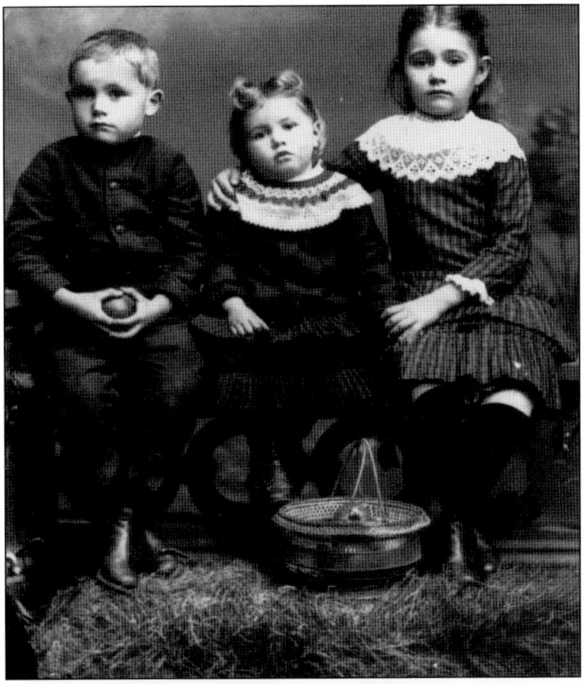

Edgar Buchannan Jr. is shown here with his sisters Kee, Kate, and Lovy. Their father was a dentist in Eagle Point. Edgar Jr. became quite famous as "Uncle Joe" in the television series *Petticoat Junction*.

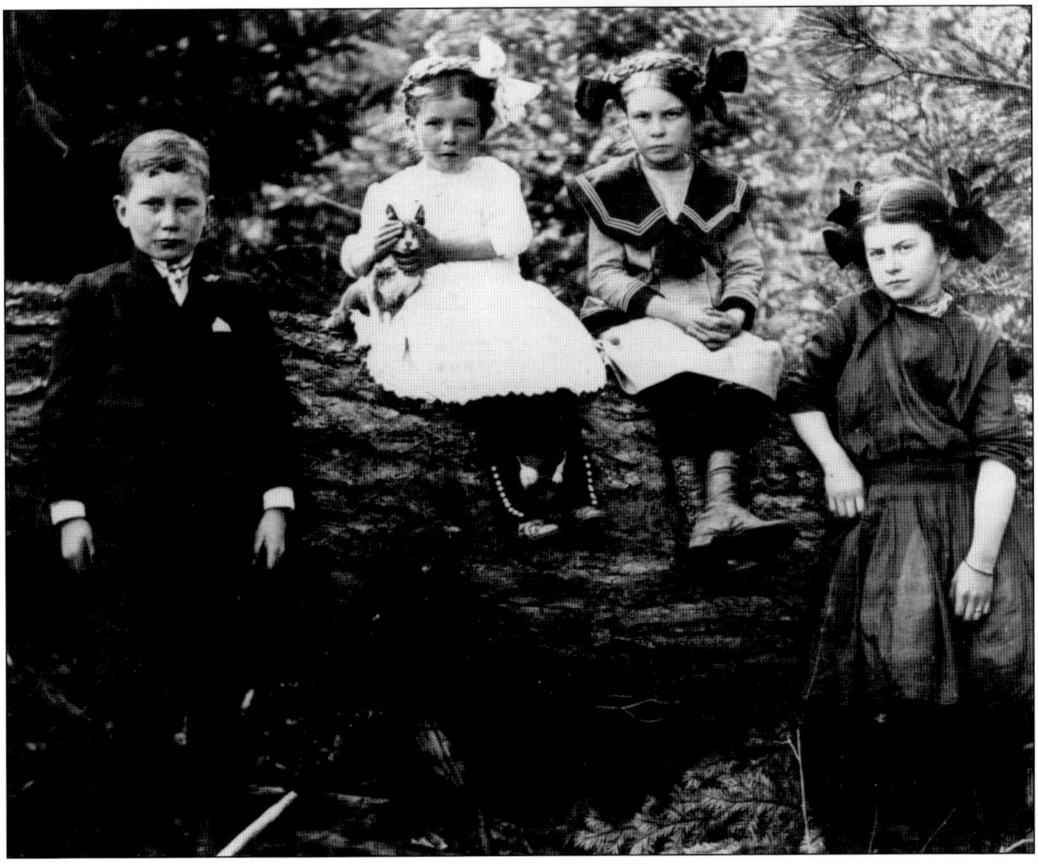

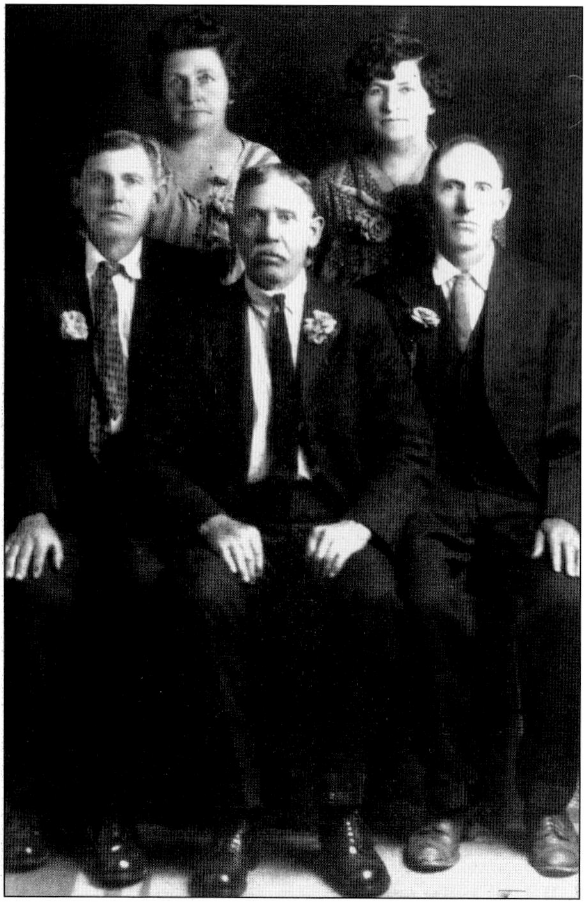

This photograph from July 1926 shows Irvin, Eli, and Zera Dahack with Ira Mathews and Dora Niepager.

Martin and Susanah Perry came to Eagle Point from Stockton, California. They had seven daughters and one son. Pictured here are all seven daughters: Nellie, Harriet, Erma, Elizabeth, Nettie, Charlotte, and Delia (in no particular order).

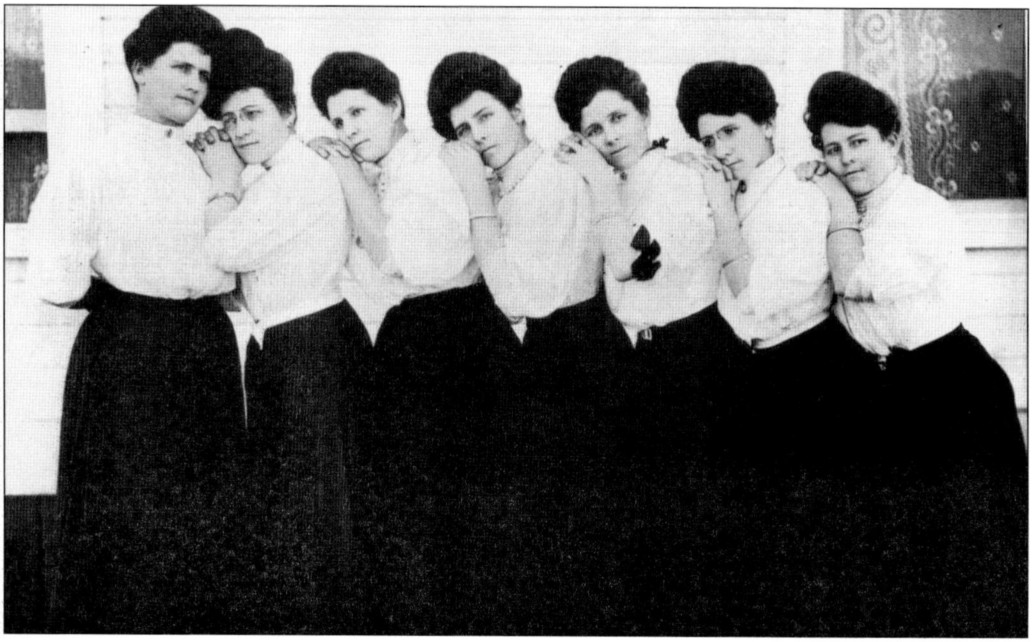

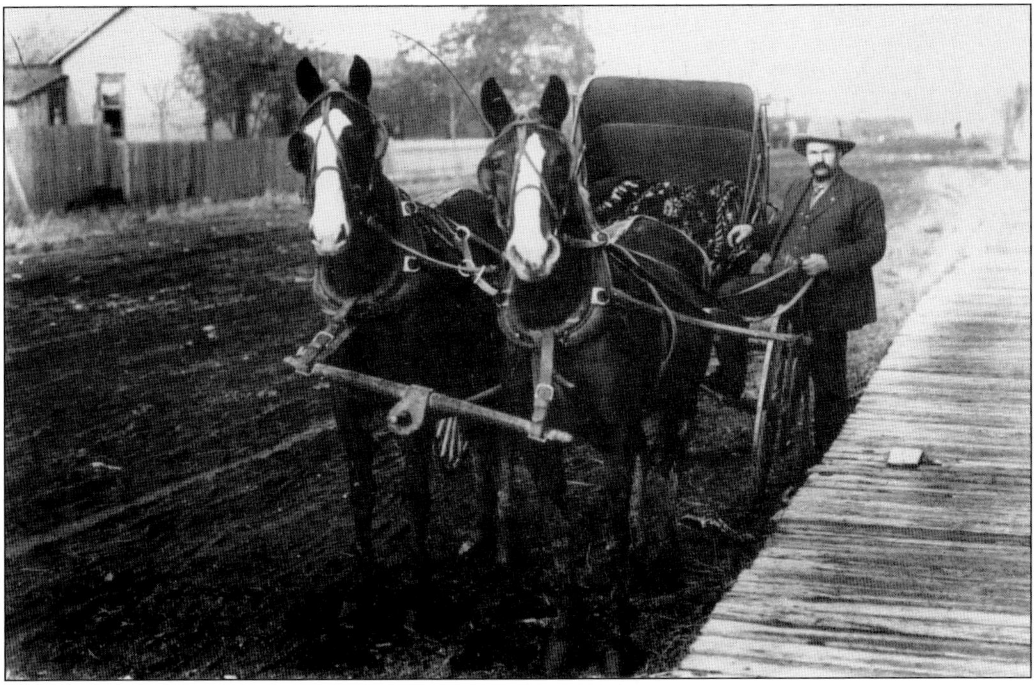

Above, John Watkins is posing with his carriage alongside a wooden sidewalk, long before the streets were paved. Below, Henry Trusty is preparing his wagon team for a busy day hauling freight.

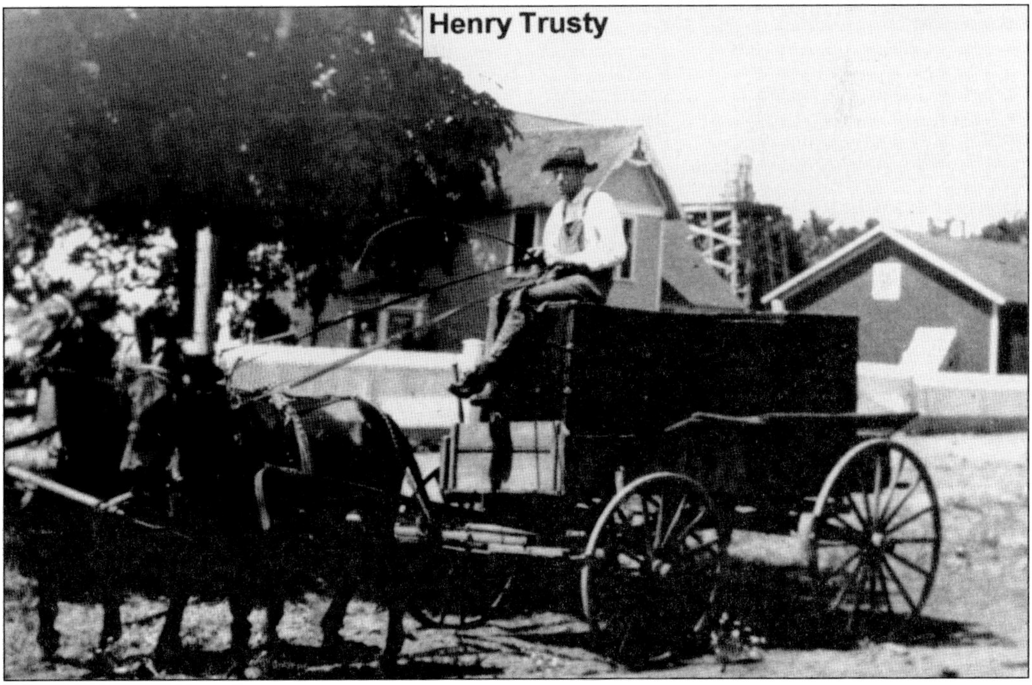

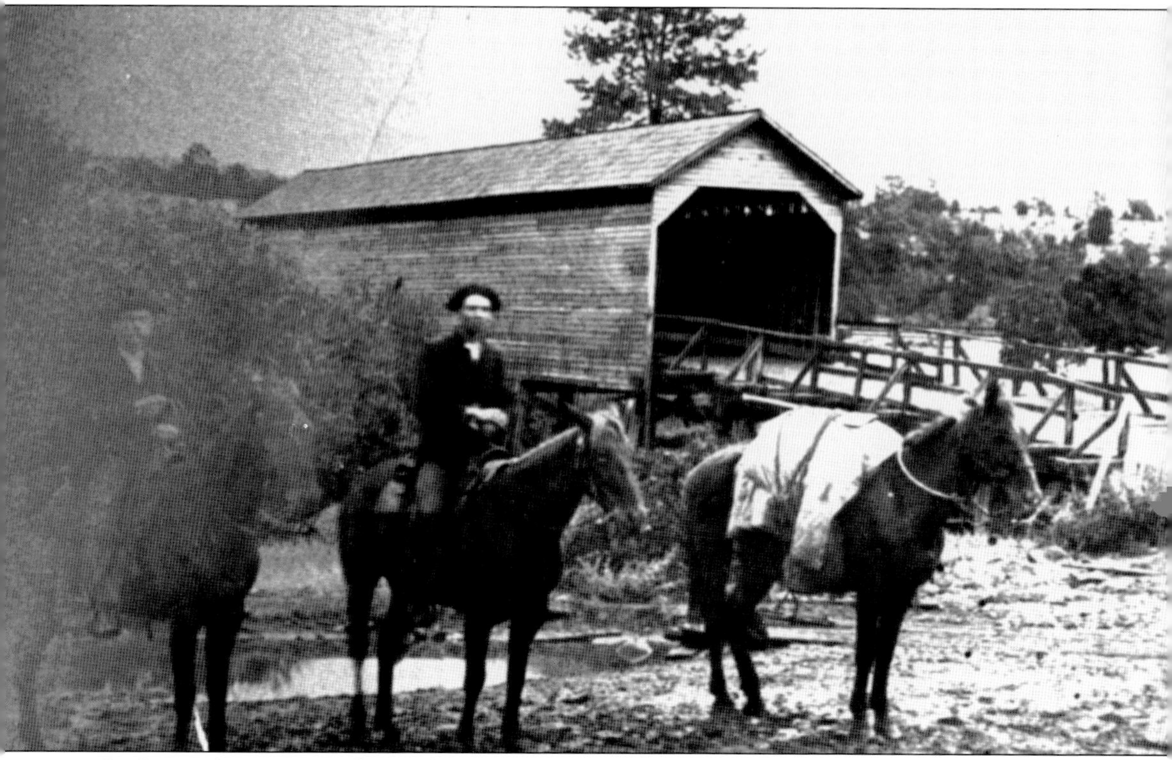

In September 1894, Wilbur Ashpole and Porter Robinett took a moment to stop in front of the covered bridge to have their photograph taken.

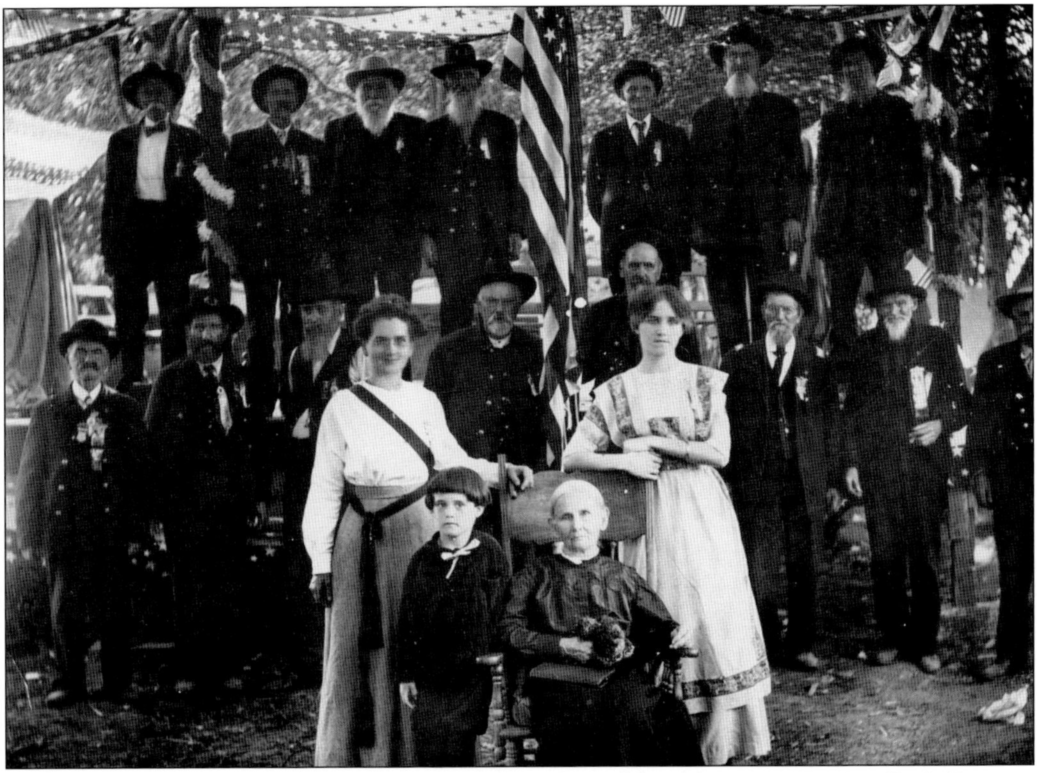

This photograph was taken on August 20, 1912 at the "Old Soldier's Reunion" in Eagle Point.

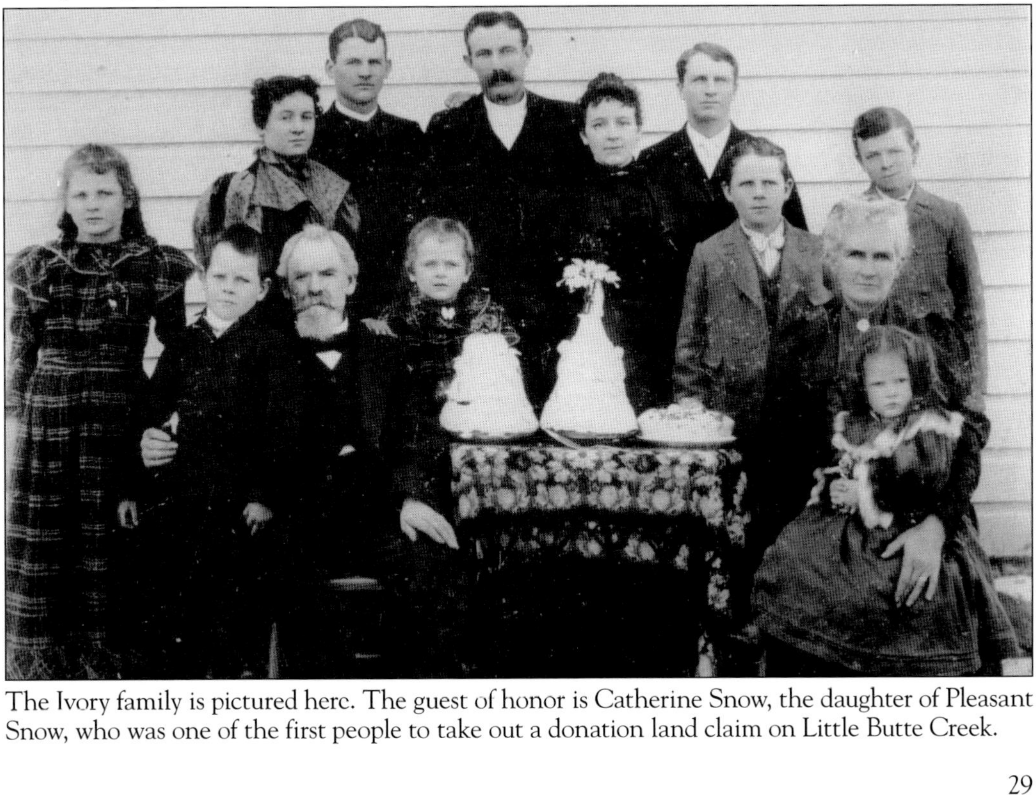

The Ivory family is pictured here. The guest of honor is Catherine Snow, the daughter of Pleasant Snow, who was one of the first people to take out a donation land claim on Little Butte Creek.

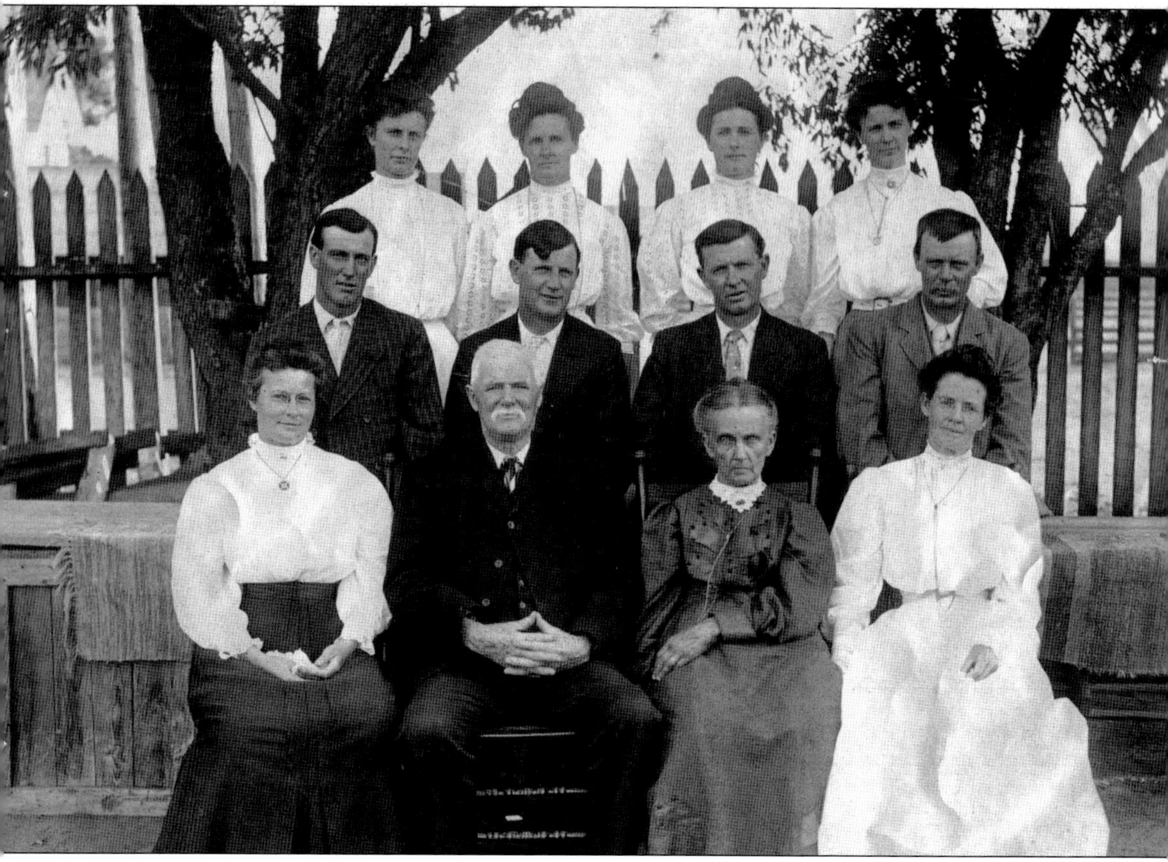

Pictured in later years is the Brown family, including (in no particular order) Cora, Cecelia, Nell, Lottie, Merritt, Will, Frank, Royal, Sarah, George, Mary, and Emily.

Lloyd Walch and George Dunlap are taking a moment out of their day to reminiscence about the good ole days in Eagle Point.

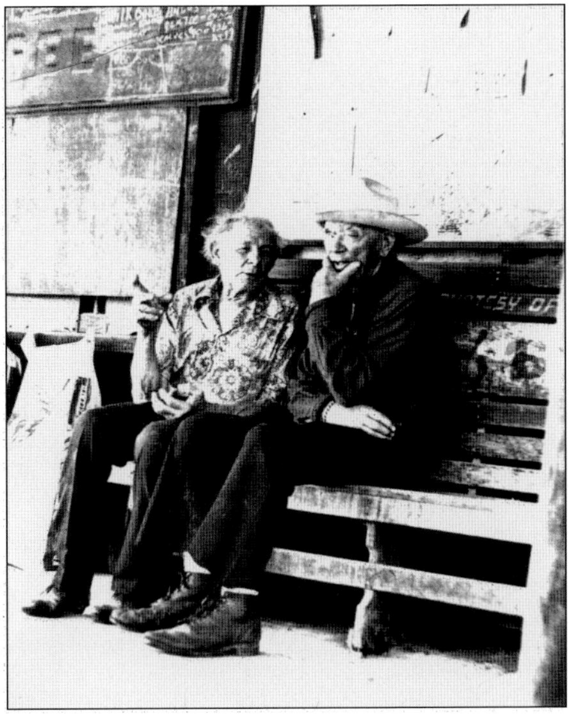

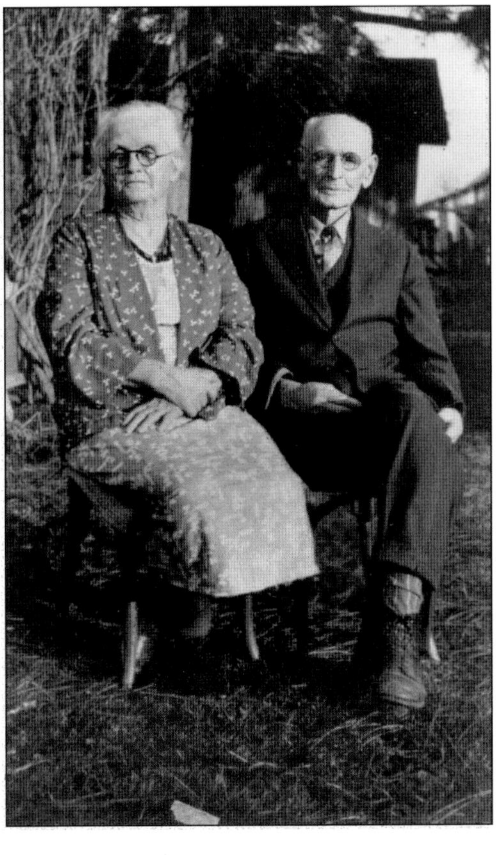

Albert and Henrietta Peachey left Oklahoma in 1900 with their eight children and made their way to Oregon by way of covered wagon. The Peacheys were rather late coming overland, as most pioneers had made the journey by the mid-1860s.

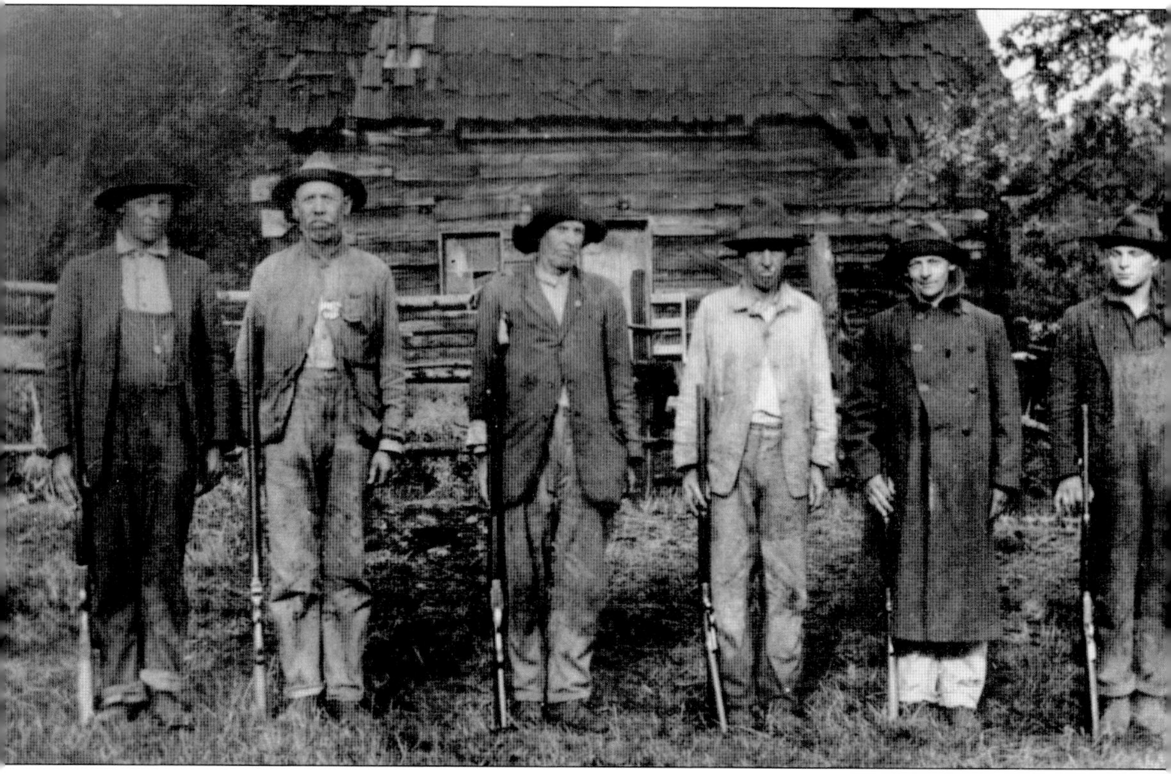

The gentlemen pictured here outside of Zera Dahack's cabin include Everett Dahack, Eli Dahack, Irvin Dahack, Zera Dahack, and Ernie Dahack.

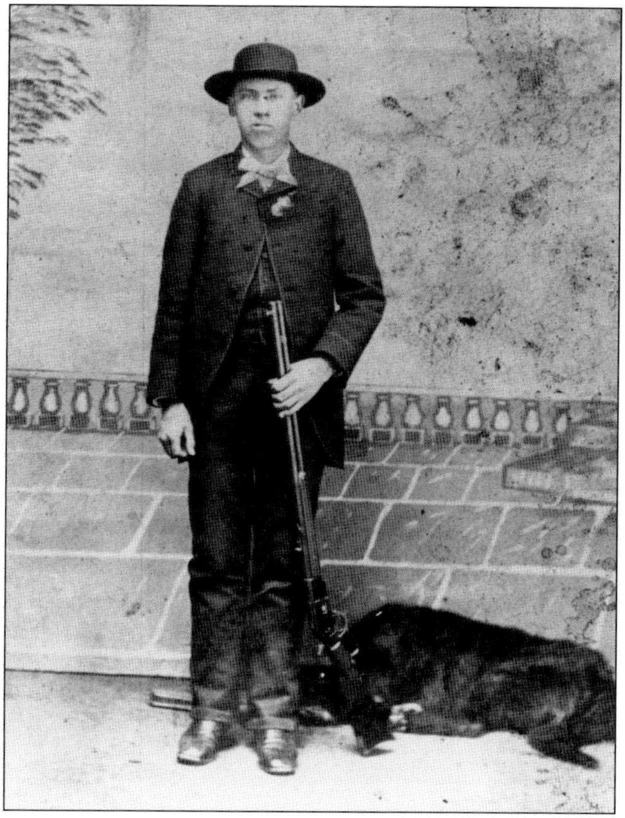

Eli Dahack is pictured (right) with his hunting buddy, and Everette Dahack is pictured in 1918 preparing to leave for World War I (below).

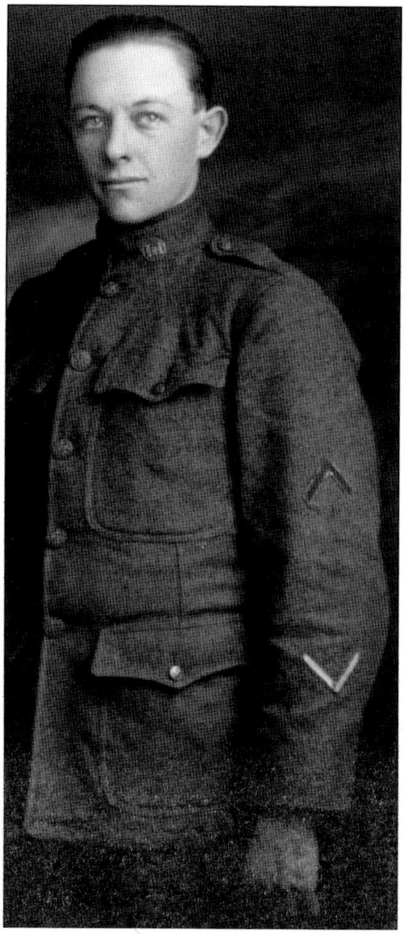

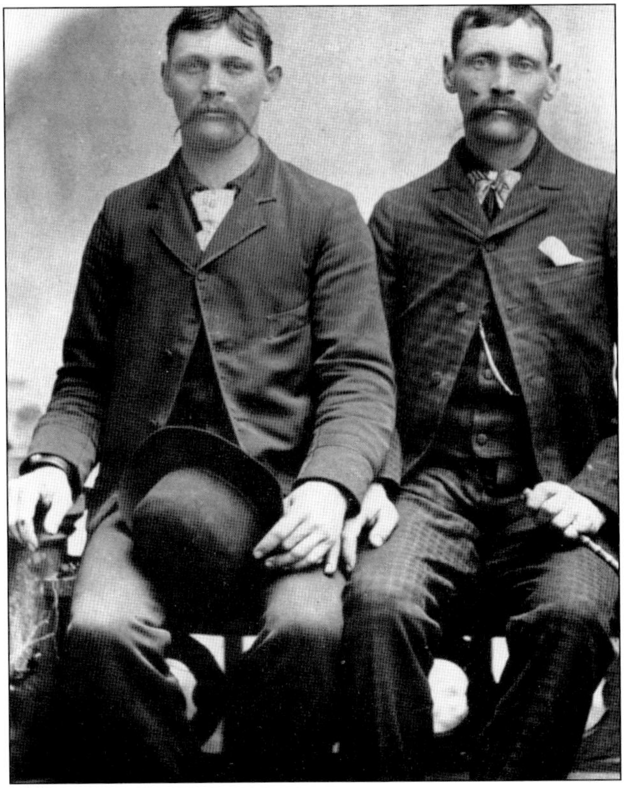

Brothers Grant and Green Mathews take a moment to pose for the camera (left), and Johnnie Mayham and Jerry Winkle strike a pose for the photographer (below).

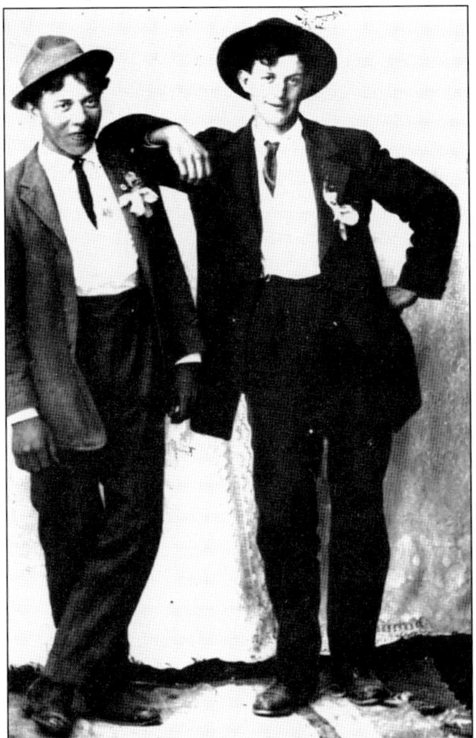

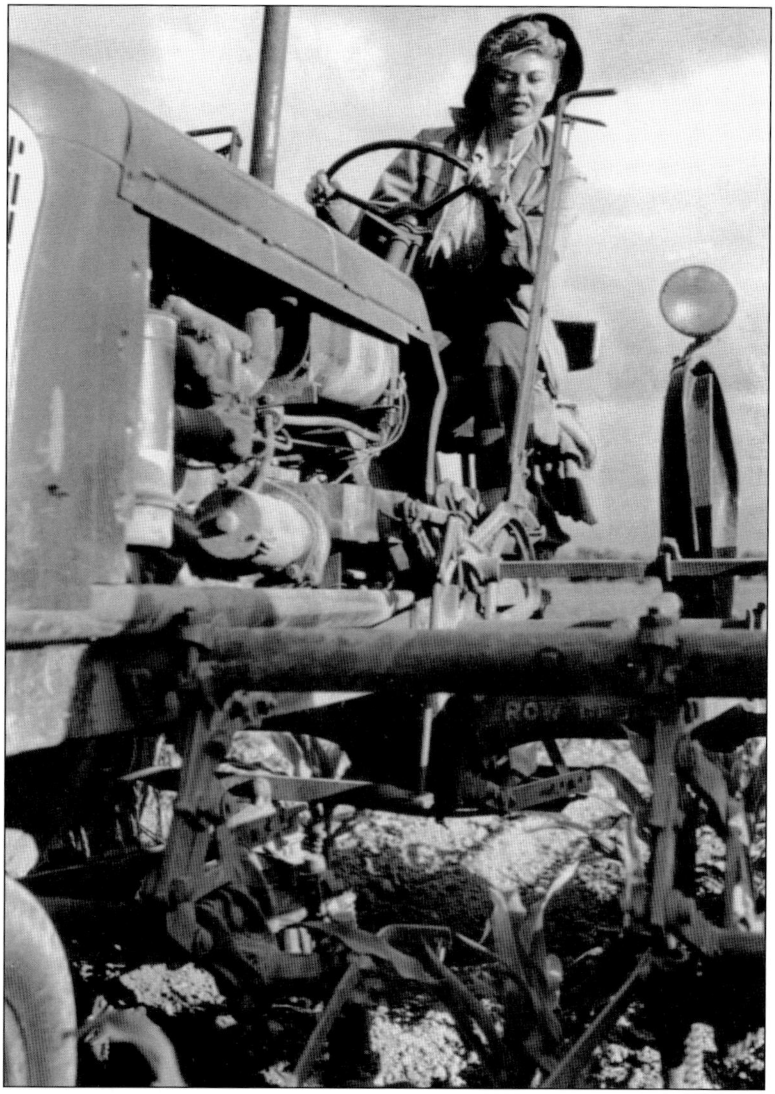

In May 1941, the Oscar-winning actress Ginger Rogers purchased more than 800 acres just outside of Eagle Point. Ginger's mother, Lela, lived on the property. She was a writer and enjoyed the peaceful surroundings. The ranch was known as Rogers Rogue River Ranch.

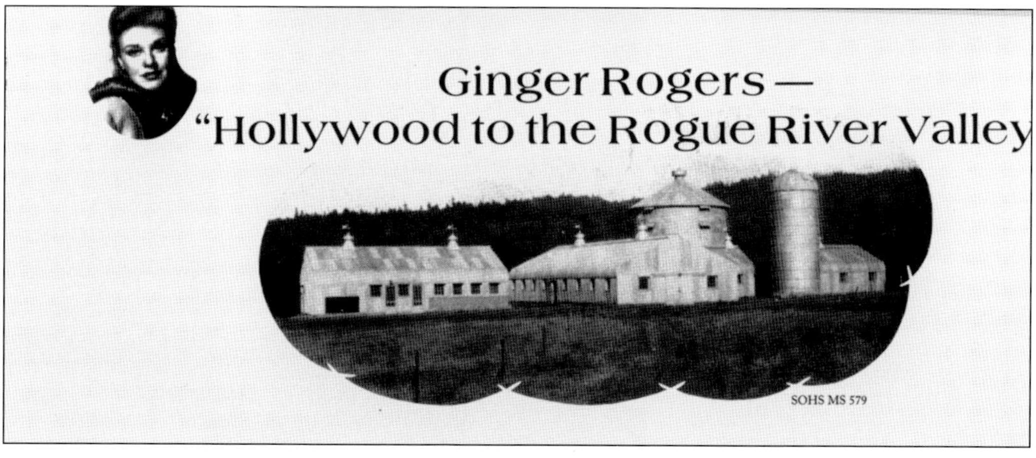

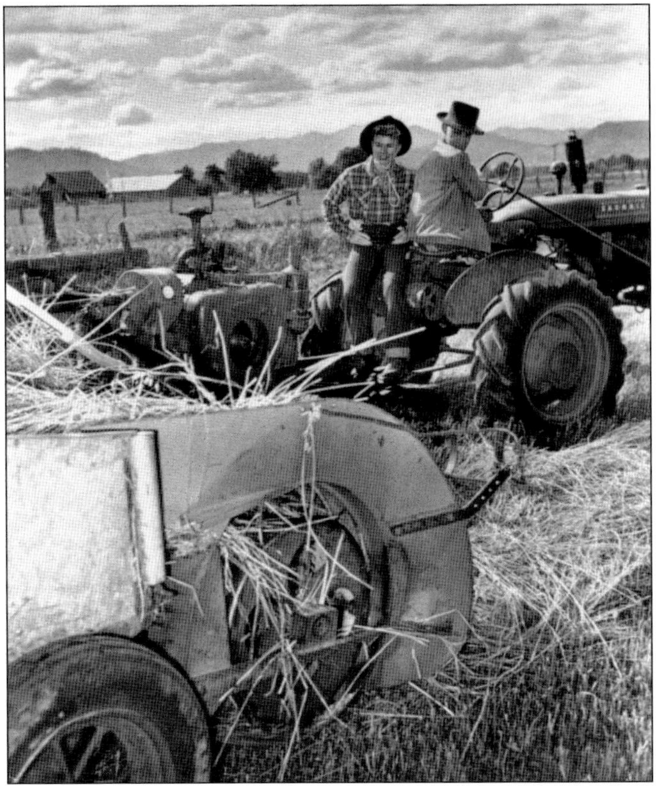

After World War II broke out, the government bought approximately half of Ginger Roger's land to be used for Camp White. Ginger entertained the troops at Camp White while she was visiting her ranch and also participated in bond rallies. Camp White purchased dairy products from the Rogers Rogue River Ranch, and the female nurses camped overnight at the ranch during their training.

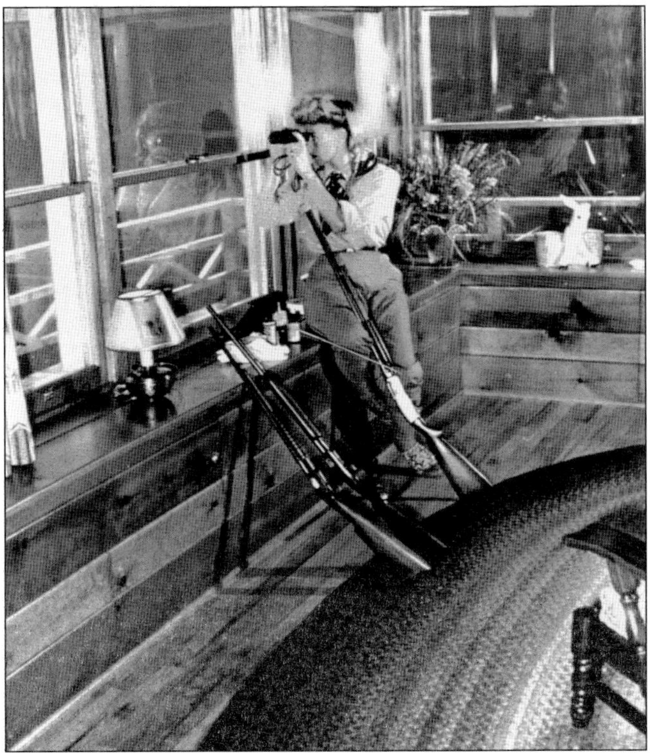

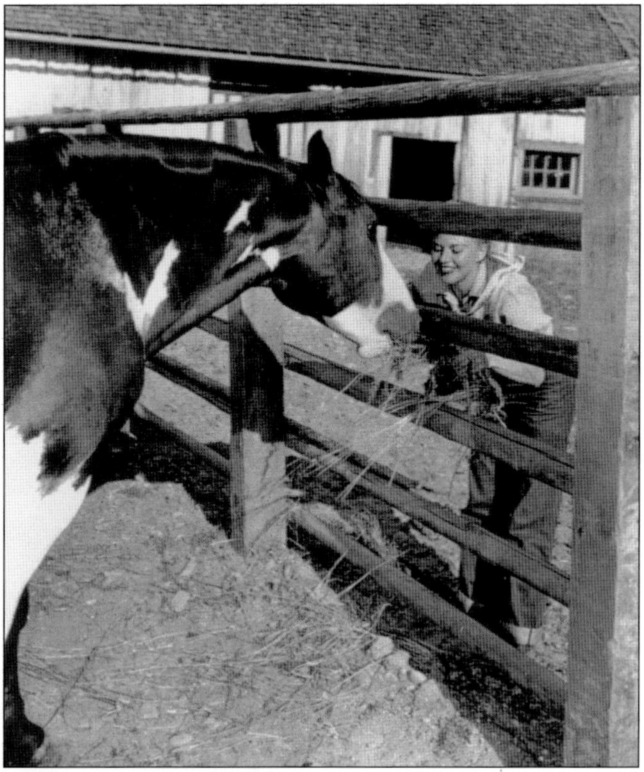

In these photographs, Ginger is enjoying the peace and quiet of her ranch. She is seen here spending time with her farm animals.

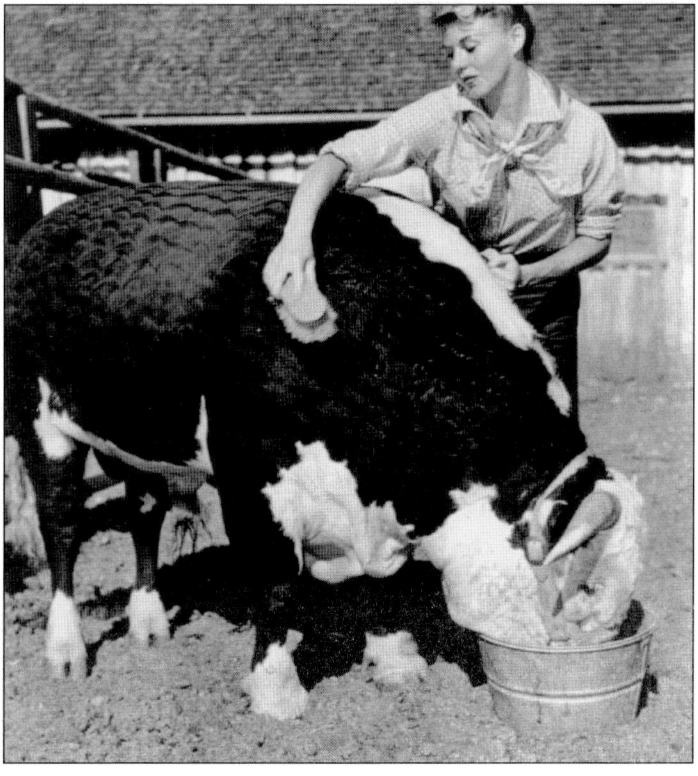

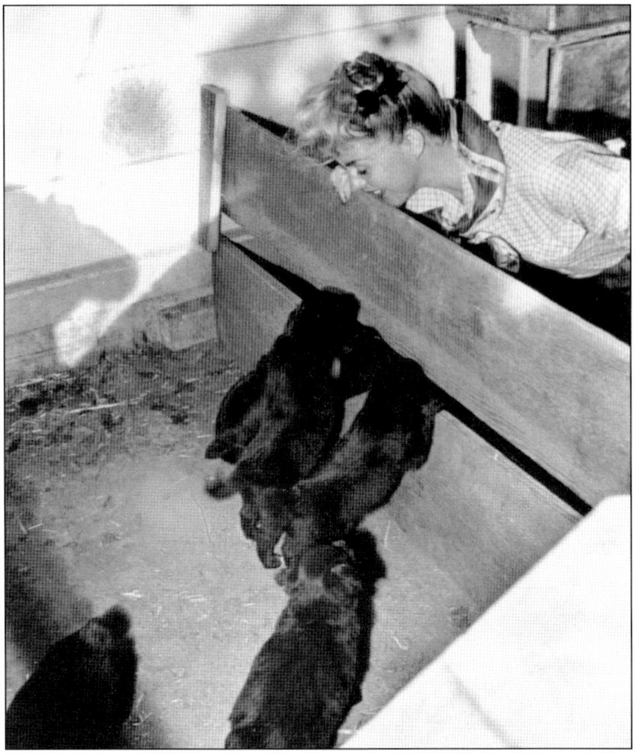

In all, Ginger Rogers made 73 films during her career. Her talents were showcased in film, stage, radio, and television as a singer, dancer, and actress. She and her dancing partner, Fred Astaire, are credited with revolutionizing Hollywood's musicals. Together, they made nine highly successful musicals. Ginger's mother, Lela, passed away in 1977 at the ranch. After Lela died, Ginger divided her time between the ranch and her other home in California. Ginger eventually sold the ranch in 1990. The Craterian Ginger Rogers Theatre in Medford is named in her honor. Ginger had performed at the Craterian Theatre in 1926 as part of a vaudeville act.

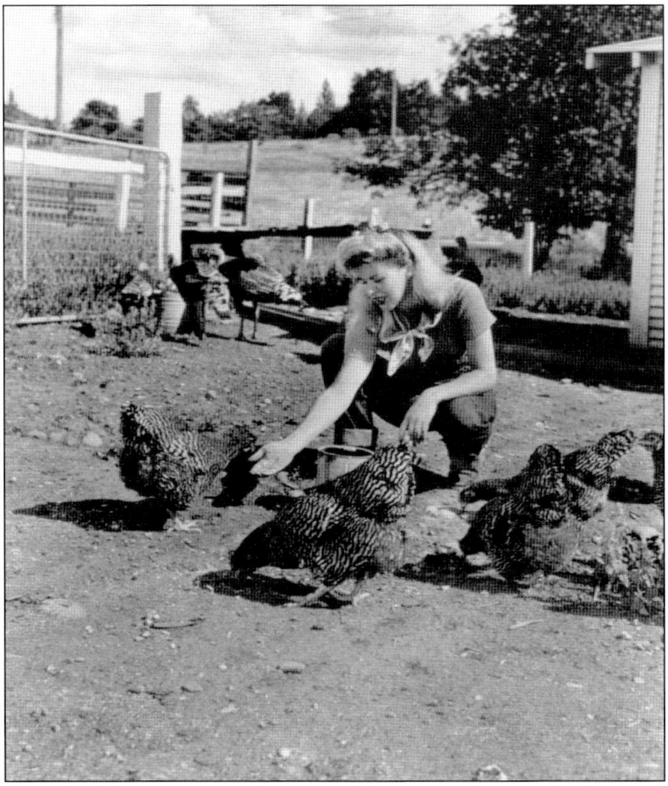

Three

BUSINESS IS BOOMING

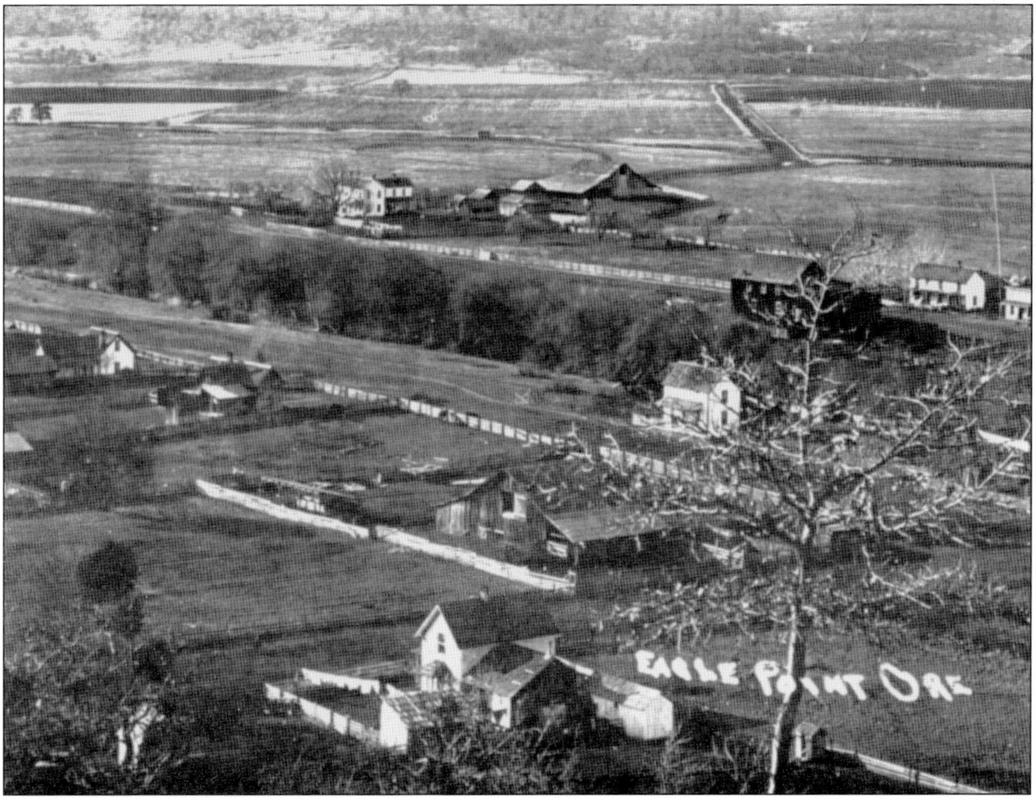

Shown is an early photograph of Eagle Point. There were very few businesses at the time, but that was about to change.

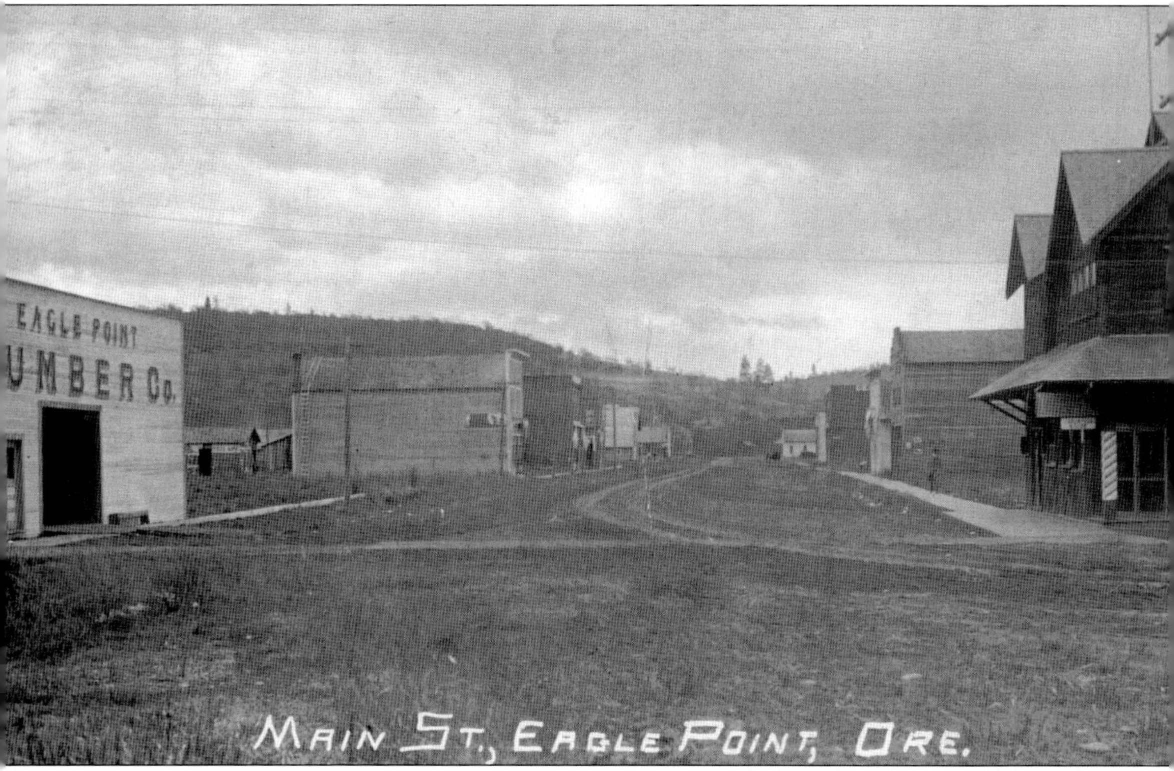

Just a few years later, the downtown area had experienced substantial growth. On the left hand side of the street is Eagle Point Lumber, Lewis Confectionery, Eagle Point Hardware, Eagle Point Bank, and the Harnish Livery. The businesses on the right include the Vogeli Hotel, Spicjers Opera and Dance House, Model Variety Store, the Brown and Sons Store, and the Eagle Point Bakery.

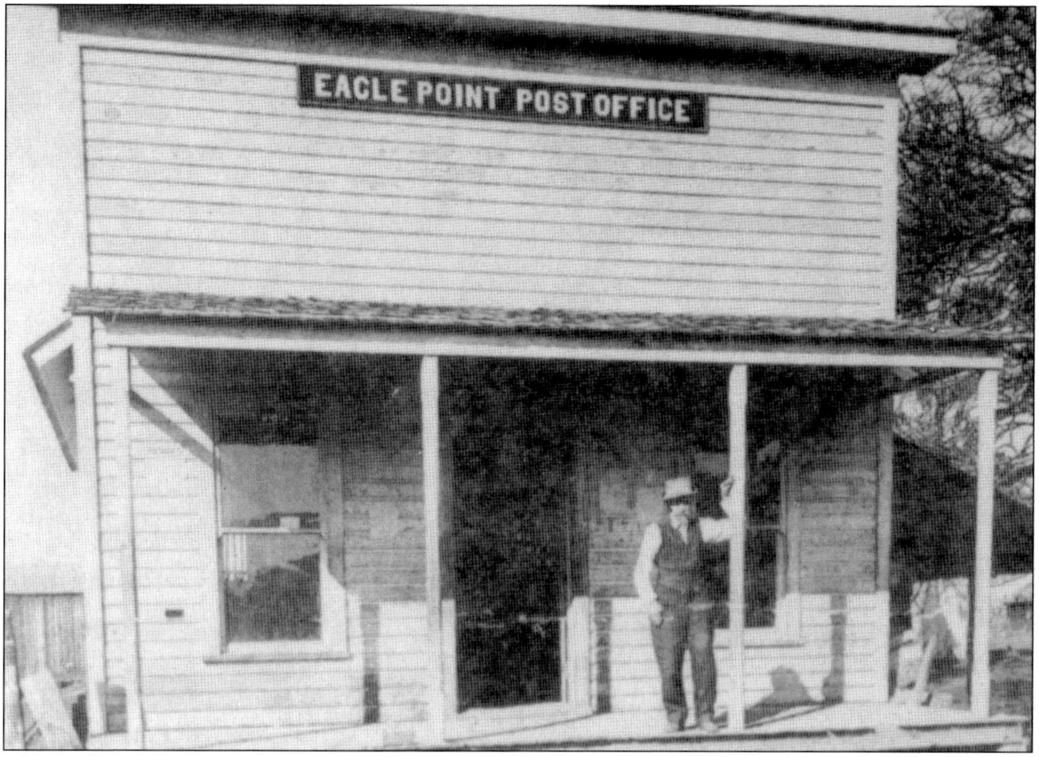

The Eagle Point post office was established on April 25, 1872, with Andrew McNeil serving as the first postmaster. The townsfolk headed down to the post office each day in hopes that a letter from home or other good news might be waiting for them. About an hour before the mail was due to be delivered, the men would wander down to the post office. Royal Brown could be heard singing "Old Father Grimes" as he walked to the post office. The post office became a favorite gathering place where the locals swapped stories and caught up on the news of the day.

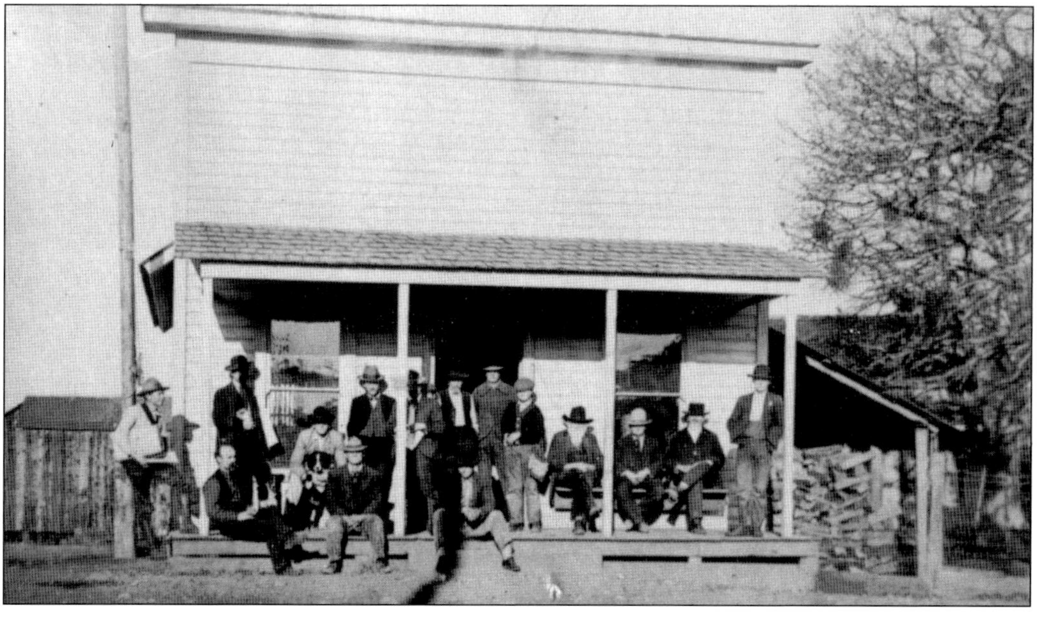

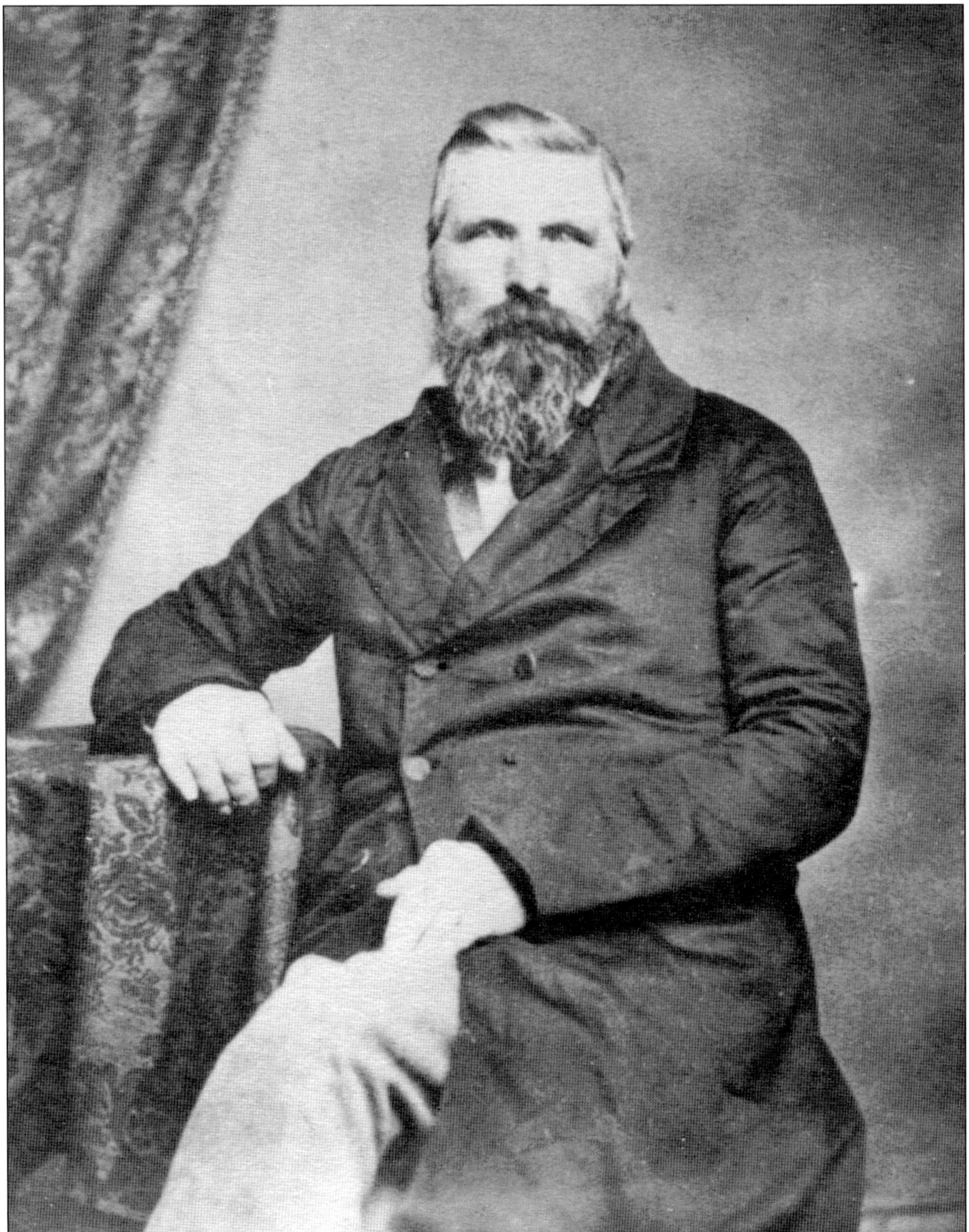

John W. Daley (pictured) and his partner Eber Emery opened the first flour mill along Little Butte Creek in 1872. The partners already owned the Ashland Woolen Mills, which was 30 miles from Eagle Point in Ashland. The flour mill was named Snowy Butte Mill and was operated by John's son Adoniram. He ran the mill for 20 years, then sold it to the Holmes brothers. Later, the Brandon brothers took over the operation. The mill then sat idle for several years until George Putnam and his sons Ed and Francis bought the mill and the surrounding quarter of an acre of land for $600 in 1932. The Putnams operated the mill for the next 40 years.

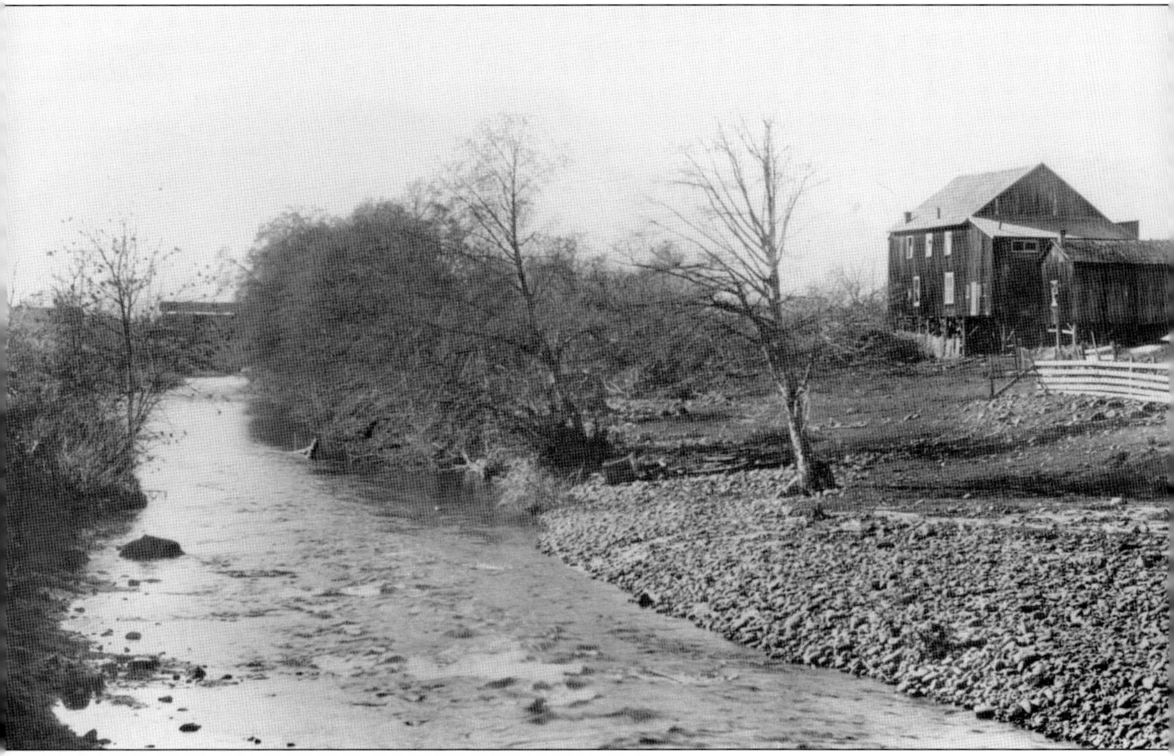

The three-story mill was built from logs felled using hand saws and double-bitted axes. Each of the 1400-pound stones for the mill were quarried in France, assembled in Illinois, and then shipped around Cape Horn. Once the stones arrived in Crescent City they were brought to Eagle Point by freight wagons. To start the milling process, the water in the millrace flows into a penstock that is 12 feet deep. At that point, its weight provides enough pressure to activate the turbine, which in turn powers the wheels, pulleys, and belts. The mill stones then begin turning and the milling process begins. By never allowing the stones to touch, the miller ensures that only the grain, the bran, and the germ are blended together. Today, the mill is known as Butte Creek Mill and still turns out a quality product.

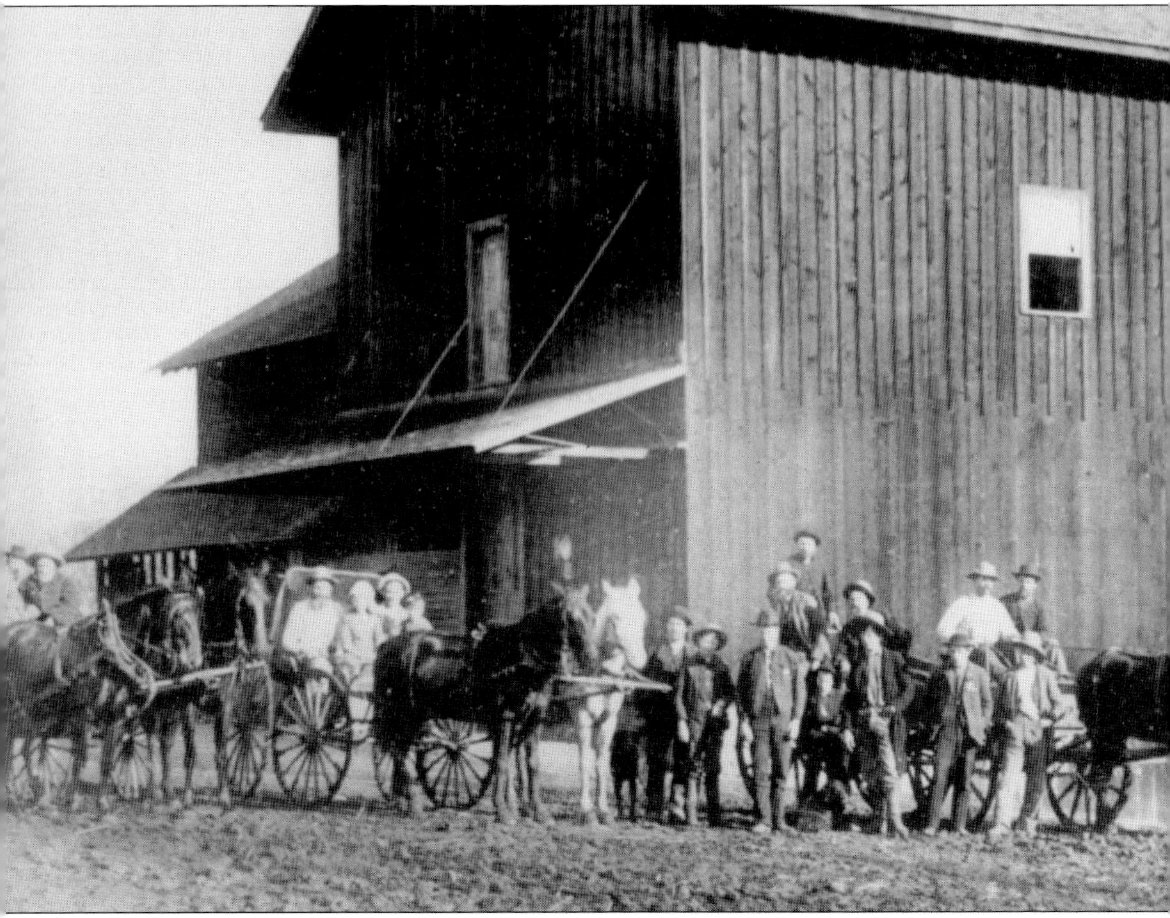

In October 1872, construction got underway on the Snowy Butte Mill. An announcement ran in the Jacksonville newspaper on August 30, 1873, stating, "Flouring mill in operation. The first wheat ran through the cleaner and dried." Just days later, the mill announced, "We are now ready to receive wheat in store and will commence grinding on the 10th. Our terms for grinding will be the eighth bushel, or exchange."

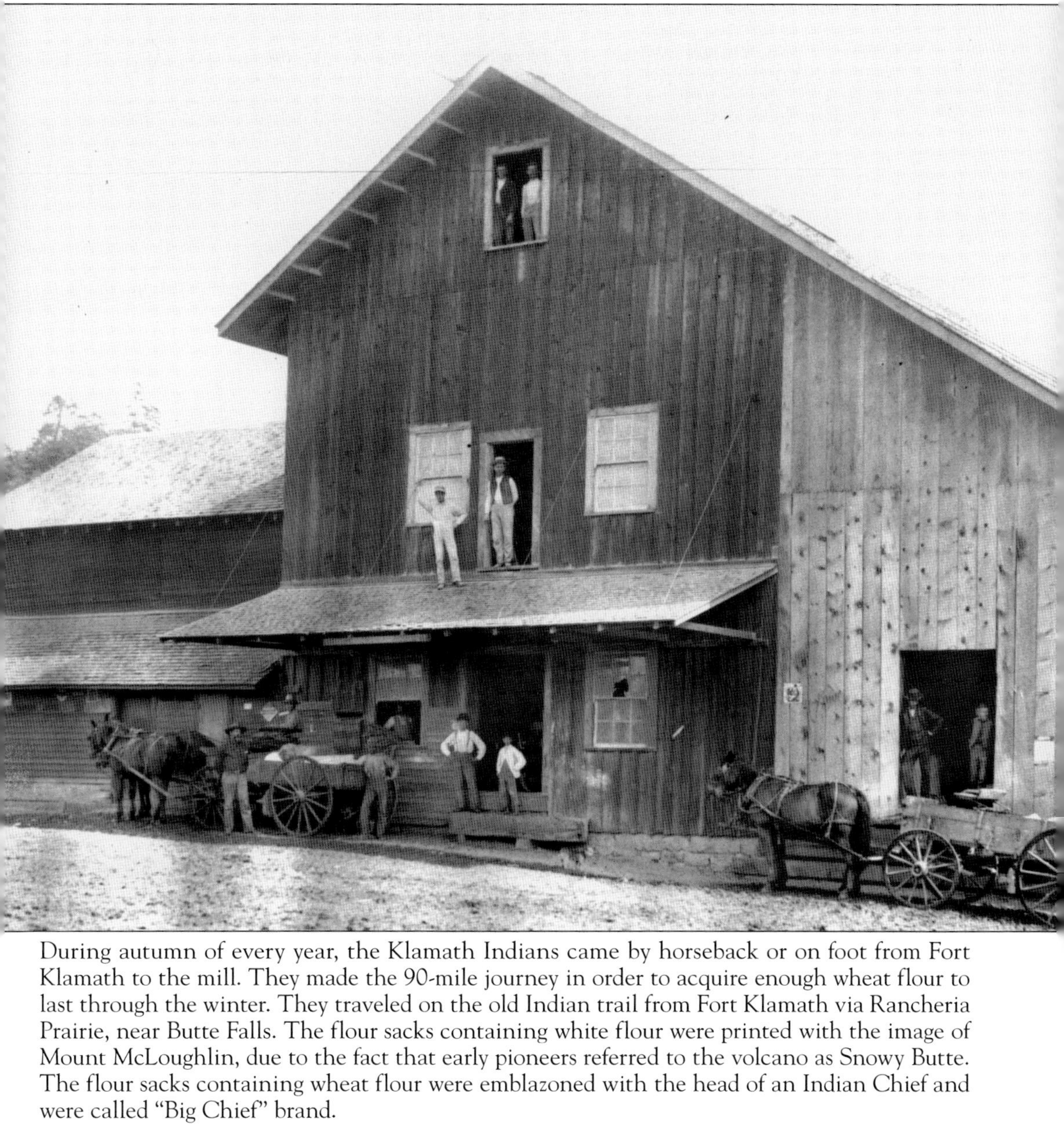

During autumn of every year, the Klamath Indians came by horseback or on foot from Fort Klamath to the mill. They made the 90-mile journey in order to acquire enough wheat flour to last through the winter. They traveled on the old Indian trail from Fort Klamath via Rancheria Prairie, near Butte Falls. The flour sacks containing white flour were printed with the image of Mount McLoughlin, due to the fact that early pioneers referred to the volcano as Snowy Butte. The flour sacks containing wheat flour were emblazoned with the head of an Indian Chief and were called "Big Chief" brand.

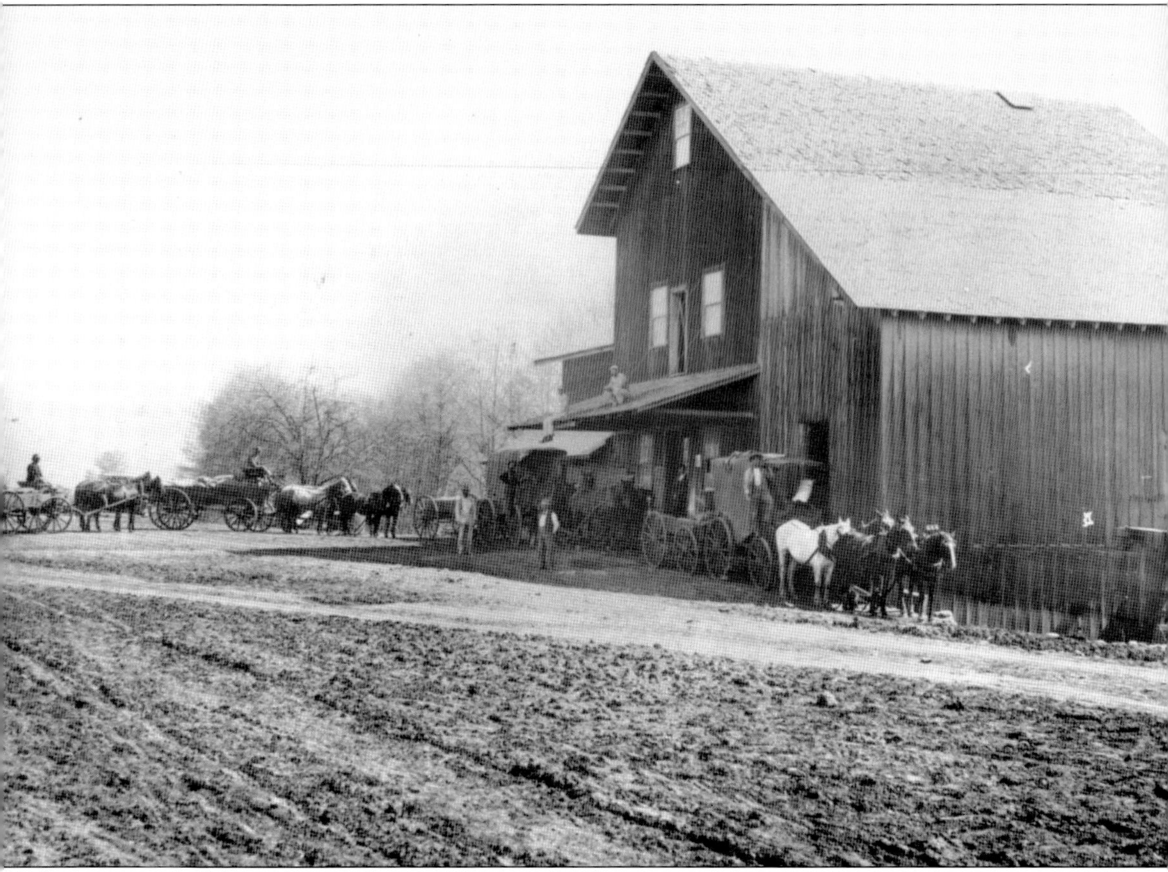

The photograph above shows the traffic jams that occurred during harvest season as the farmers lined up to unload their wheat at the mill.

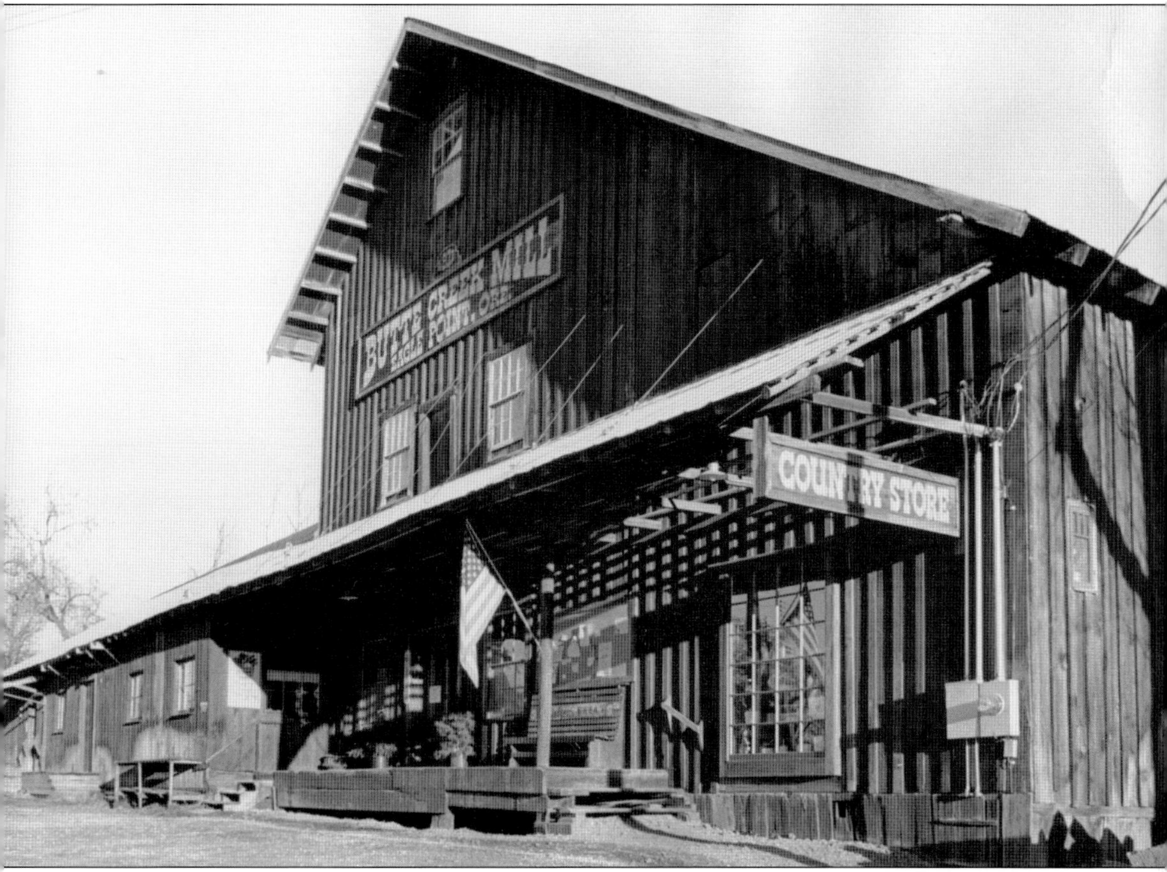

The Branden brothers owned the mill during World War I, and on May 3, 1918, the *Medford Mail Tribune* reported, "Branden brothers have recently received 3,000 bushels of wheat from Sam's Valley and have been running the Snowy Butte Mill full capacity day and night to fill a government contract for 70,000 bushels of flour." The Branden brothers filled many orders for the government during World War I.

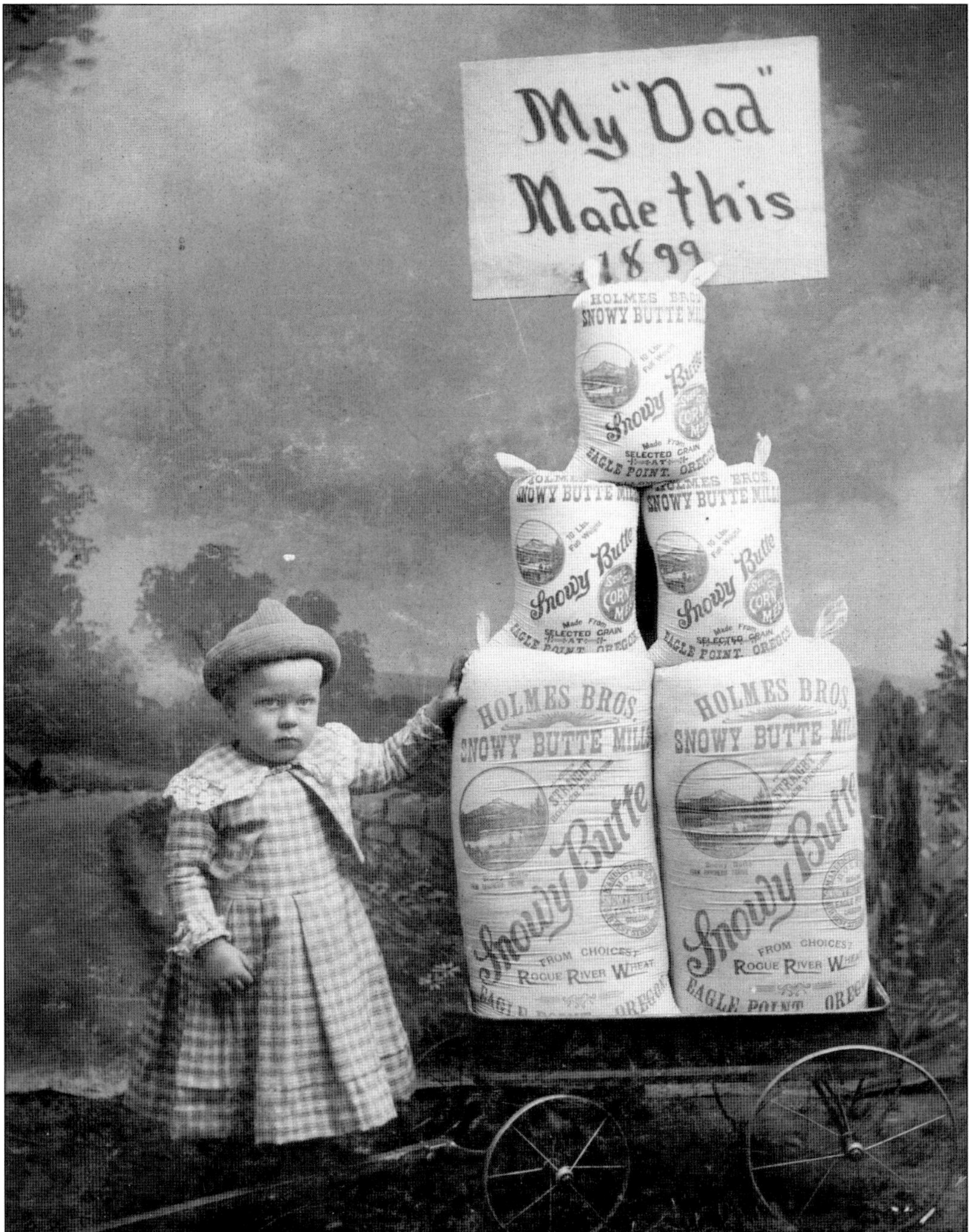

When the Holmes brothers operated the flour mill, they had the best salesperson around.

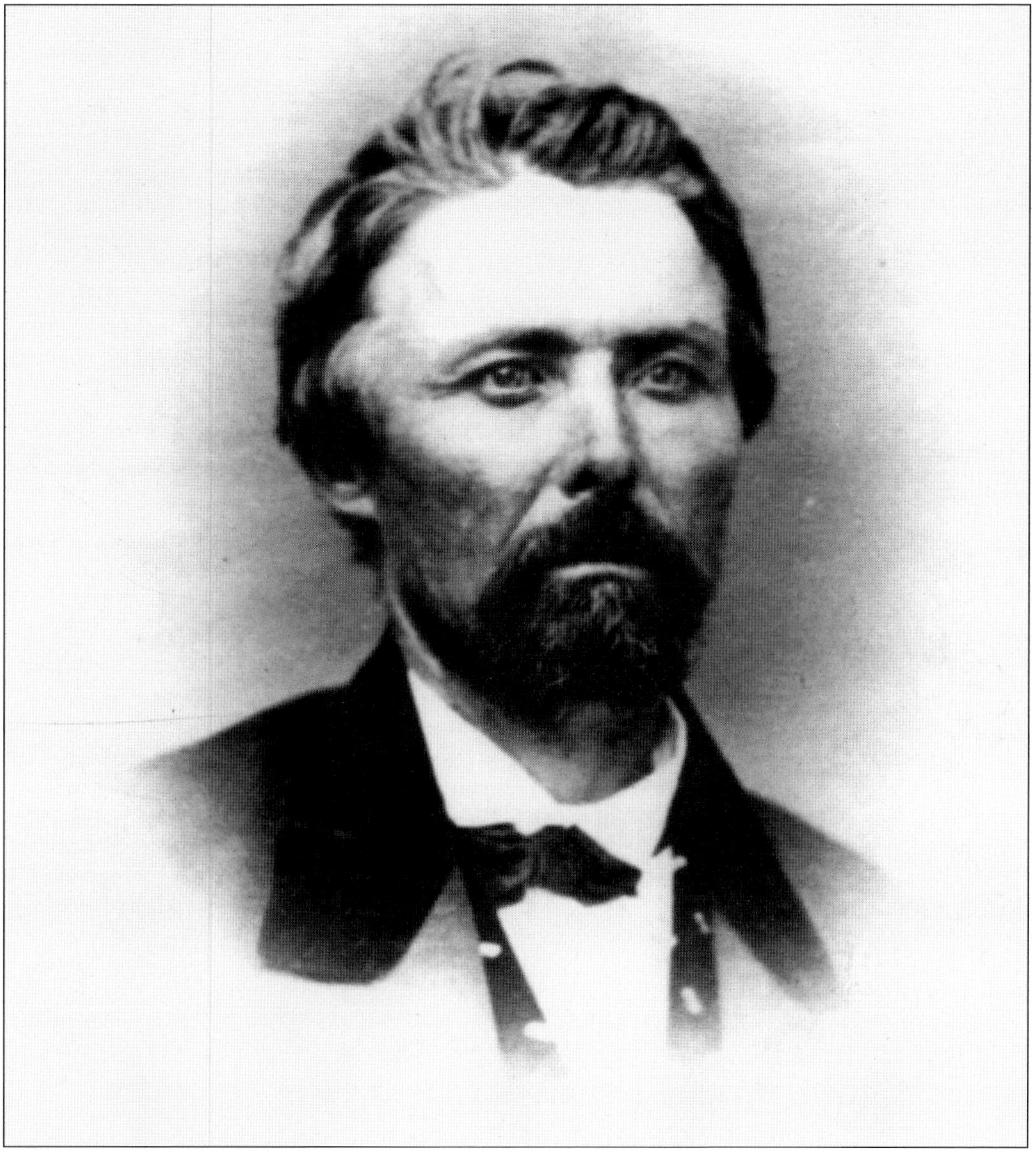

In 1852, Henry Brown sailed around Cape Horn with his brother Robert in search of a new beginning out West. Henry first began mining outside of Jacksonville but then took out a donation land claim along Little Butte Creek in 1854. The area was just outside of Eagle Point, and the brothers named the area Brownsboro. Henry built his home and barns, and soon began ranching and farming. In 1859, he made a trip back to Wisconsin to fetch his mother and bring her to Oregon. Before leaving Wisconsin, Henry married Martha Mary Beamsley. Henry's description of the opportunities and beauty in Oregon made his other brothers Richard, George, and William decide to join him in Oregon as well. Henry and his bride were joined on the trip overland by Henry's mother, Celia (age 70), his brothers, George's wife, Mary Jane, their newborn baby, Emily, and Henry's sister Annie. Henry also brought along 12 Morgan mares and two stallions.

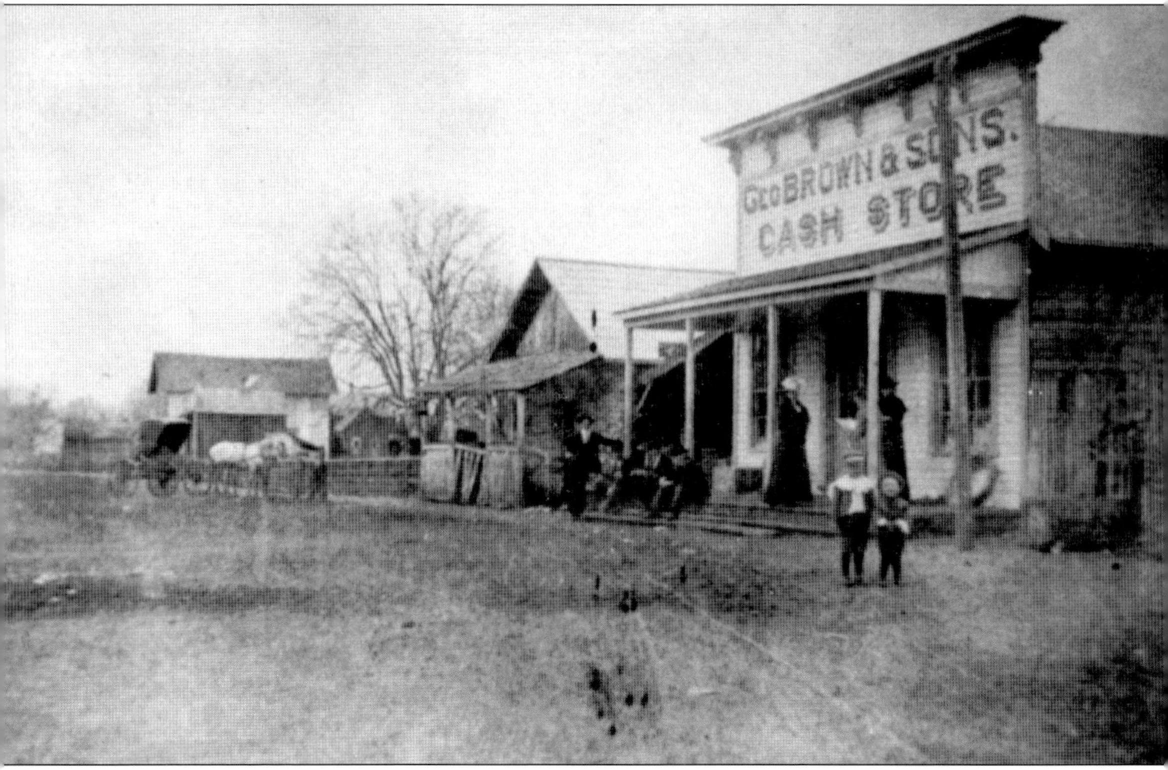

In the early 1870s, Henry and Robert operated Brown's General Merchandise in Brownsboro. It wasn't long before Robert noticed business was booming in Eagle Point. The brothers decided to move their store to Eagle Point. In 1885, Robert sold his share of the business to his brother George. George and his wife, Mary, had 11 children. Over the next few years, George's sons Frank and William joined the business and the store was renamed Geo. Brown & Sons Cash Store. The store remained in the family until 1952.

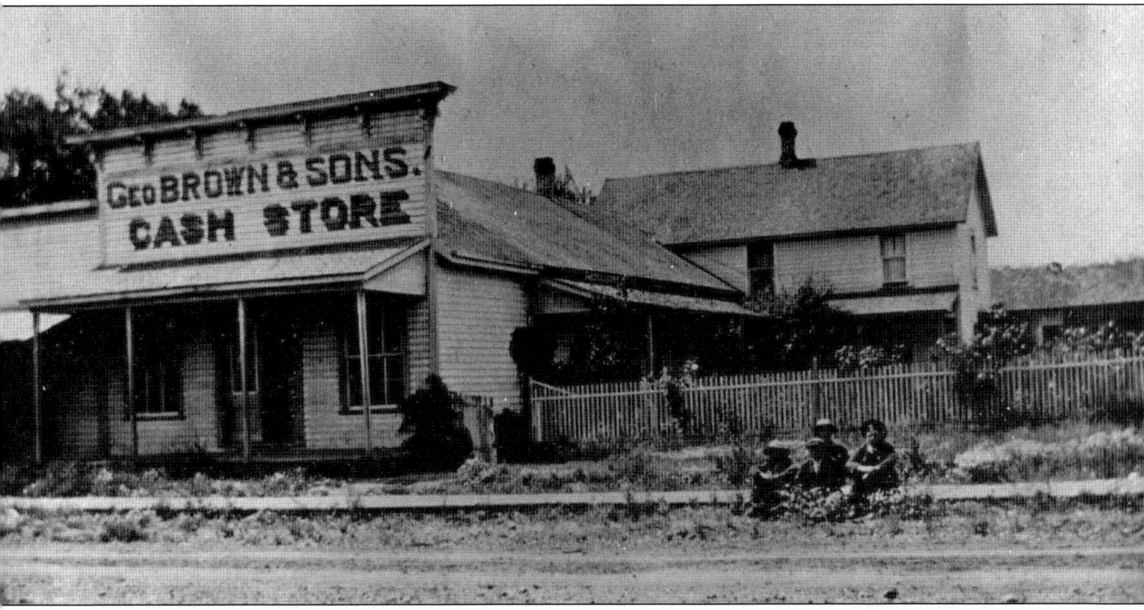

A glance through Mr. Brown's store ledger from 1875 shows that Aaron Wyland purchased 15 yards of dress material, buttons, thread, some lead, and a slate for $4.43; five days before Christmas, Mr. Wooley purchased some whiskey at a cost of $1.25; Mr. Ragsdale sold four pounds of butter to Mr. Brown and received $1; Mr. Lewis received $3.75 for 300 pounds of potatoes; Mr. Simpson paid $2 for 50 pounds of salt; and Mr. Farlow bought seven pounds of nails for 75¢.

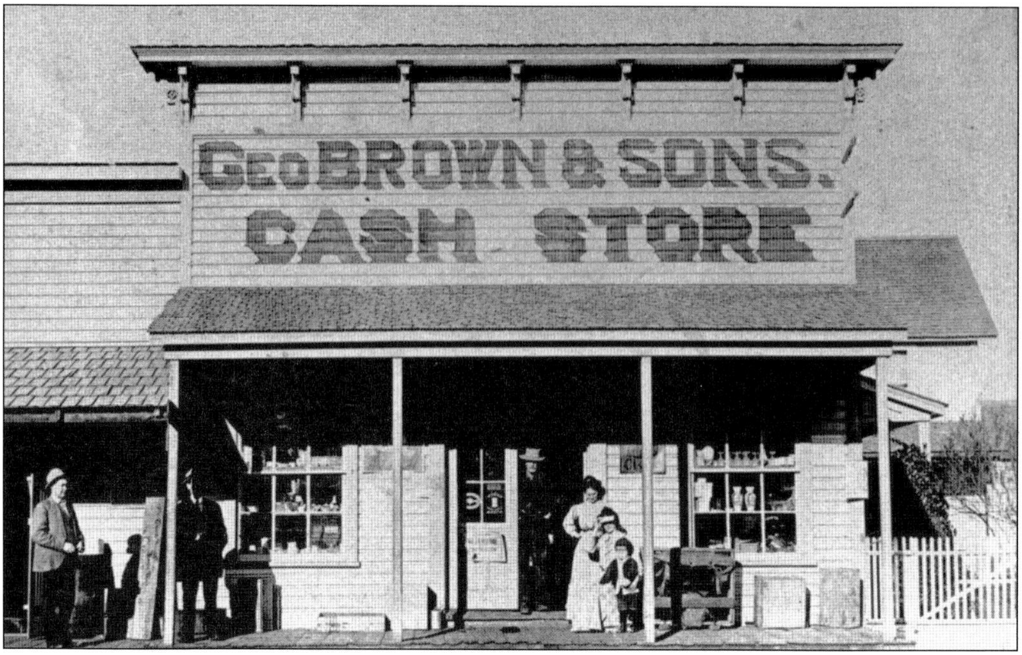

The Geo. Brown & Sons store was a favorite of the locals. On one side of the store, George's sons Frank, Royal, and Bill sold groceries. The other side of the store was dedicated to dry goods. Frank's wife, Amy, and Bill's wife, Mattie, ran that half of the operation. Two black cats, Tom and Jerry, kept a watchful eye on the store when they weren't snoozing by the large pot-bellied stove. Women in town would gather at the store in the afternoon to relax for a few minutes before returning home to finish their chores.

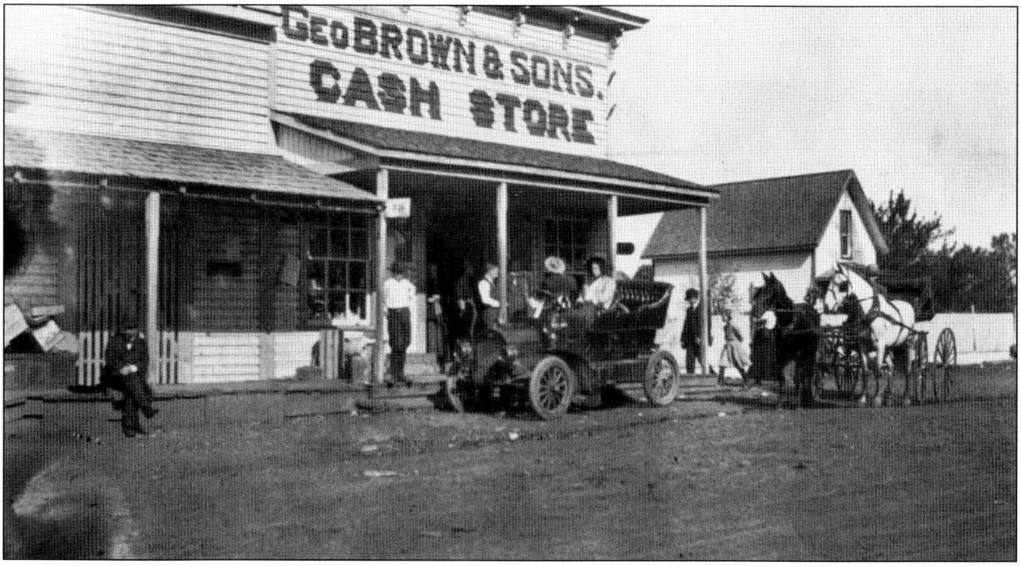

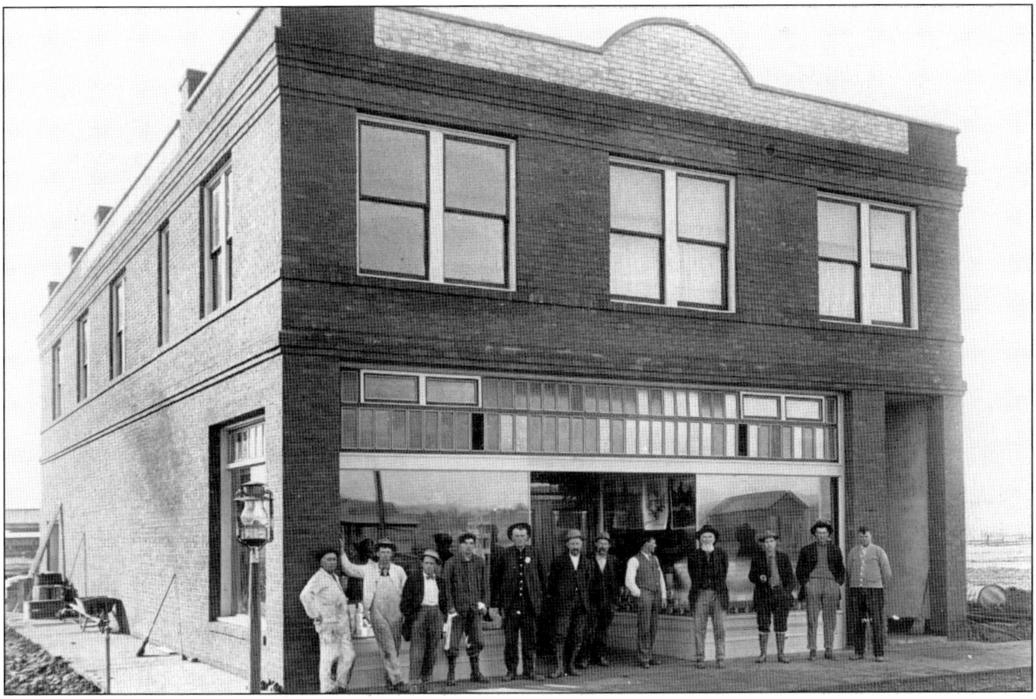

When Geo. Brown & Sons' newest store (above) was still under construction in 1911, the Browns took a break outside with two of the painters and several of their friends. Below, the Rock Building, as it is known, still stands on North Royal Avenue. It was originally built by the Browns to be used as a cold storage facility for their nearby store.

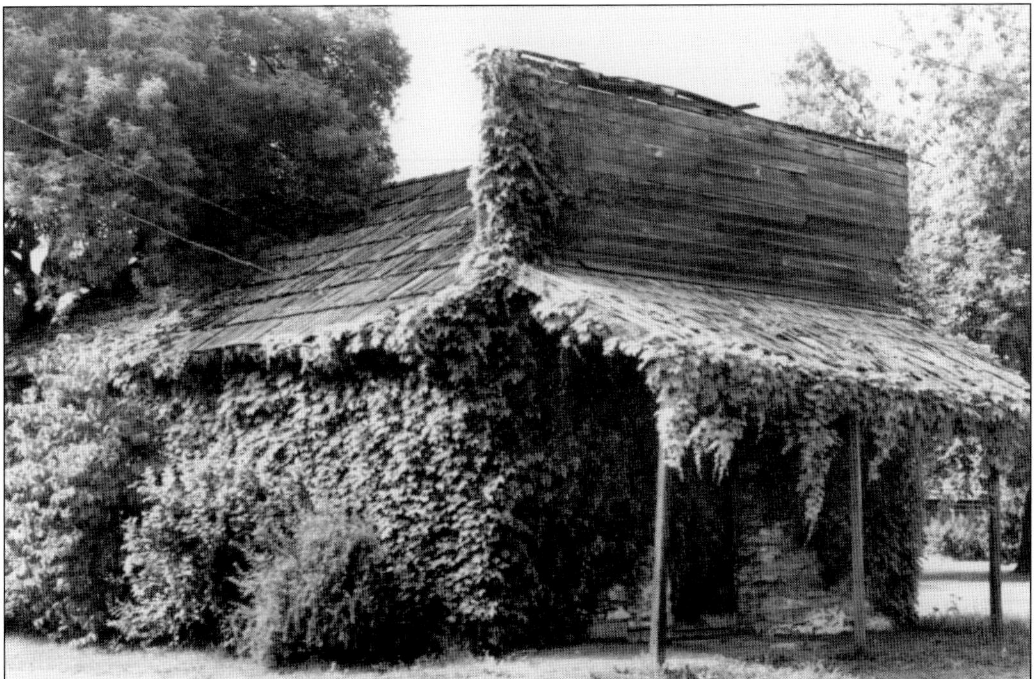

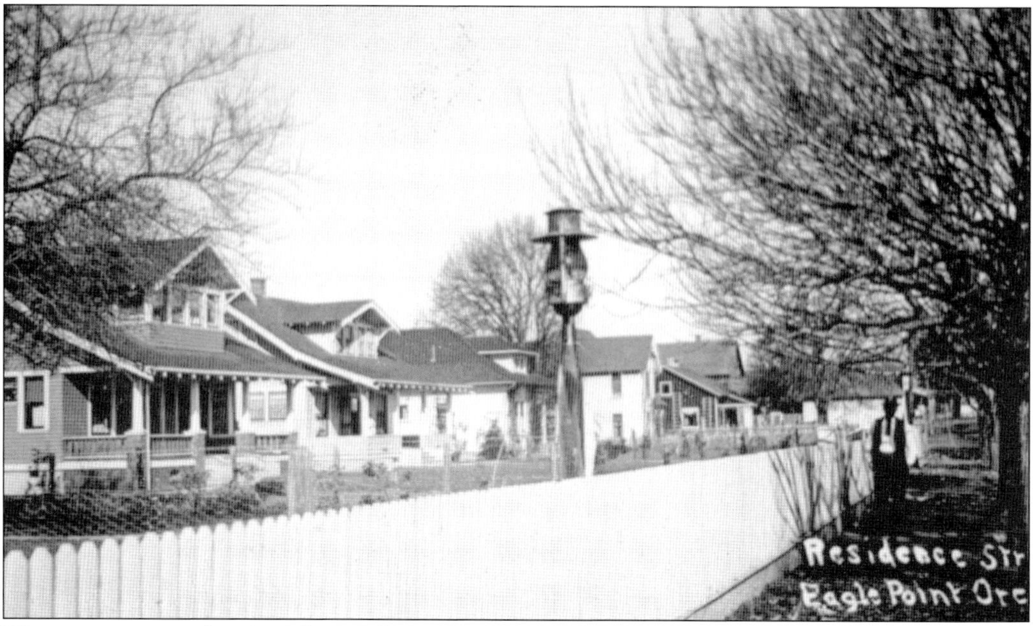

There was a time when North Royal Avenue was known as "Millionaire's Row" due to the stately homes that lined the street.

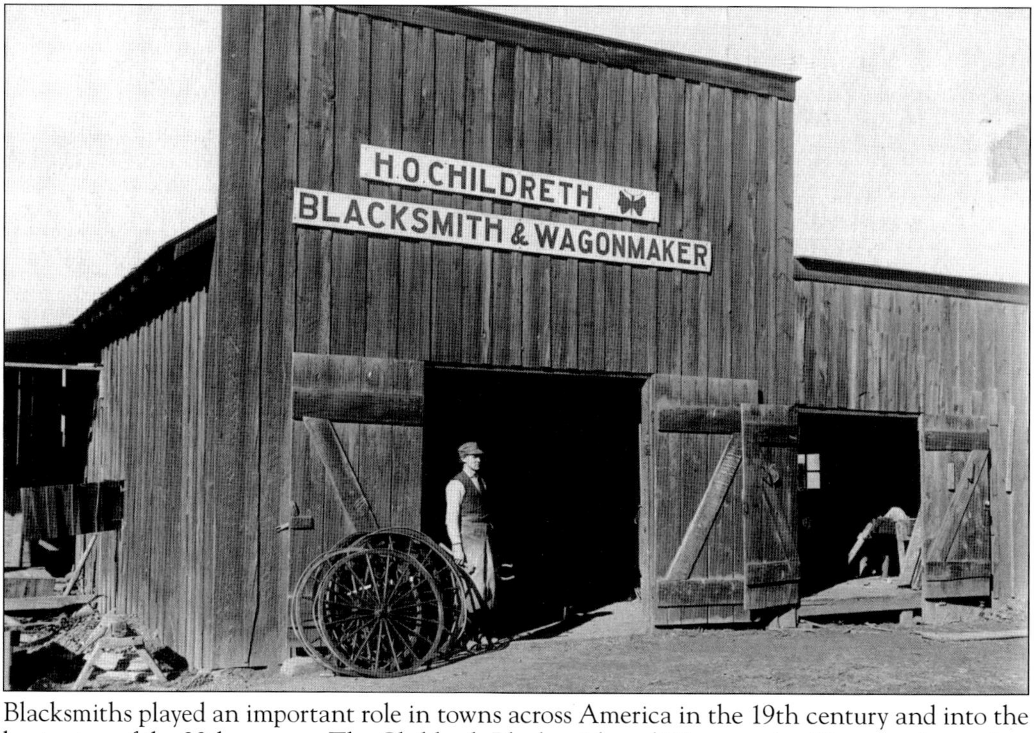

Blacksmiths played an important role in towns across America in the 19th century and into the beginning of the 20th century. The Childreth Blacksmith and Wagonmaker Shop was located on Main Street. In what was a true sign of the times, Wes Childreth received training as an automobile mechanic and began a new career repairing automobiles when they began replacing horses.

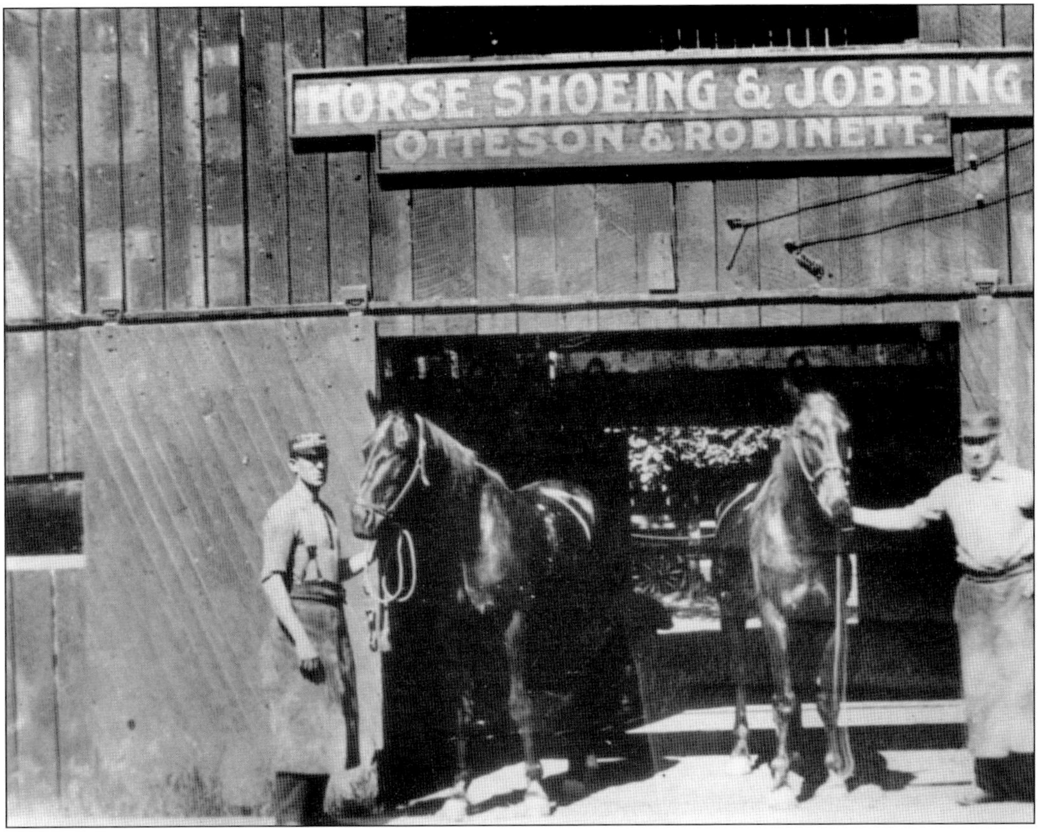

Otteson and Robinett Horse Shoeing & Jobbing did a brisk business before the invention of the automobile. Below, these men are hard at work inside Samuel Robinett's Blacksmith Shop.

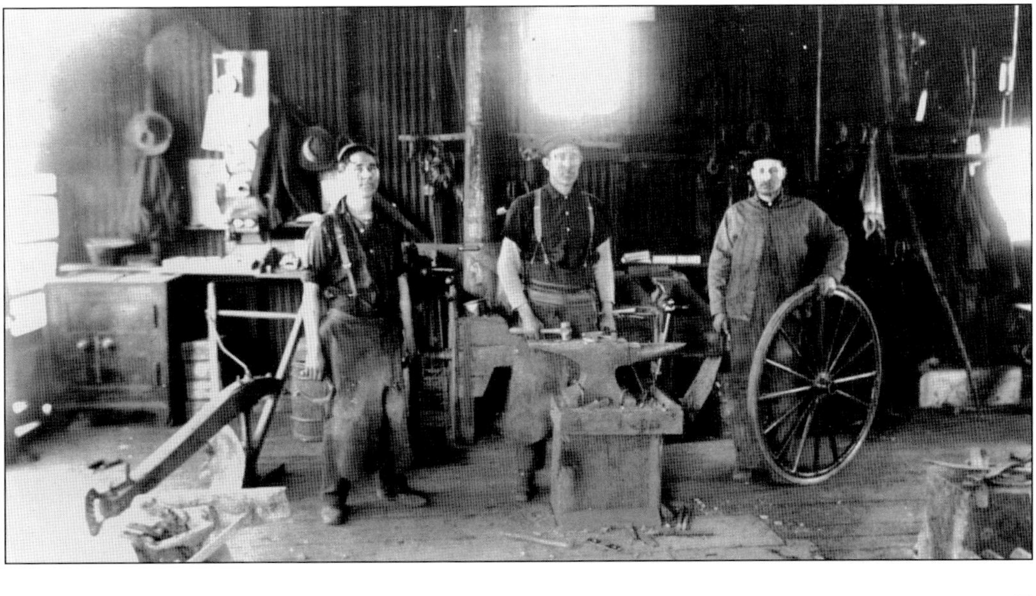

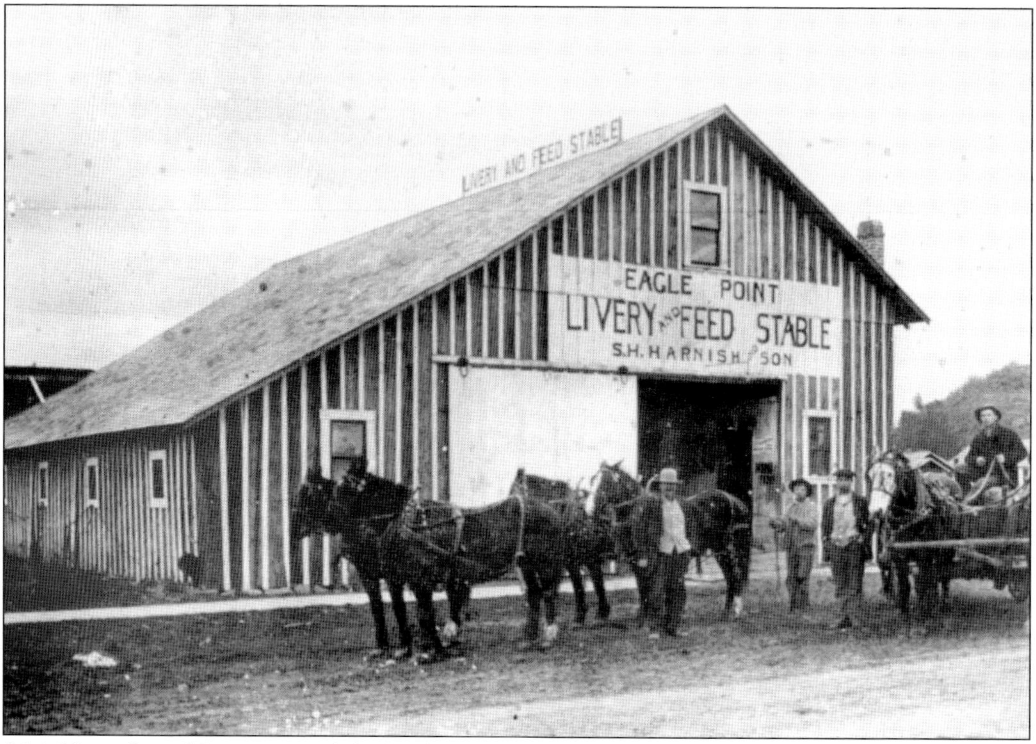

S.M. Harnish and Son operated the Eagle Point Livery and Feed Stable. Previously, Sam Harnish had operated a freight hauling business between Central Point and Eagle Point. He also worked as a mail carrier hauling mail between Eagle Point and Butte Falls with his wagon team. In the 1920s, Sam's wagon teams played an important role in hauling gigantic water pipes from Butte Falls to Medford. In later years, Sam ran a jitney automobile service transporting people between Eagle Point and Medford. His ad read, "S.H. Harnish auto leaves Eagle Point at 8 a.m. and 1 p.m. daily except Sunday. Leaves Medford 9 a.m. and 5 p.m. Calls for passengers at the hotels in Medford, and business houses in Eagle Point."

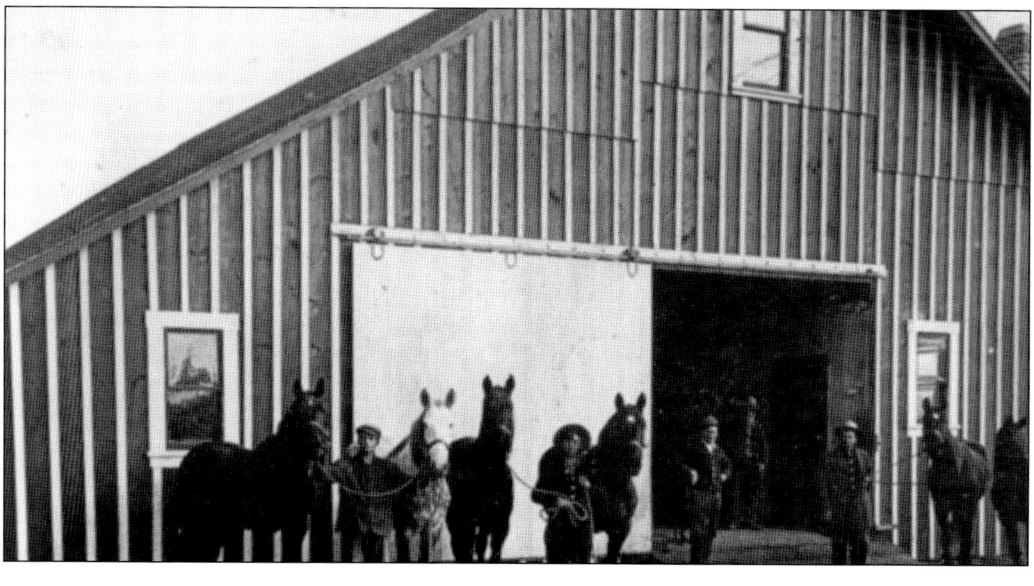

Frank Lewis operated the Lewis Confectionary Store. In addition to fine candy, there was also a large soda fountain. Frank had previously owned a pool hall. Soon after acquiring the business from his brother-in-law Jerry, the *Medford Mail Tribune* reported, "Mr. Lewis promises to keep a respectable house, and says that he will not allow any gambling, and no whiskey." Pictured here are Ray Harnish, Jerry Lewis, and Ed Cingcade.

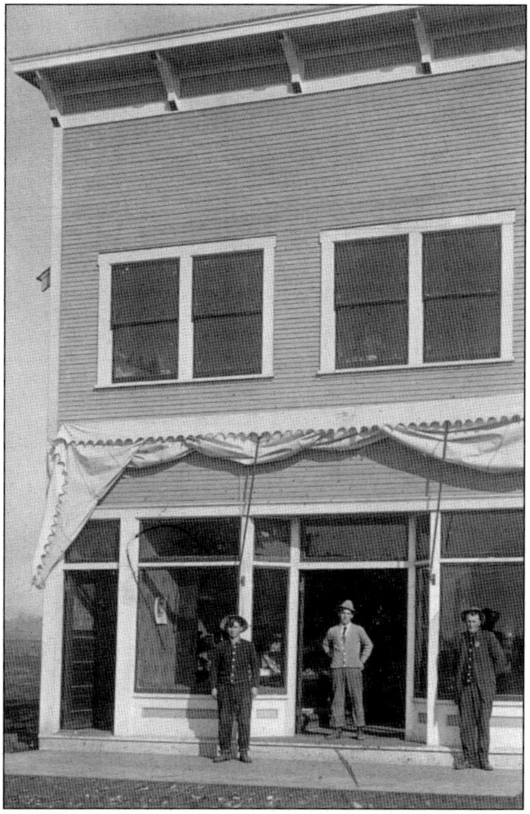

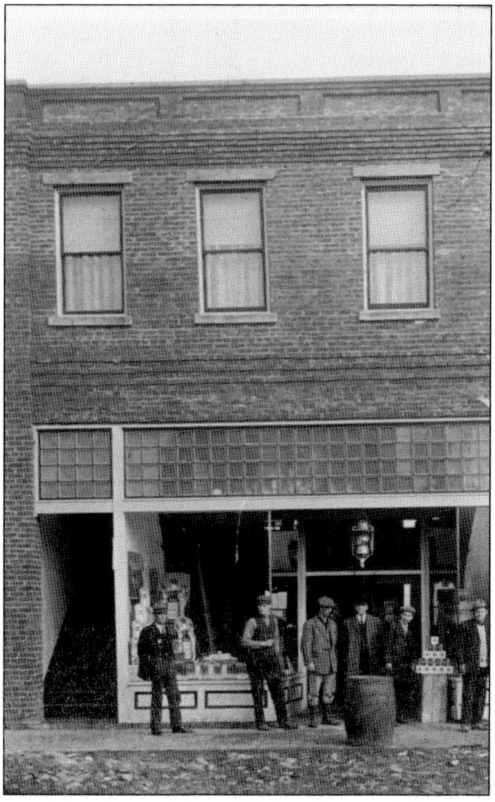

The Von der Hellen's Hardware store is pictured in 1911. The hardware store was a popular place for the local men to discuss politics and the happenings of the day. For a time, the Von der Hellen Hardware Store rented space to Doctor Holt. He saw patients upstairs and shared the downstairs with the hardware store. In addition to selling patent medicines, he sold schoolbooks, perfume, and rock candy.

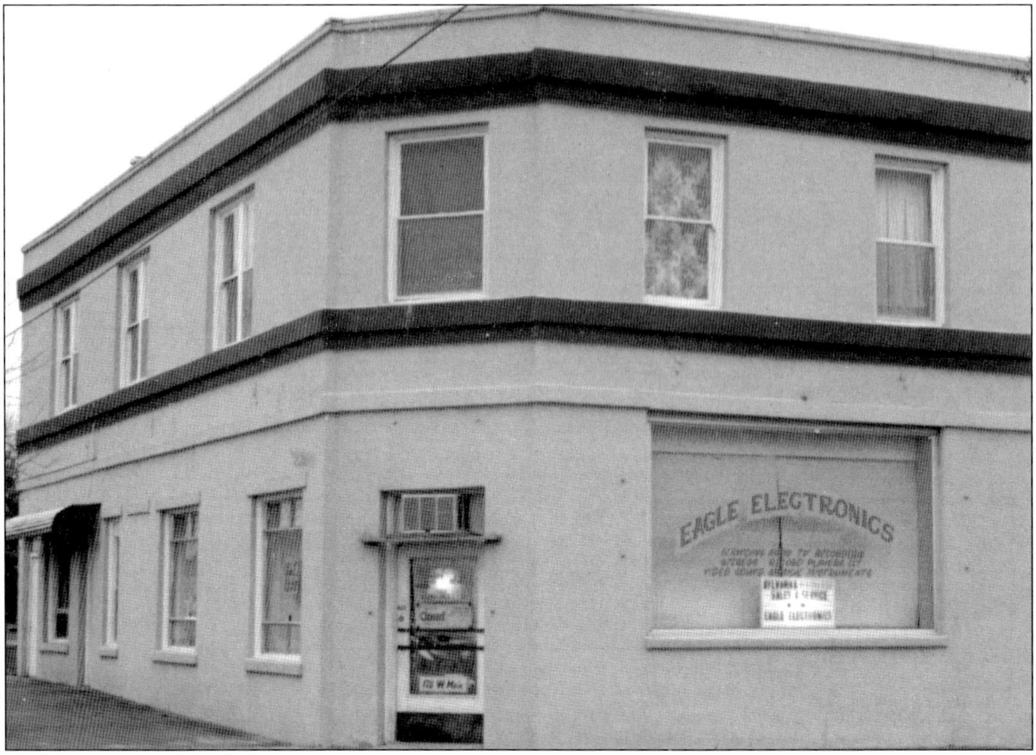

The First State Bank (formerly housed in the building pictured above) opened in 1911 in downtown Eagle Point. It may have been a small-town bank, but it was one of only three banks in Oregon that did not need to close down during the national banking crisis of 1933. While the rest of the country was experiencing banks defaulting and shutting their doors, this little bank proved it was stable. The First State Bank applied for and was accepted as the 24th bank in the United States to become a member of the Federal Deposit Insurance Corporation. In later years, the bank moved to Medford.

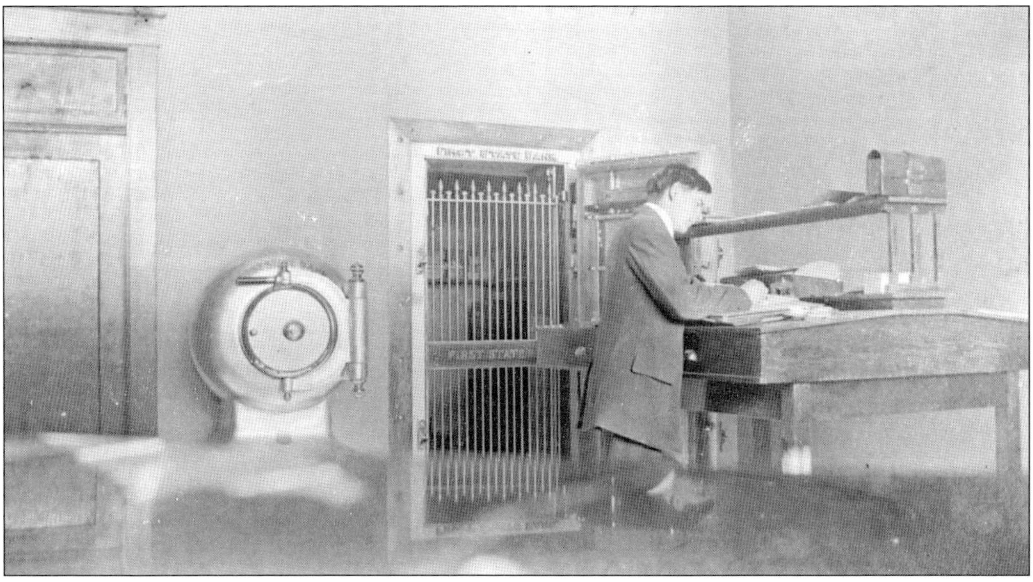

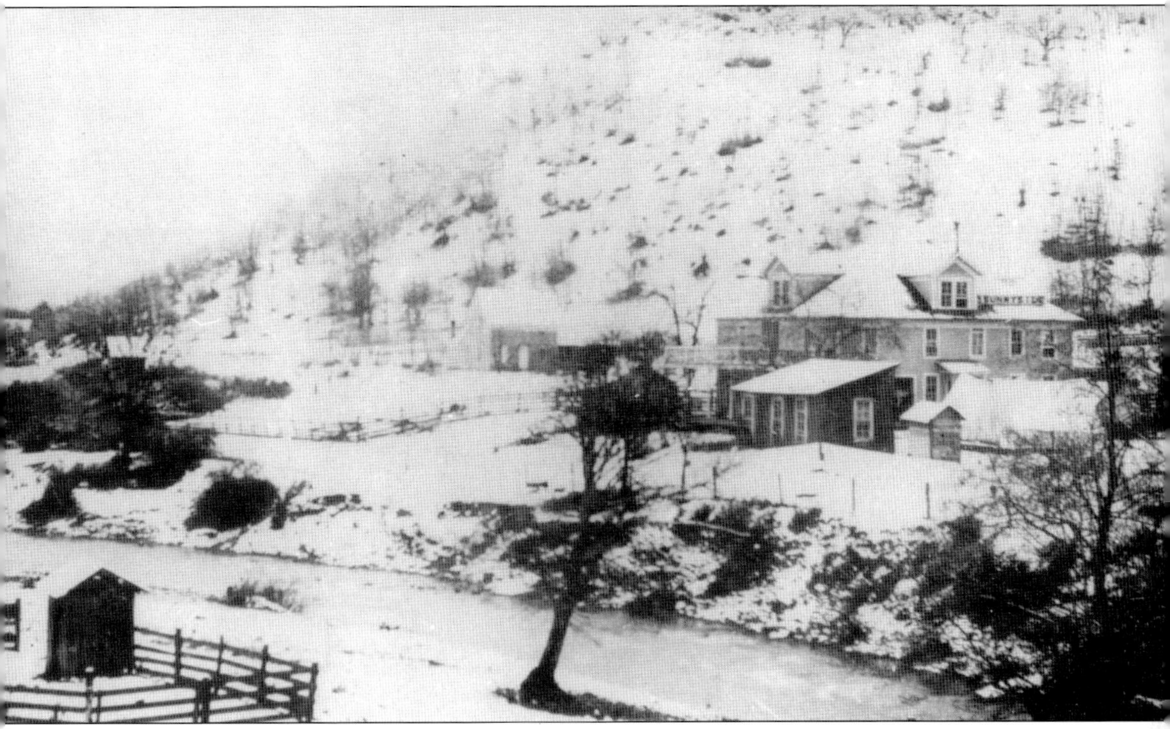

One of the most successful businesses in Eagle Point was the Sunnyside Hotel. Alfred and Sarah "Ma" Howlett built a small house on Little Butte Creek. One evening, a gentleman showed up unannounced and asked if he could spend the night. The Howletts welcomed him into their home, and the next morning Ma fixed him a big breakfast followed by a full lunch. By the time dinner rolled around, the stranger announced he would be moving in. Before Ma knew it, a friend of his moved in, followed by yet another friend. Soon Ma realized that she was running a boardinghouse, and she began charging 25¢ per meal.

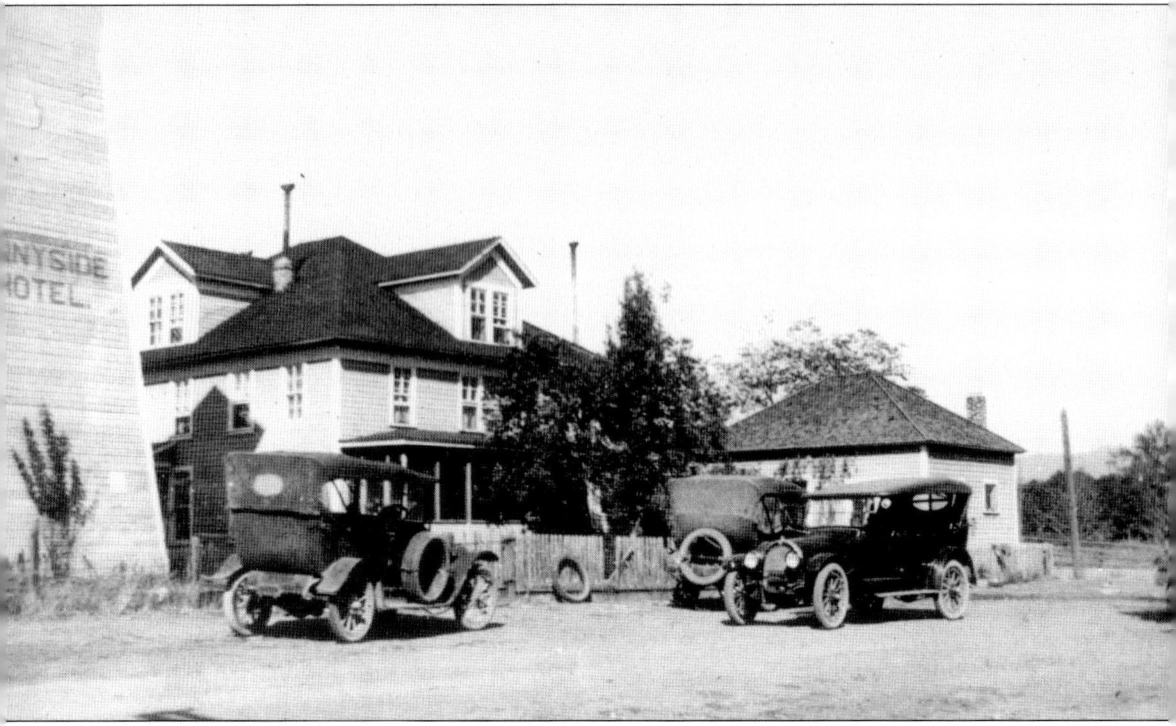

Realizing the demand for a good hotel, the Howletts opened the Sunnyside Hotel on North Shasta Avenue. The three-story hotel offered 18 rooms for visitors. Since the hotel was near the train depot, the Howletts built a wooden sidewalk in front of the hotel so women would not drag their dresses through the mud when going to and from the train. Ma Howlett became quite famous around town for her Sunday meals, and soon the hotel became a popular dining room. It wasn't just dinner that brought the locals out, since the Sunnyside Hotel became quite the social scene as well. There were dances, taffy pulls, husking bees (when folks showed up and husked their corn together), carpet rag tacking (when people made rag rugs together), quilting bees, parties, and weddings. On the Fourth of July in 1912, more than 225 people enjoyed an afternoon meal and festivities at the hotel.

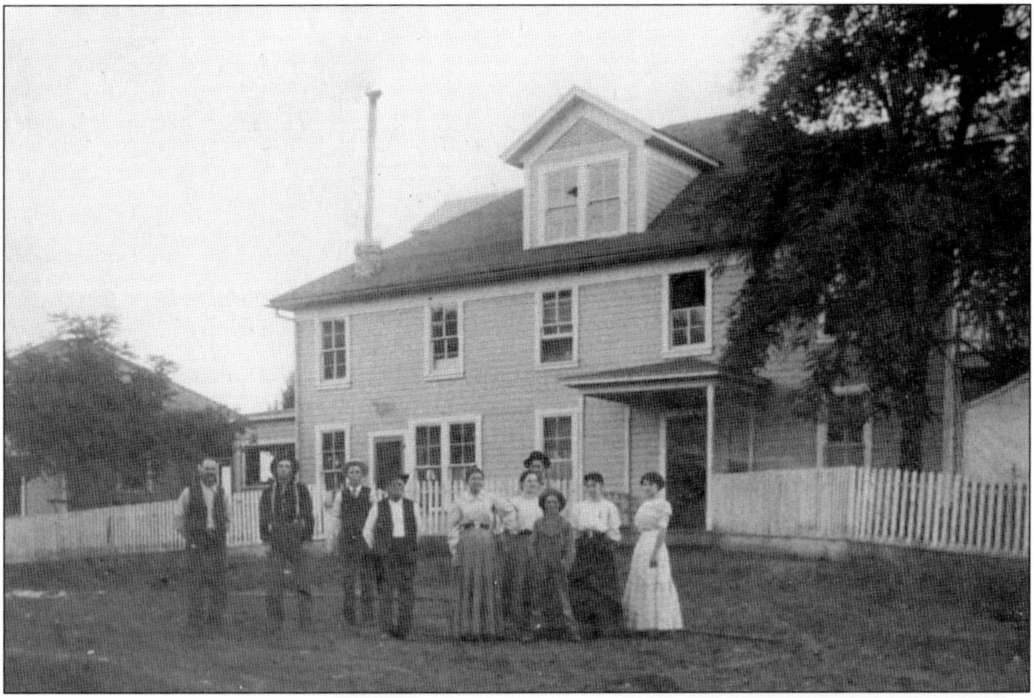

Above is a photograph of the Sunnyside Hotel and on the right is a family portrait. Alfred Howlett wrote a newspaper column that ran in the *Medford Mail Tribune* for many years. He also had a career as a minister and a teacher. Over the years, the Howletts had 13 children. Ma operated the hotel by herself for 12 years after Alfred died. Her children and neighbors helped out during the busy times. After Ma died, the hotel, a barn, nine lots, and 20 acres were sold for $1,500.

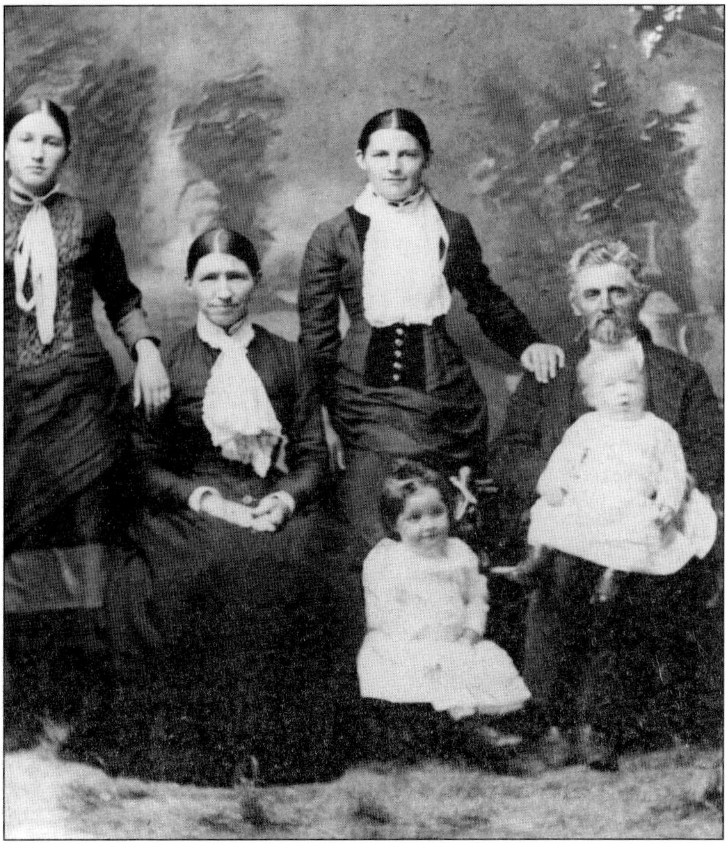

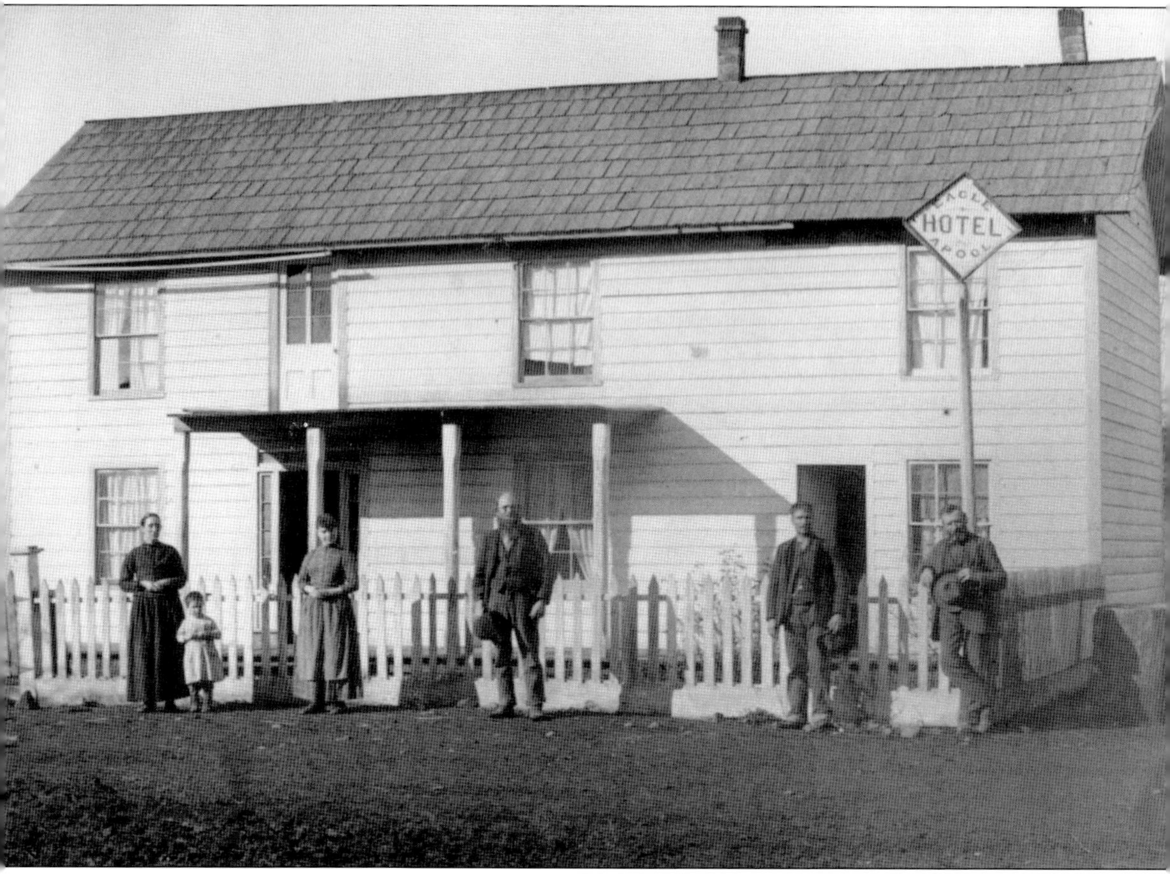

Art Poole and his first wife, Alletta, had 11 children. After Alletta's death, Art married Laura Safford, who already had one daughter. Art operated a livery and a blacksmith shop near the Snowy Butte Mill. In 1880, Art was appointed town marshal, and years later, he served as justice of the peace for Eagle Point. Together, Art and Laura ran the Eagle Hotel. Laura was well-known for her fresh huckleberry pies. The Eagle Hotel was a popular place for the locals to enjoy games, socials, and dances.

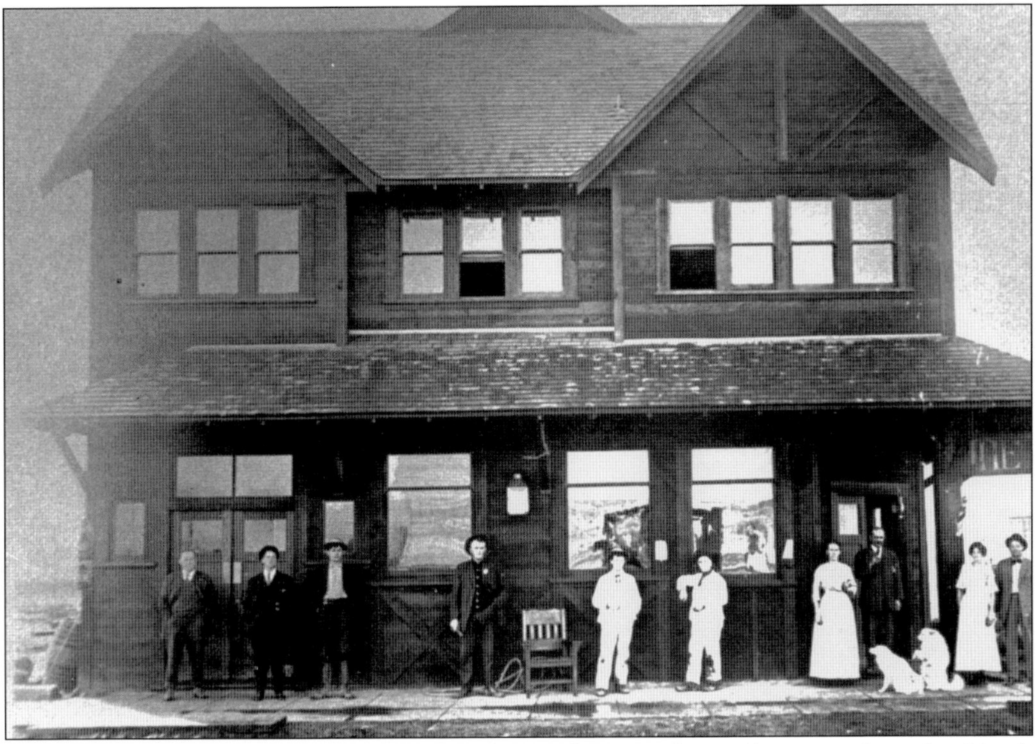

In 1911, the Vogeli Hotel and Saloon opened near the train depot. Four years later, Jim Vogeli closed the hotel, as it was no longer profitable. The saloon remained opened and was renamed the Tavern. The entire building burned to the ground soon after. After the fire, Jim operated the saloon out of an old bakery.

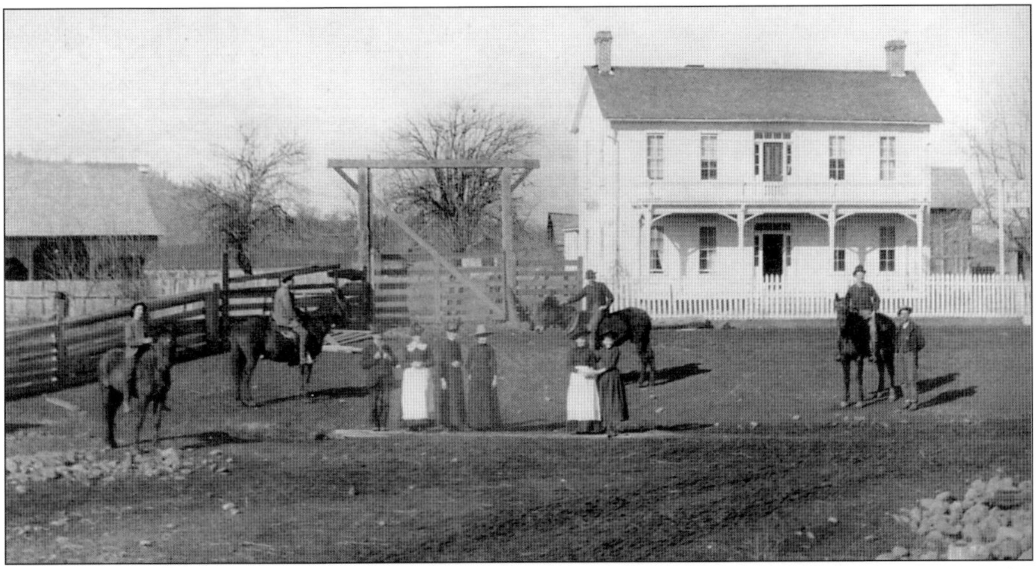

Peter Simon and his wife, Anna, were originally from Germany and arrived in Oregon in 1853. The Simons had 13 children. Peter engaged in ranching, operated a successful bartering and trading business, and had a livery business for a time. The Simons built this beautiful hotel in 1884 and named it Pioneer Hotel. It was a popular place for dances, weddings, and reunions.

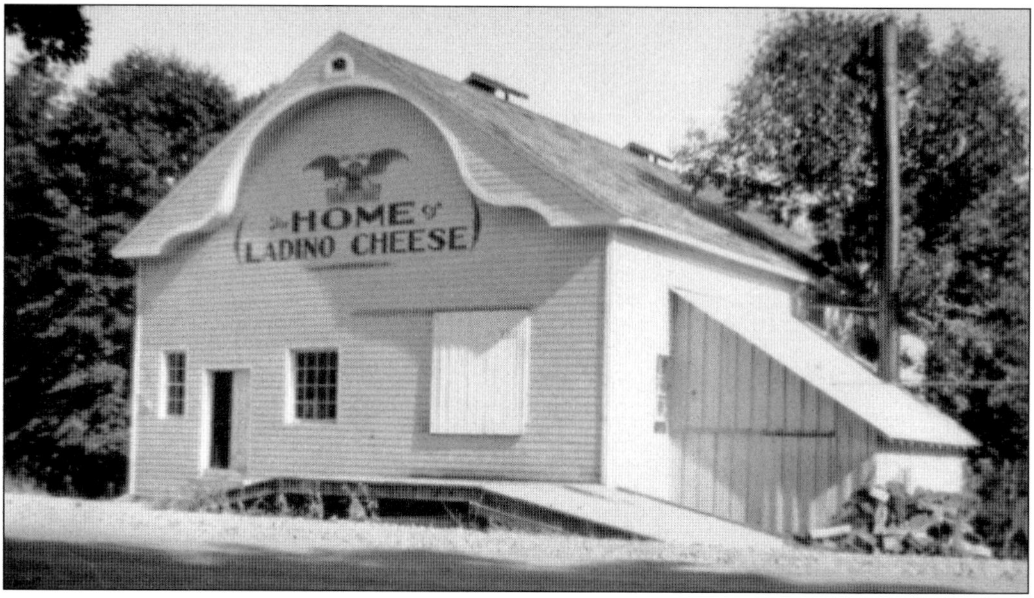

The Ladino Cheese Factory opened in 1895 and was an immediate success. Farmers had a place to sell their cow's milk, and it also provided jobs in the community. The building was originally constructed to serve as a granary for the mill. Since the cheese factory closed, the building has been used by fraternal organizations and has been a movie house, a thrift store, a church, a meeting hall, and an antique store. Known as "Mr. Eagle Point," Sam Coy was born in Eagle Point in 1889. In 1912, Sam married a young lady by the name of Ethel. He worked as a mail carrier for many years, operated a ranch, drove a truck for the Ladino Cheese Factory, and later owned Coy's Ice Cream Place, pictured below. He worked for the City of Eagle Point, serving as the city recorder, treasurer, judge, and even the town marshal.

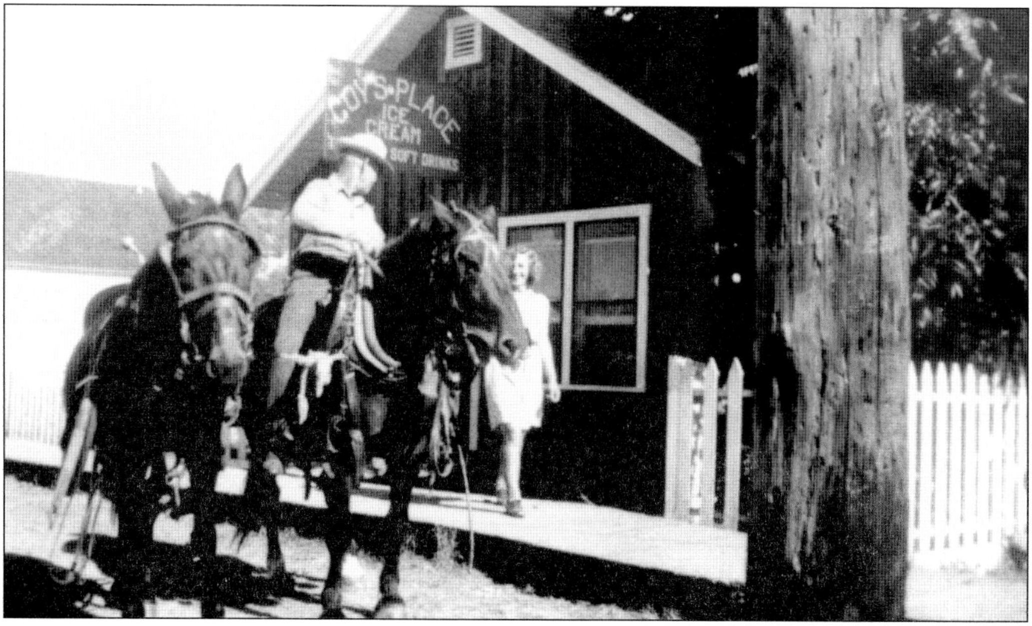

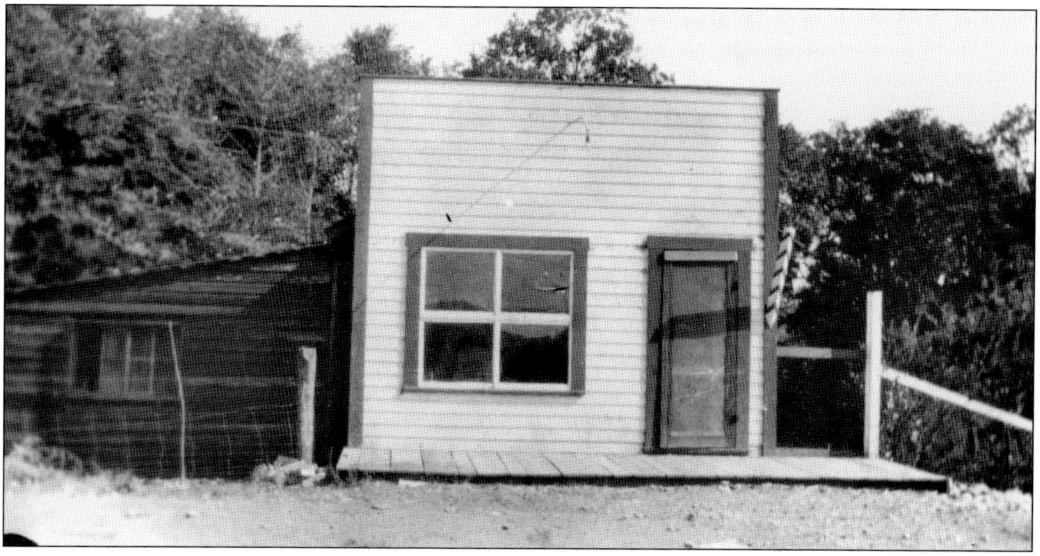

Before Ernie Dahack opened his own barbershop in Eagle Point, he apprenticed in a barbershop in Medford. After finishing work on Saturday, he would walk from Medford all the way home to Eagle Point. On Sunday night, he would leave his house and begin the journey back to Medford. Ernie's first barbershop is pictured above. It started out on one side of Royal Avenue, but one night, he and his friends picked up the building and set it down on the other side of the street. During the Great Depression, Ernie gave free haircuts to little boys before they headed back to school in the fall. In the late 1930s, Ernie had a two-story building constructed. It had a barbershop and a tavern downstairs and living quarters upstairs. The tavern was a favorite of the Camp White soldiers.

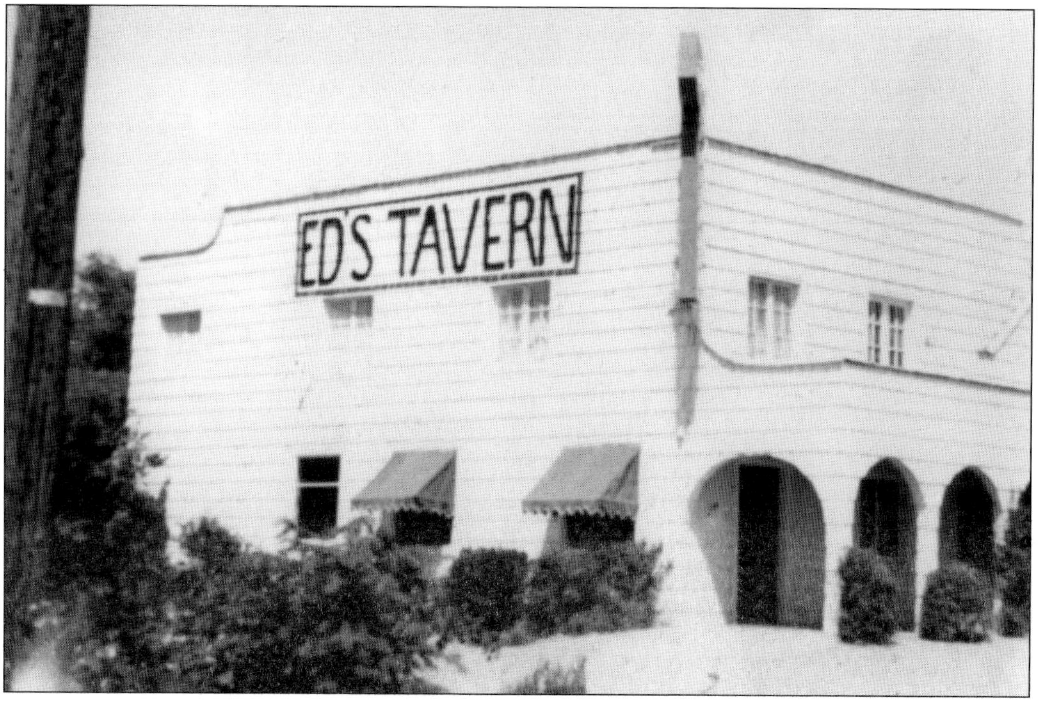

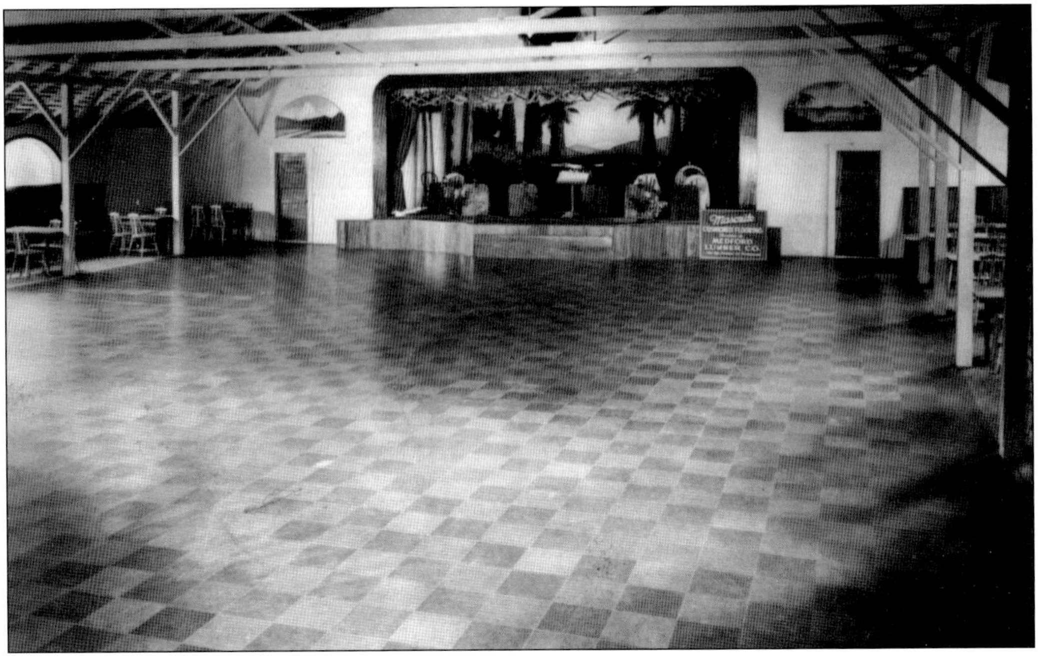

The Cingcade Dance Hall became Ed's Oasis after Ed Dahack took over the business. Ed's Oasis quickly became the most popular spot in town. Ed installed 90 springs underneath the dance floor. Many entertainers made a stop at the Oasis on their way to larger cities. Anna (Carson) Zander recalled, "It was overrun with soldiers during World War II. There were just gobs of soldiers in there." But they weren't just on the inside, as Billy Carlson remembered, "This was a big place during the war. The Army guys used to maneuver and a lot of them liked to get killed near the tavern so they could stop and get a beer."

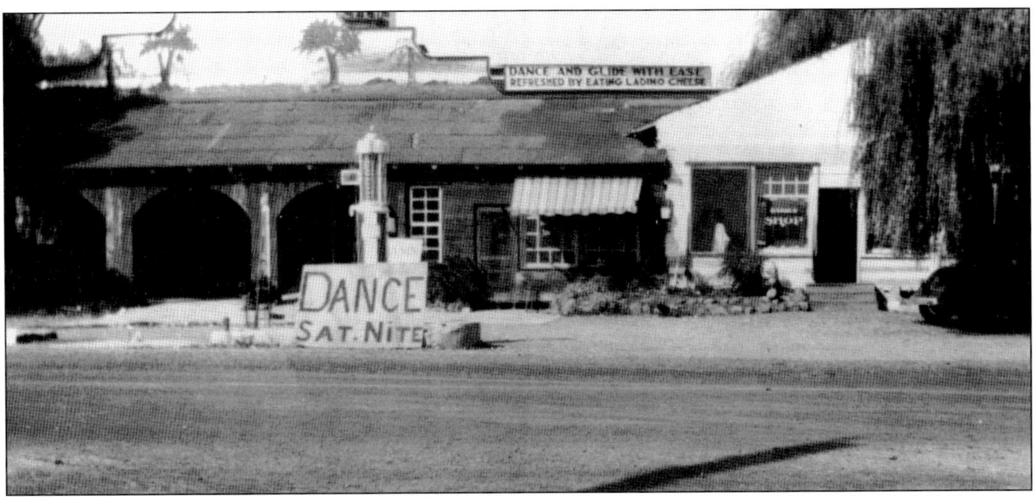

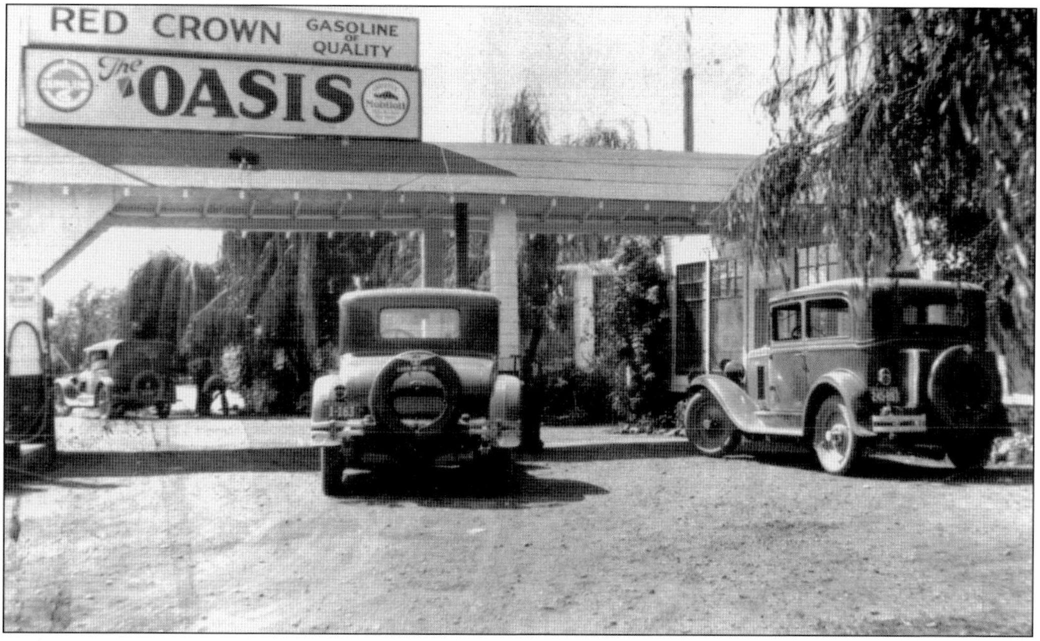

In later years, Ernie Dahack owned the Oasis Gas Station, from which he ran his barbershop. Haircuts cost 50¢ and a shave cost 25¢. Inside the gas station, Ernie displayed a large collection of agates collected locally.

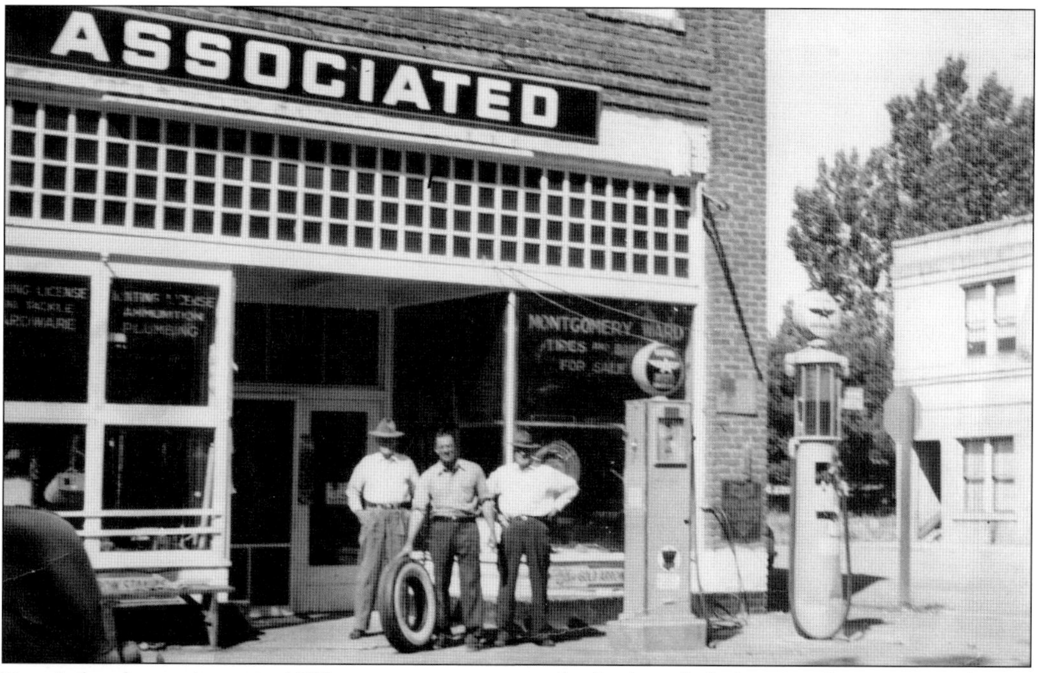

Roy Ashpole was born in 1887 to pioneer parents who had settled along Little Butte Creek. His father, John, was a merchant in Eagle Point. Roy opened a pool hall with his partner, Charles Cingcade, on the corner of Royal and Napa Streets. Later, he and his son Donald operated the Eagle Point Hardware Store and sold gas outside.

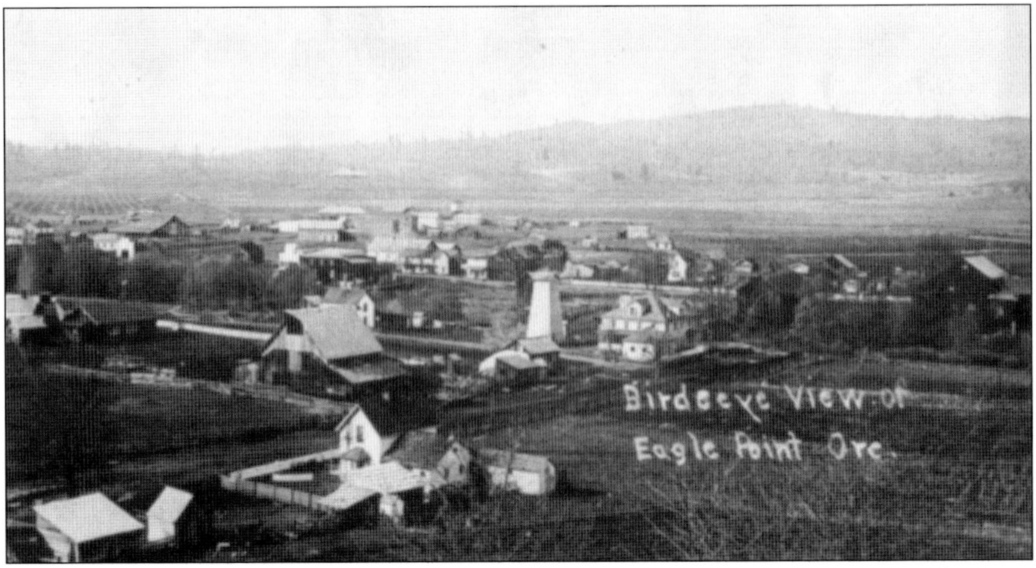

This bird's-eye view from 1912 shows the town of Eagle Point taking shape. By this time, there was a thriving downtown with many businesses and the area had become well-known for its superior farming, ranching, and agriculture.

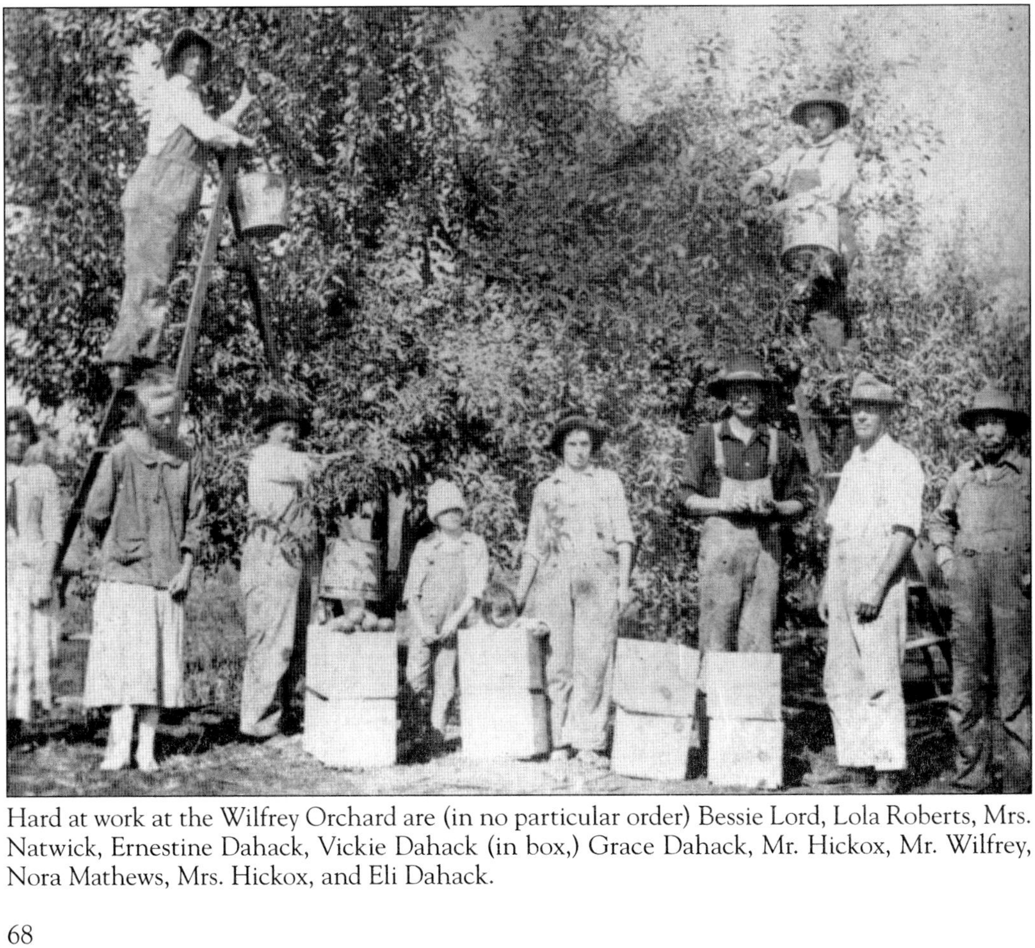

Hard at work at the Wilfrey Orchard are (in no particular order) Bessie Lord, Lola Roberts, Mrs. Natwick, Ernestine Dahack, Vickie Dahack (in box,) Grace Dahack, Mr. Hickox, Mr. Wilfrey, Nora Mathews, Mrs. Hickox, and Eli Dahack.

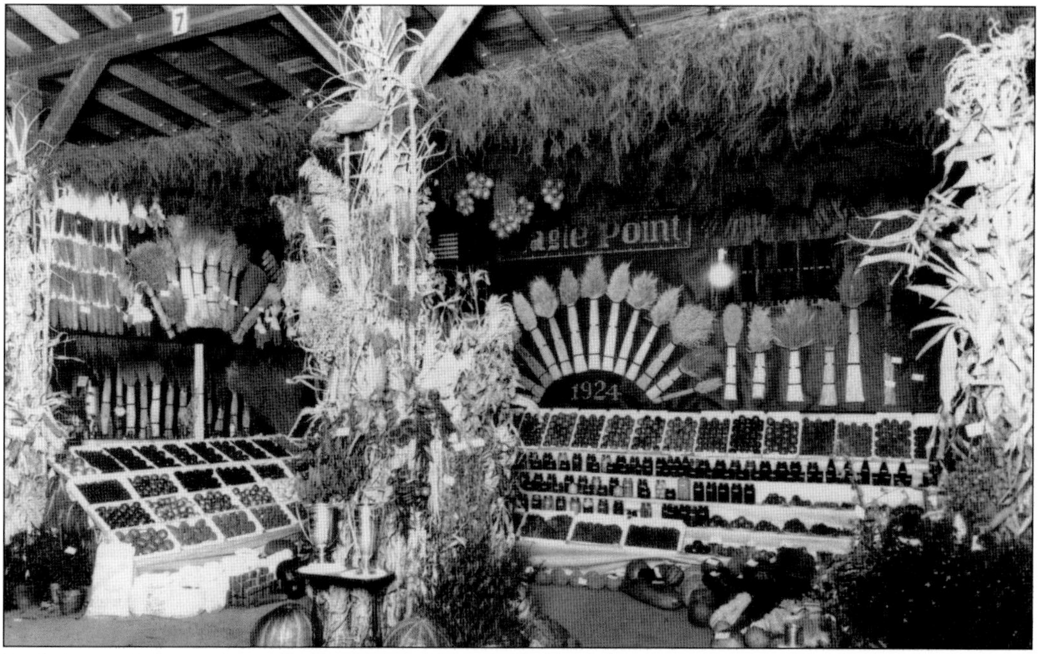

Eagle Point became known for its fine fruits. When apples from the Bradshaw orchard won top prize at the Spokane Apple Show in 1909, Eagle Point was labeled the "Apple Kings of America." Eagle Point was also known as the "onion capital." Michael Hanley's farm on Little Butte Creek received the highest compliment when the king of England placed an order for his Bosc pears. King George ordered 45 boxes of the delicious fruit.

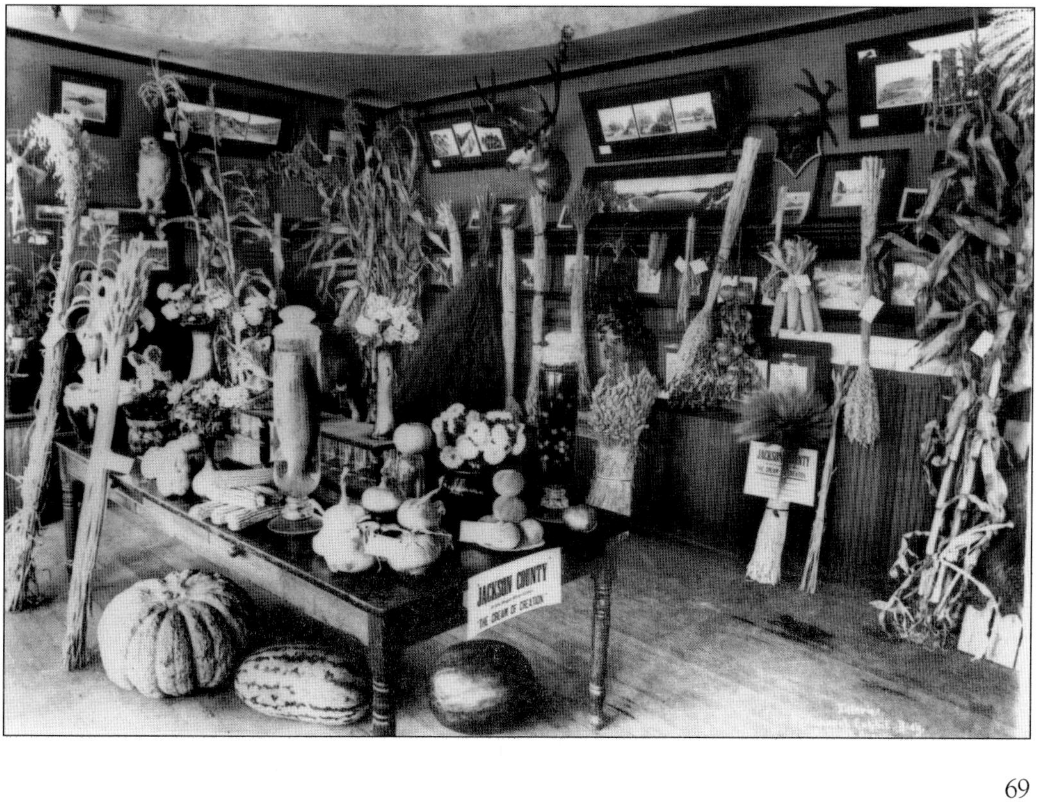

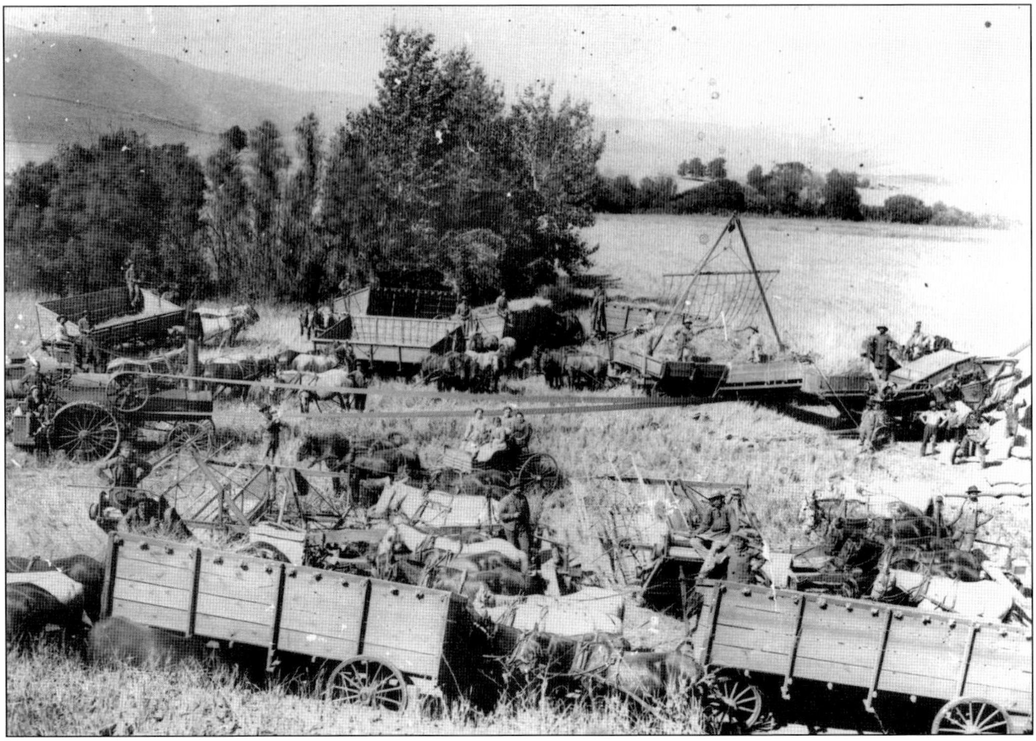

Farming has always been hard work. For these farmers, who did not have the benefit of today's technology, it could be downright treacherous. These hay farmers are bringing in one of Eagle Point's most valuable crops. Schools in rural areas frequently postponed the opening of school until after harvest, since everyone in the family was involved.

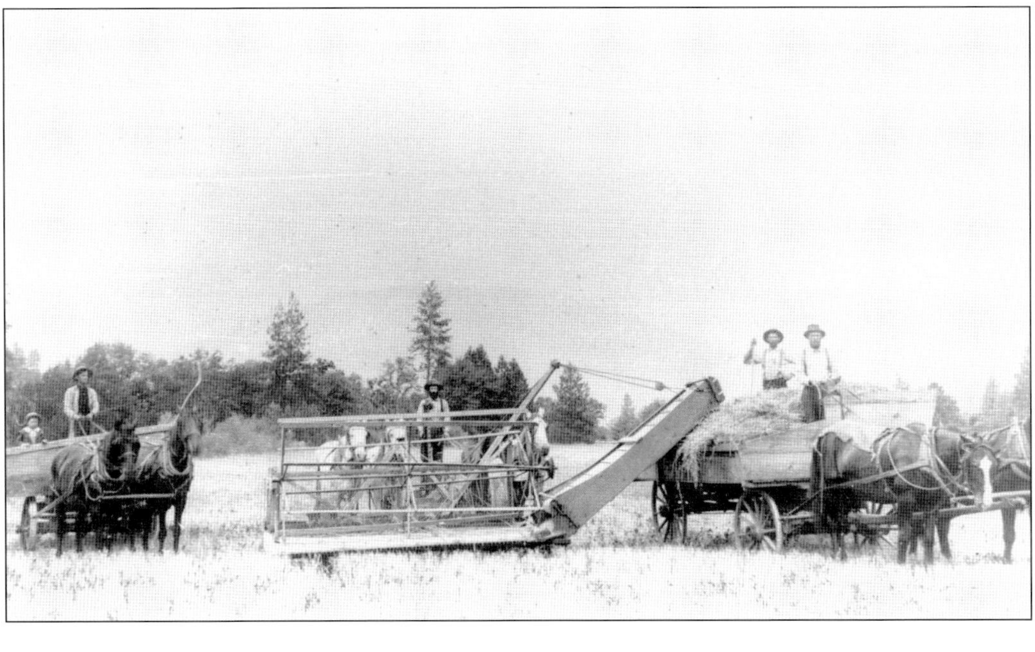

Four

Schools and Sports

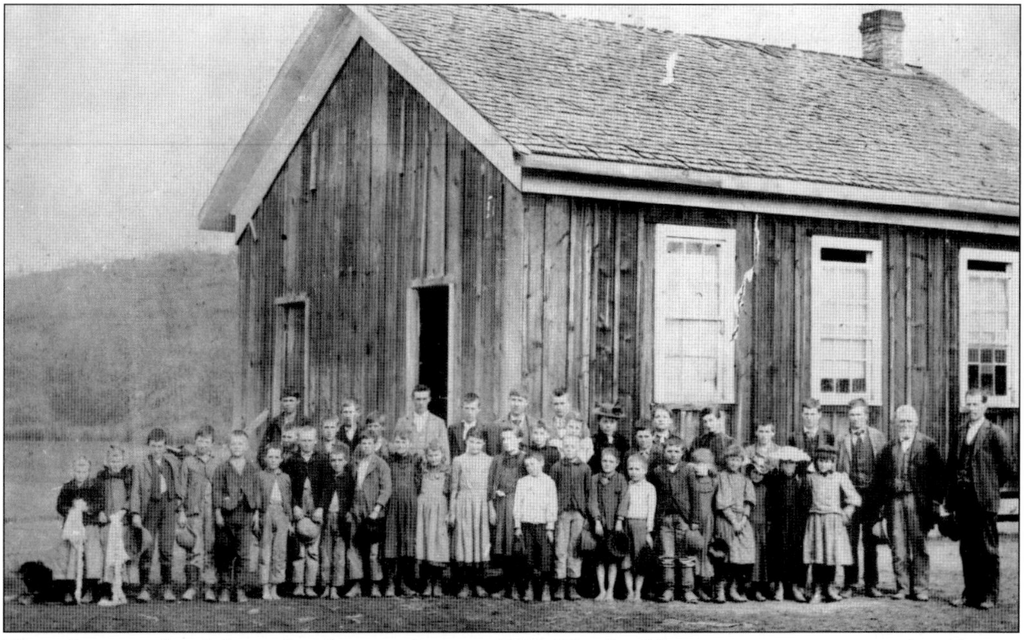

The photograph of this school was taken in 1898. The building was a one-room schoolhouse located on "C" Street. An article ran in the Jacksonville newspaper stating that the townsfolk in Eagle Point were complaining about the condition of their school, saying, "The old shack we have is not fit for winter school."

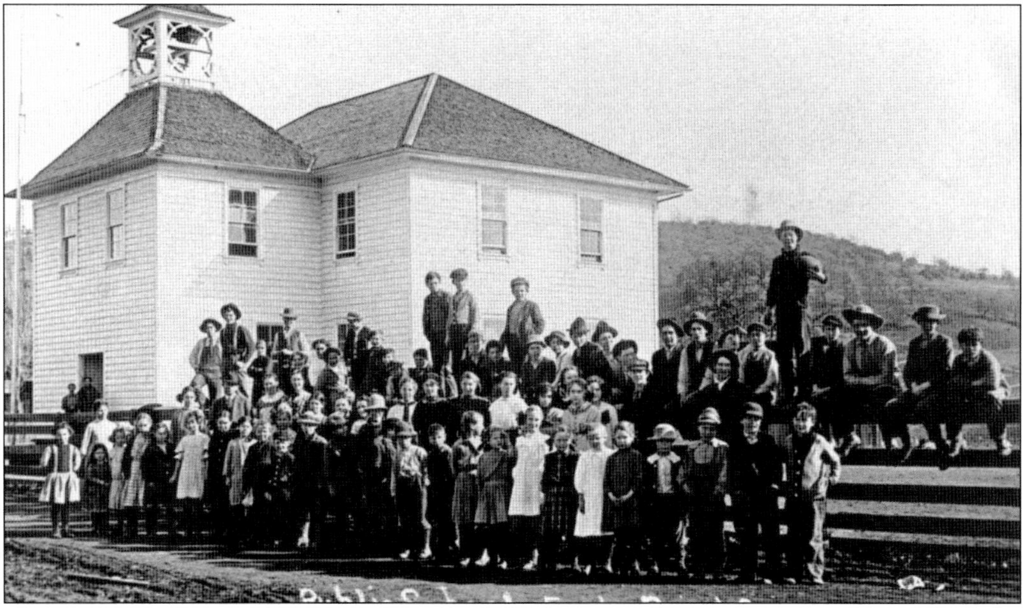

The following year, a new school was built. It was located on "B" Street and had a bell tower. On September 8, 1899, the locals held a community dance in the school even though the second story was not completed. The school opened on October 27, 1899. The old school was sold for $25 and later used for a church. Below, Mrs. Derick's class of 1925 included (first row) Gladys Nichol, Edward Crotser, Clyde Rigsby, Tommy Dewes, Angela Rosalap, Verna Cingcade, Clara Thompson, Rachel Mayham, and Ida Dewes; (second row) Opal Grove, Garrett Dewes, Victoria Dahack, Donald Ashpole, Lyle Cingcade, Thelma Mayham, Lucile Hurst, and Josephine Rosalap; (third row) Mrs. Derick, Vance Pierce, Hazel Smith, Zetta Rigsby, Verta Mathews, Glenn Winkle, and Robert Boyd.

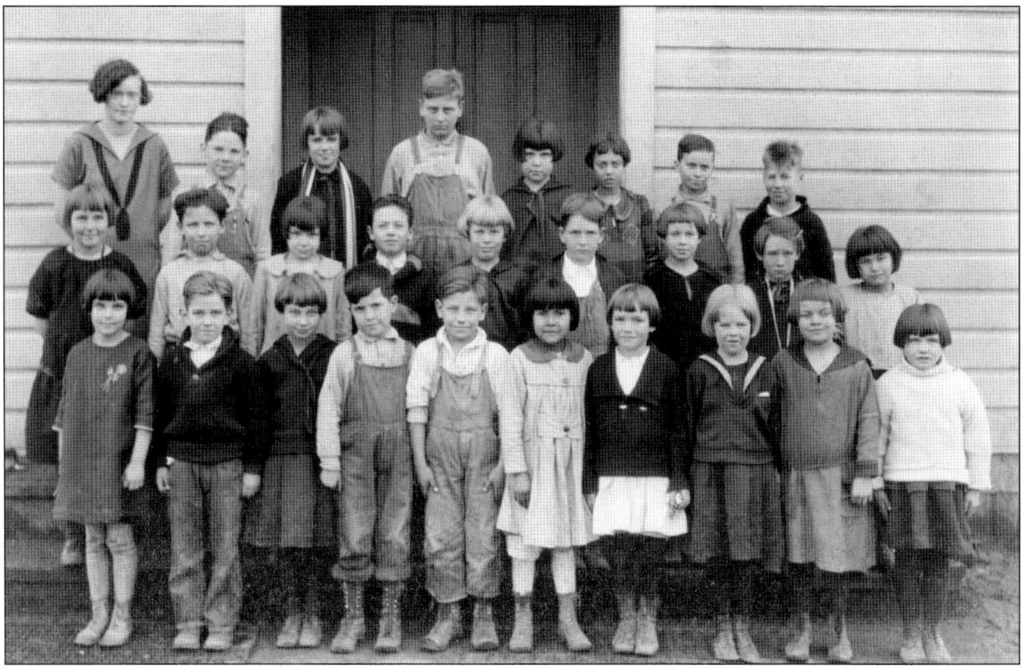

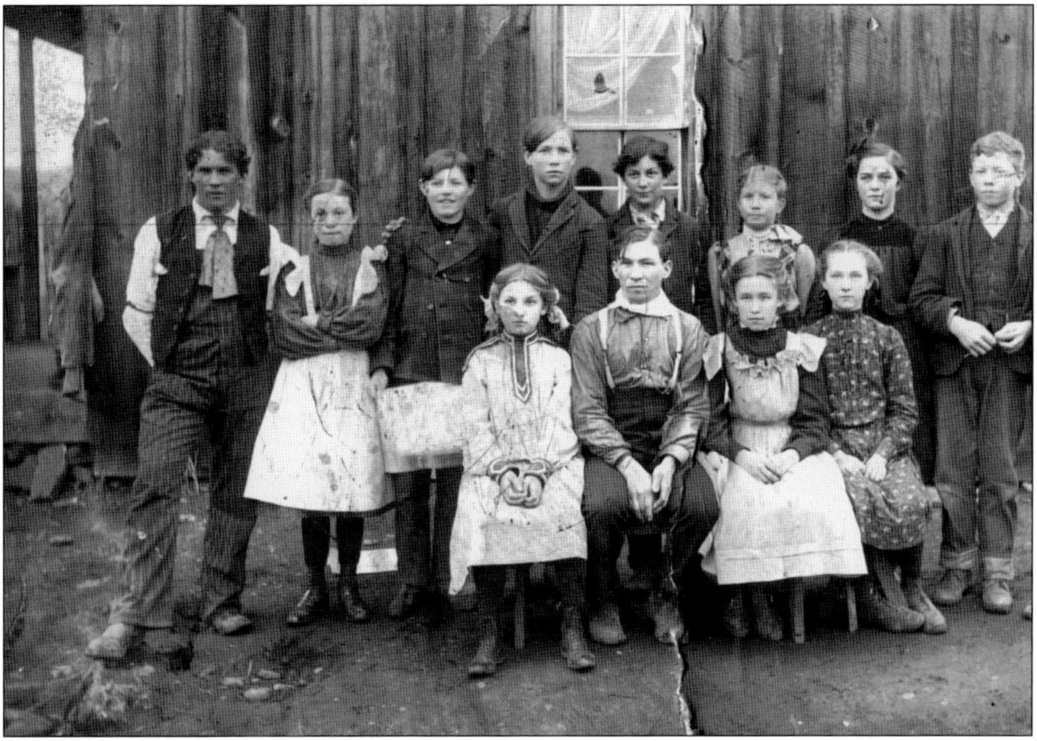

The Little Butte Creek School in Brownsboro just outside of Eagle Point is pictured above before it fell on hard times. The rural school supervisor reported in the early 1900s that the school was "Located in a prosperous farming district, good land, but a poor school—old building with rundown equipment, small salary paid to teacher, and seemingly not much local pride, small school population. About seven miles from Eagle Point." The 1917 photograph below shows the new Brownsboro School, which replaced the old, dilapidated one.

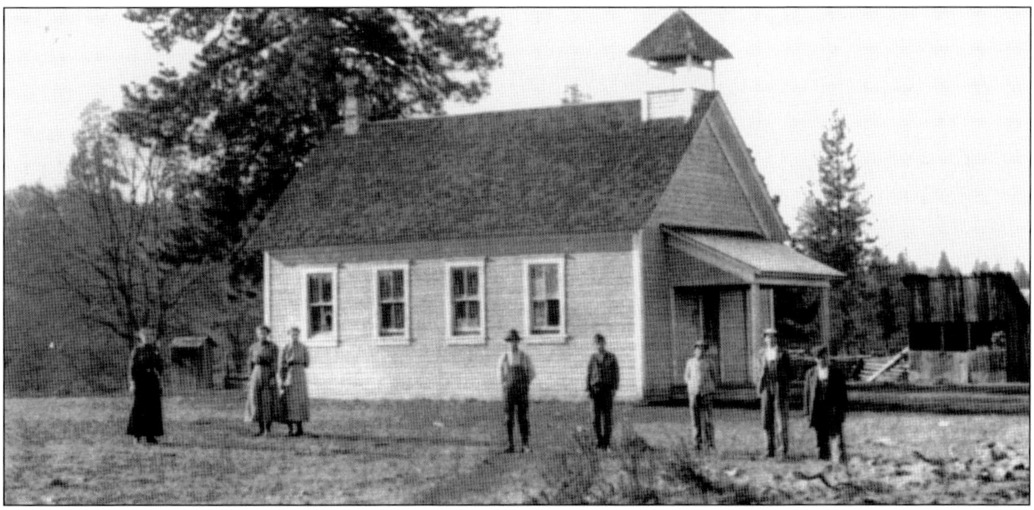

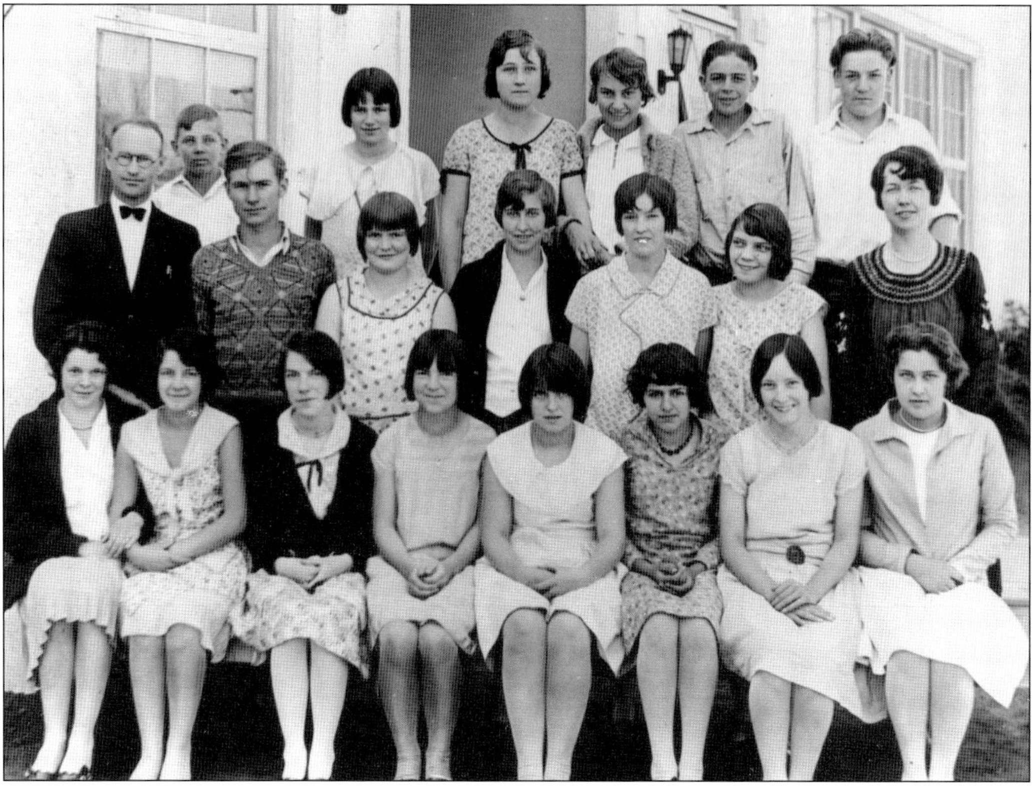

The students in this 1928 photograph include (first row) Davies Philbrook, Dorothy Coy, Catherine Philbrook, Mary Hannaford, and Fred Compton; (second row) Donald Young, Freda Chambers, Sybil Caster, Elsie White, Glady Cowsden, and Mildred Burt; (third row) Ernestine Dahack, Margaret Brophy, Dorothea Pearce, Mrytle Grisby, Donna Brown, Dorotha Wihite, and Isalee Brown. The 1932 photograph below shows Eagle Point students.

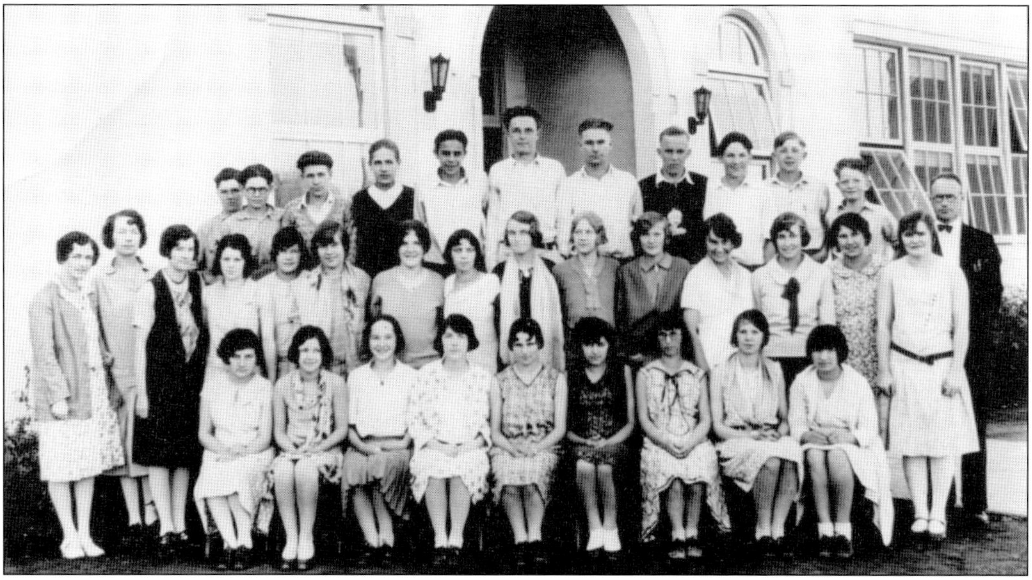

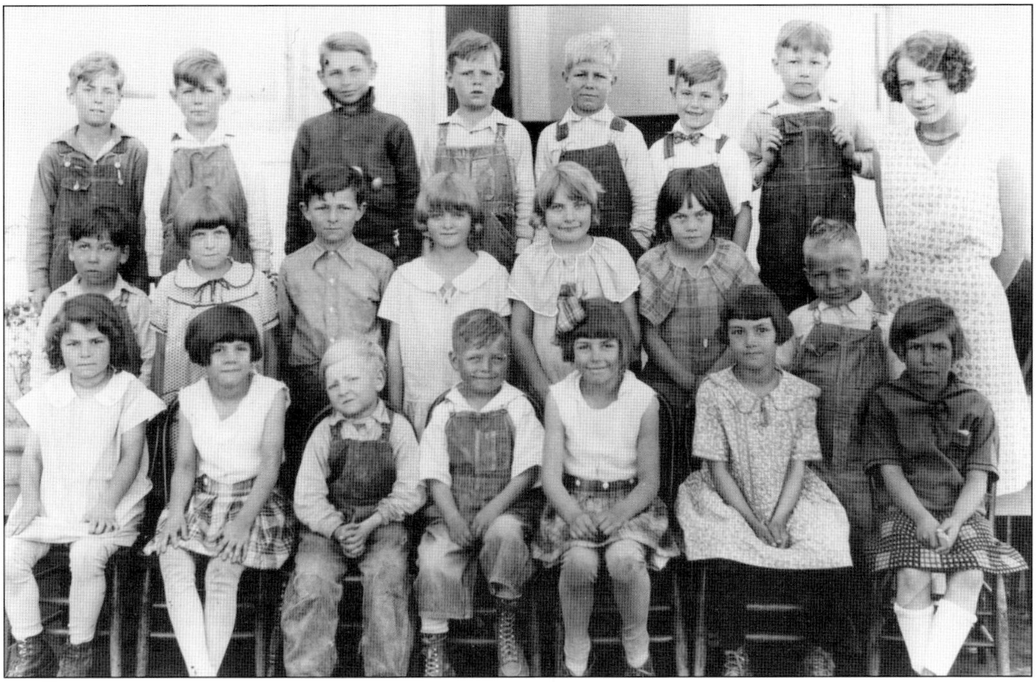

The young students above are pictured in 1931 standing in front of their school. Below, Coach Melvin Smith is pictured with his seventh- and eighth-grade football team in 1947.

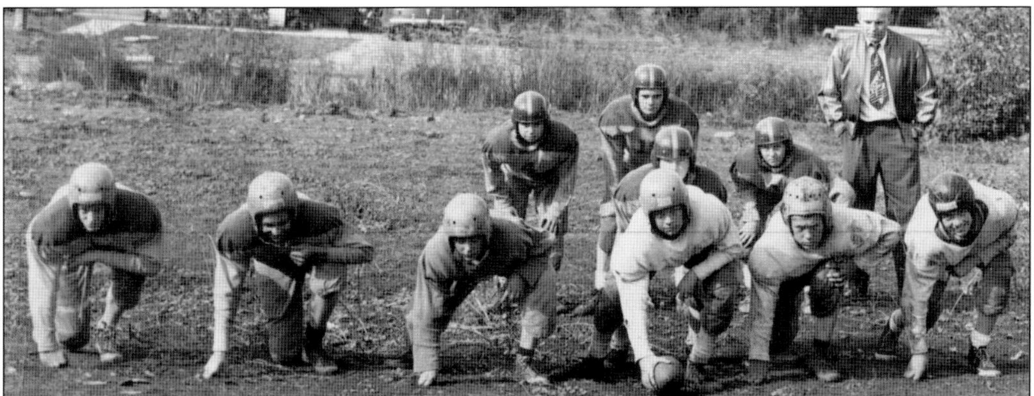

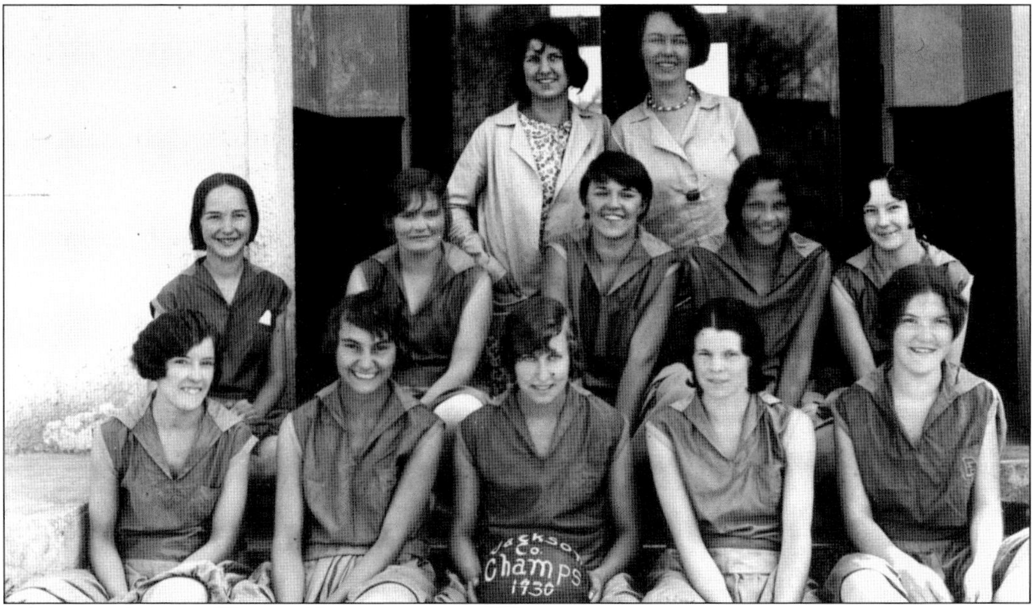

The girls' basketball champion team of 1930 includes (first row) Elsie White, Mary Hannaford, Sybil Caster, Ernestine Dahack, and Truth Peile; (second row) Norma Peile, Freda Chambers, Hazel Smith, Hazel Helms, and Dorothy Wilite; (third row) Margeurite Marshall and coach Mildred Burt. The 1936 boys' basketball team is pictured below and included Dale Throckmorton, Harry Gallop, Chester Smith, Bill Marshall, Earl Harnish, Ray Chamberlain, and coach Ray Neugart.

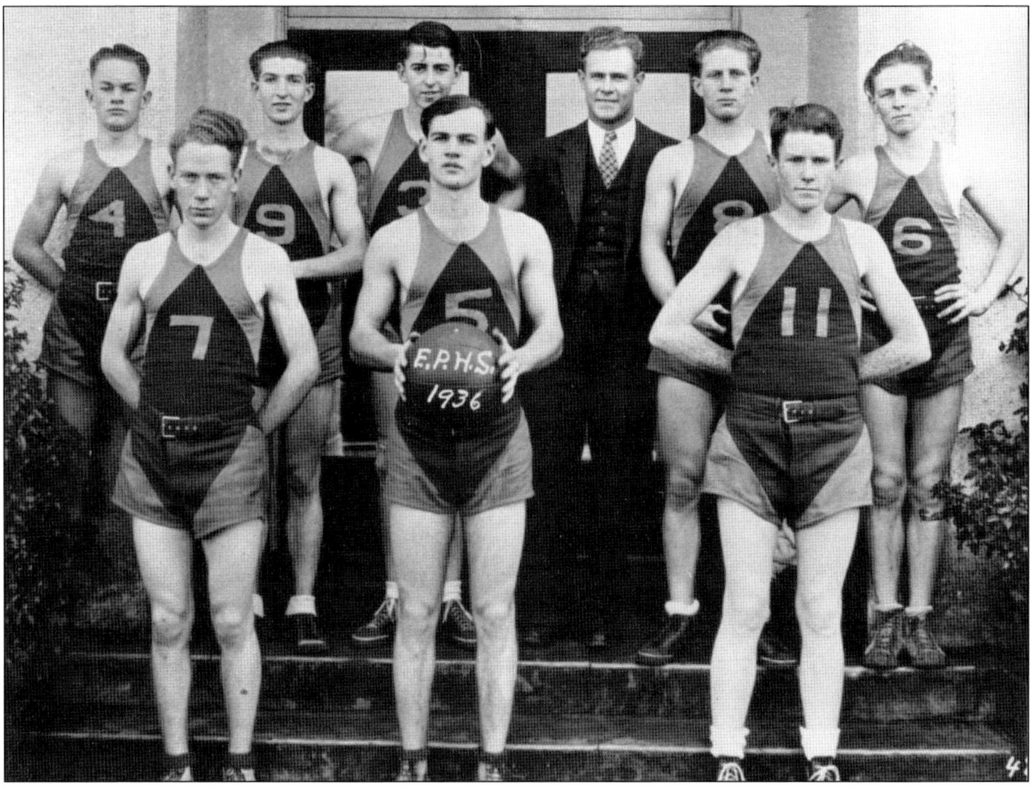

Five

Recreation

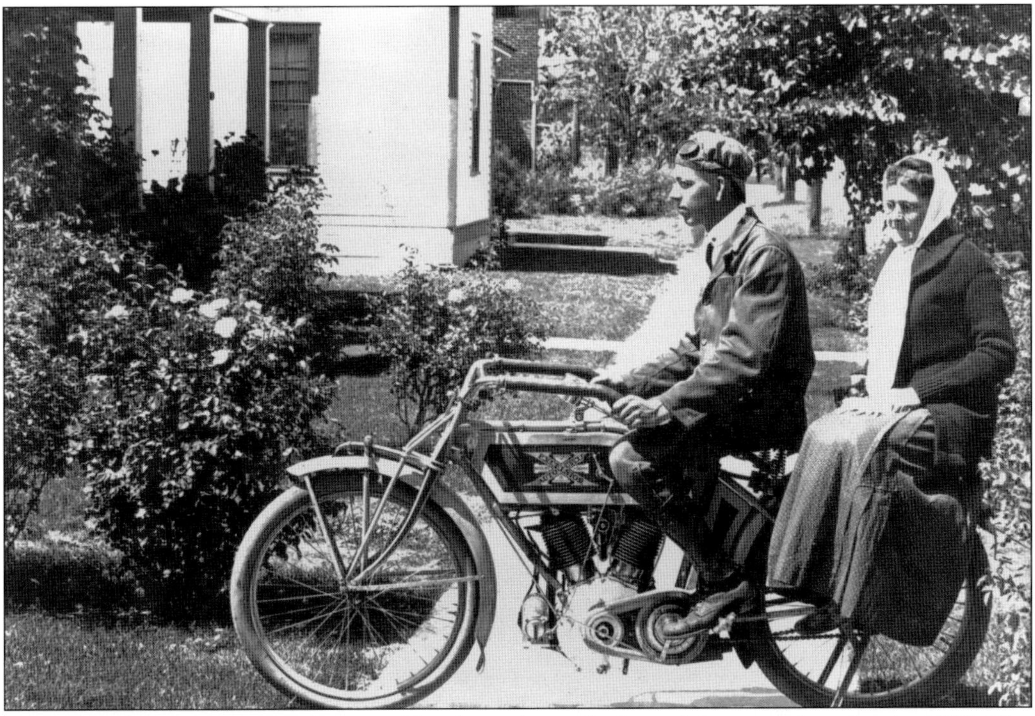

George Daley is testing out his new Excelsior Auto Cycle with his grandmother in 1913. The Excelsior Company got its start in 1876 by manufacturing bicycles in Chicago, Illinois. In 1909, they produced their first motorcycle. It had a single-cylinder engine with a leather belt drive. The following year, the Excelsior Company came out with a twin-engine motorcycle. The company was bought out by the Schwinn Bicycle Company.

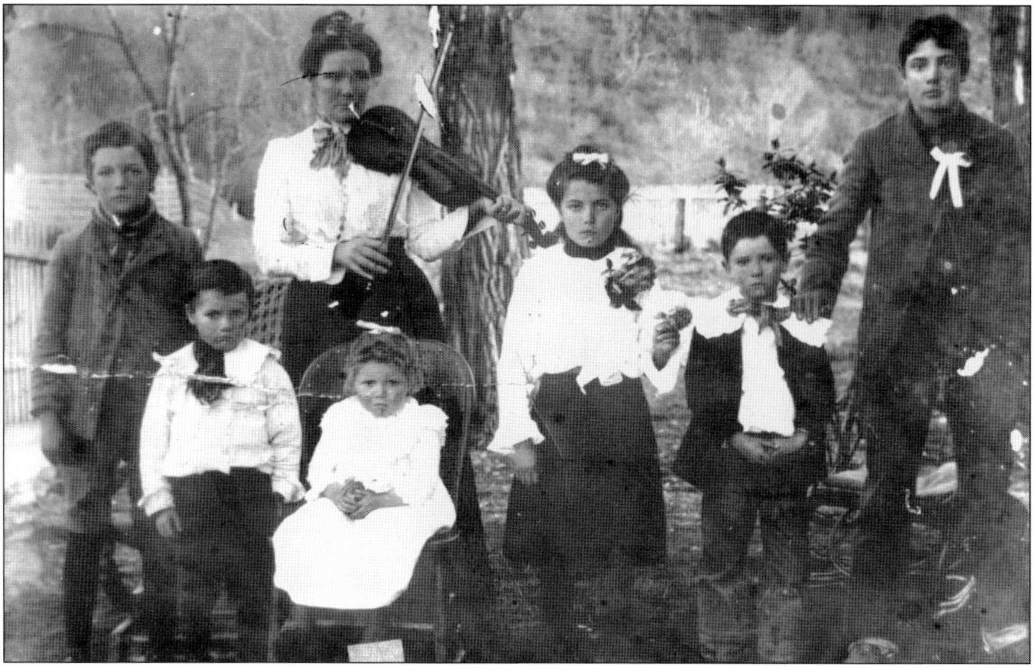

The Smith children are pictured above in 1900. Included in the family photograph are (in no particular order) Dave, Corbett, Mary, Viola, Polk, Harvey, and Nellie. Below, Polk, Corbett, Mary, Viola, Maggie, and Nellie are pictured in their Sunday best.

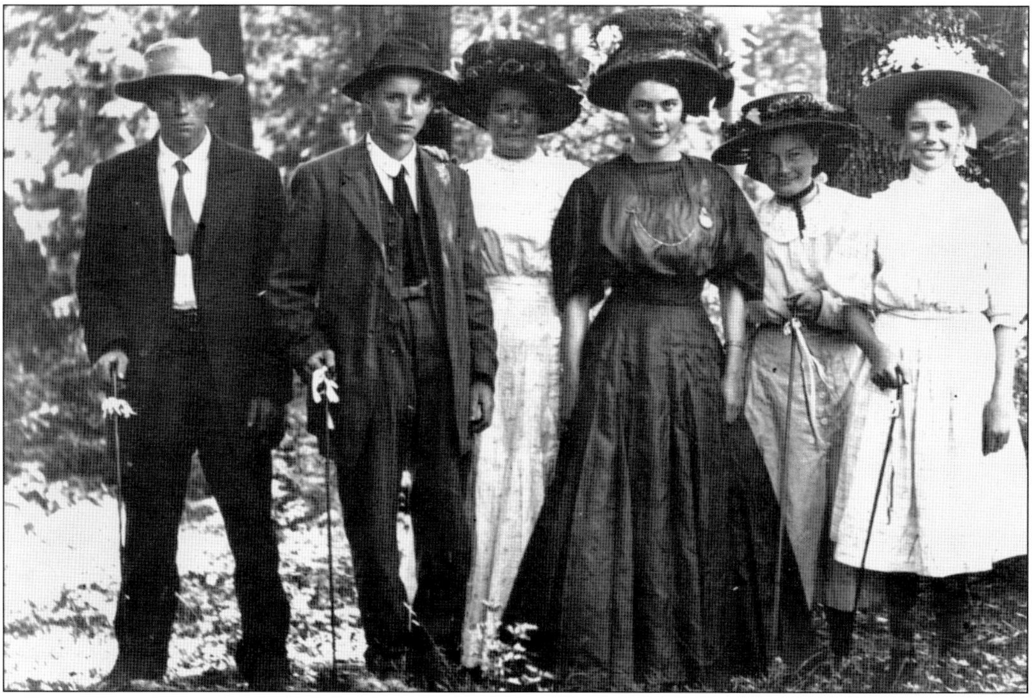

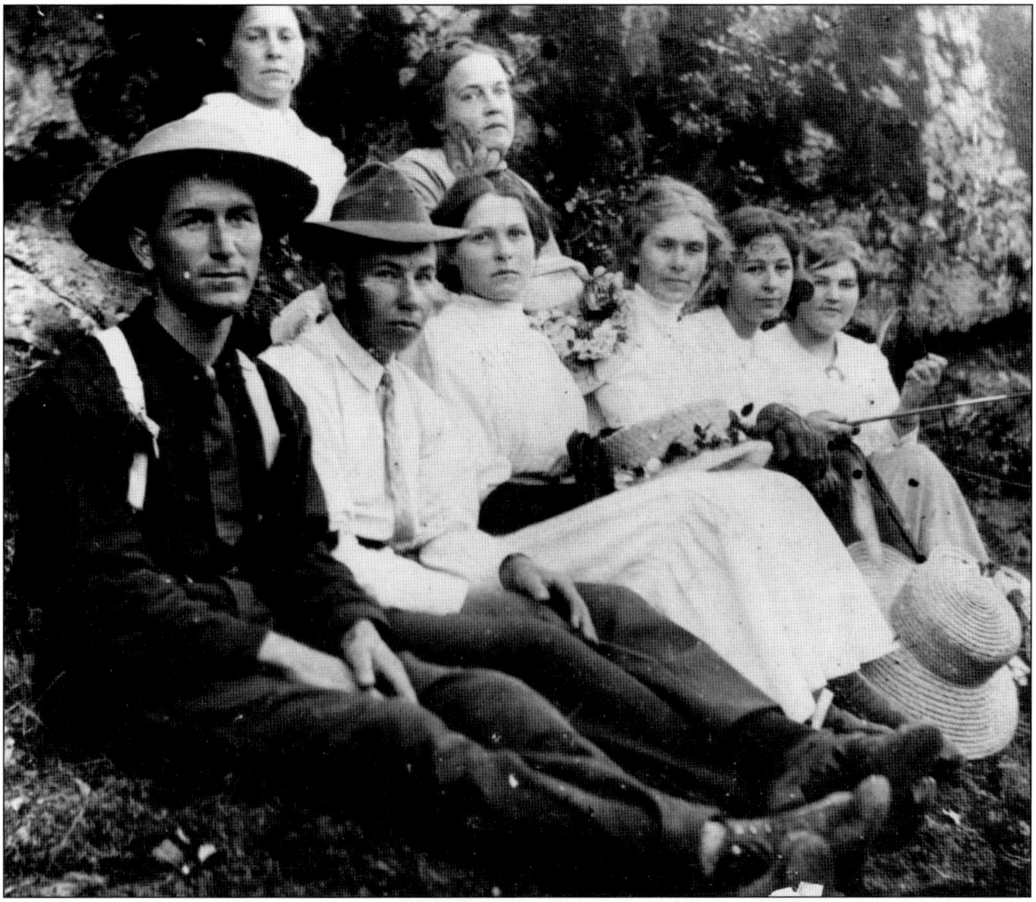

Some of the young people pictured above include Janie and Arnie Johnson, Alvin Connor, Amos Ayers, Polly Johnson, Mattie Minter, and Clara Carter. On the right, Francis Simon and her prized horse are ready for an outing.

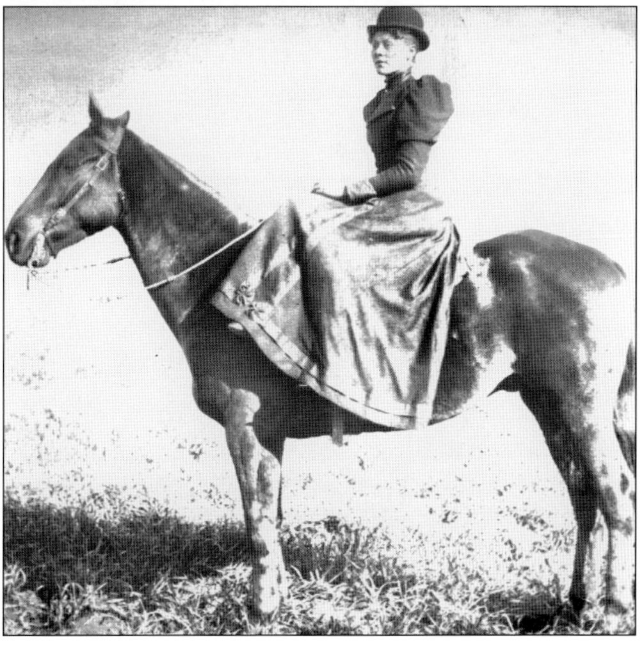

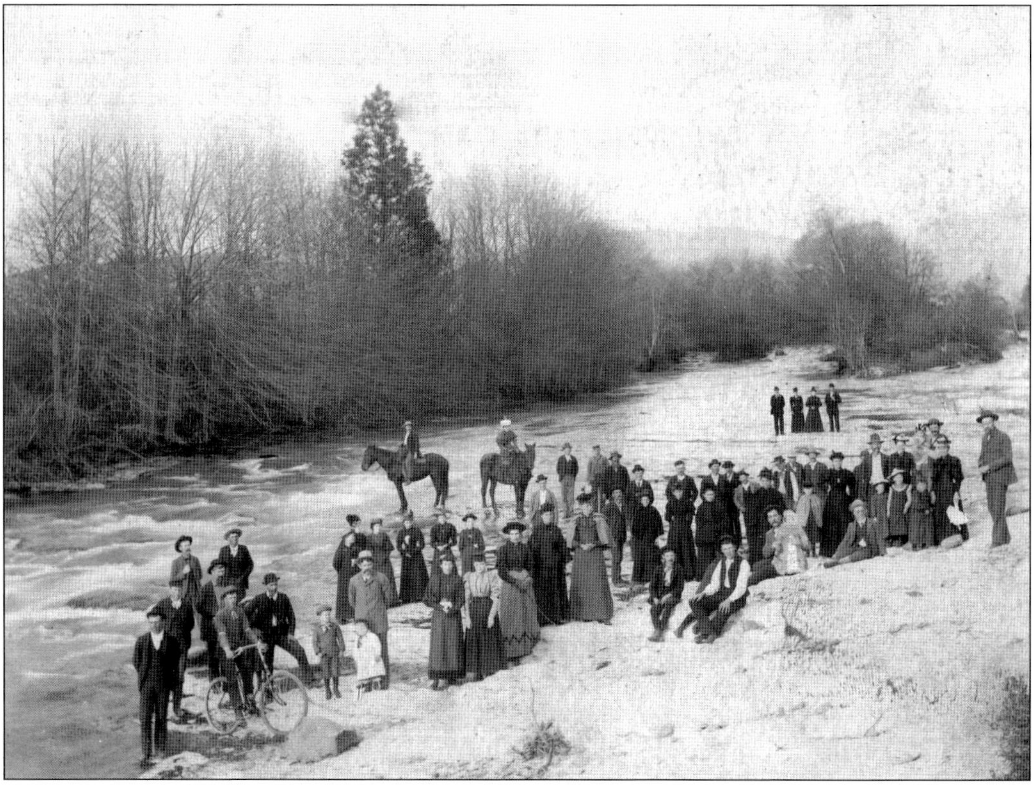

In the photographs above and below, townsfolk are all dressed up and enjoying some leisure time along the banks of Little Butte Creek.

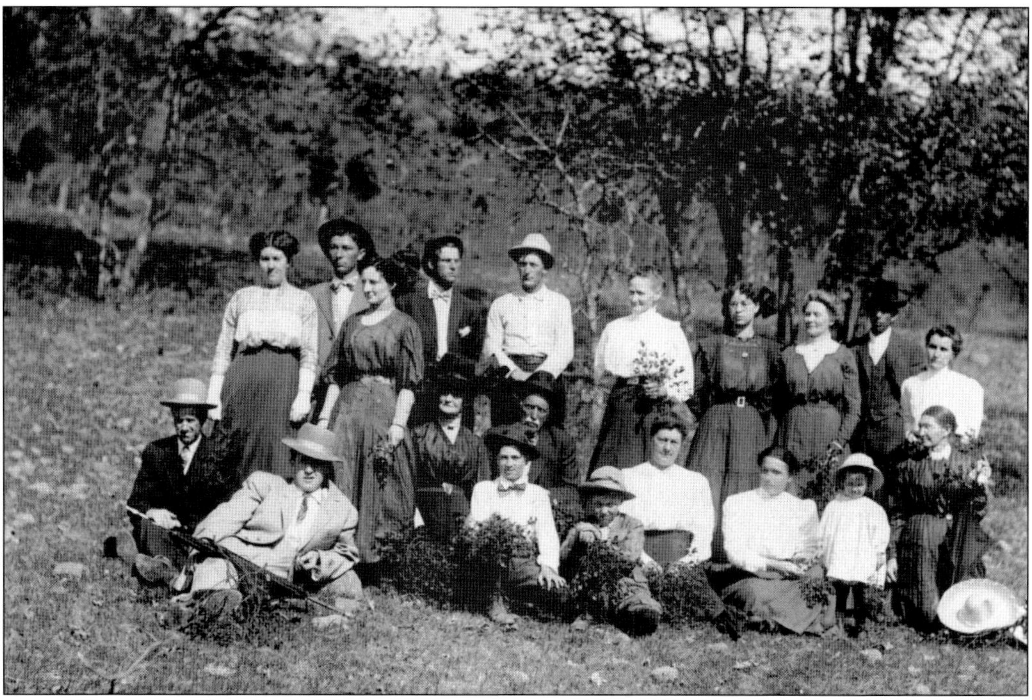

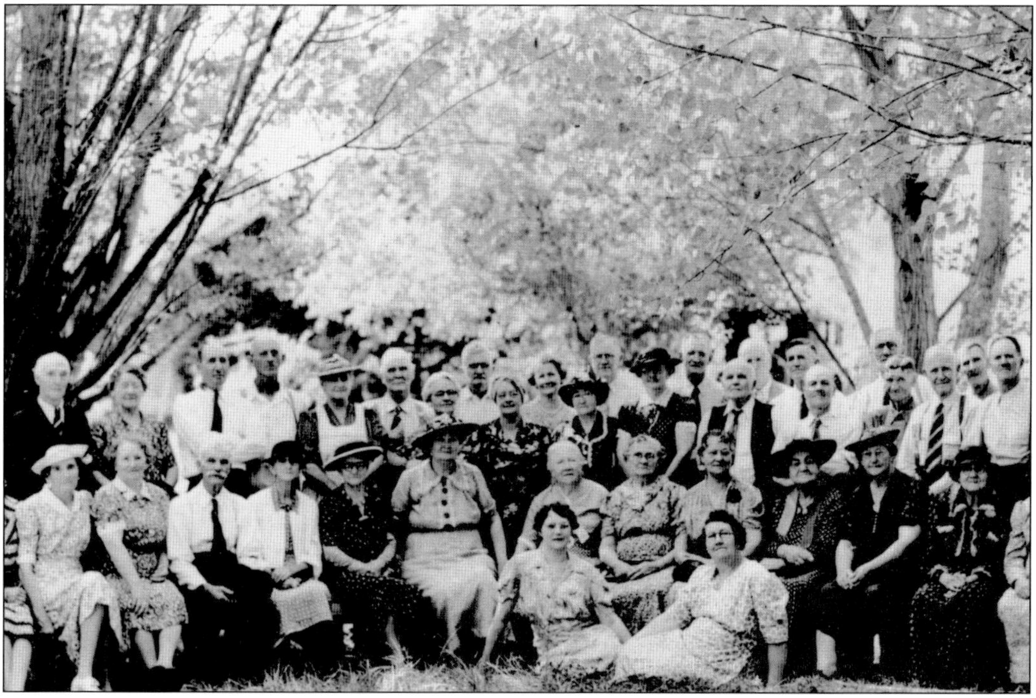

They referred to themselves as the "Old Timers Club" and are pictured above in 1939 enjoying a picnic. Granges have played an important part in farming communities across America. In March 1874, Deputy Master Buick organized the first Eagle Point Grange. Over the years, the grange has provided Eagle Point farmers with social, educational, and business connections. Members of the grange enjoyed picnics, dances, and dinners. This building was constructed in the 1920s when Eagle Point boasted the fourth-largest number of grange members in Oregon, with approximately 200 members.

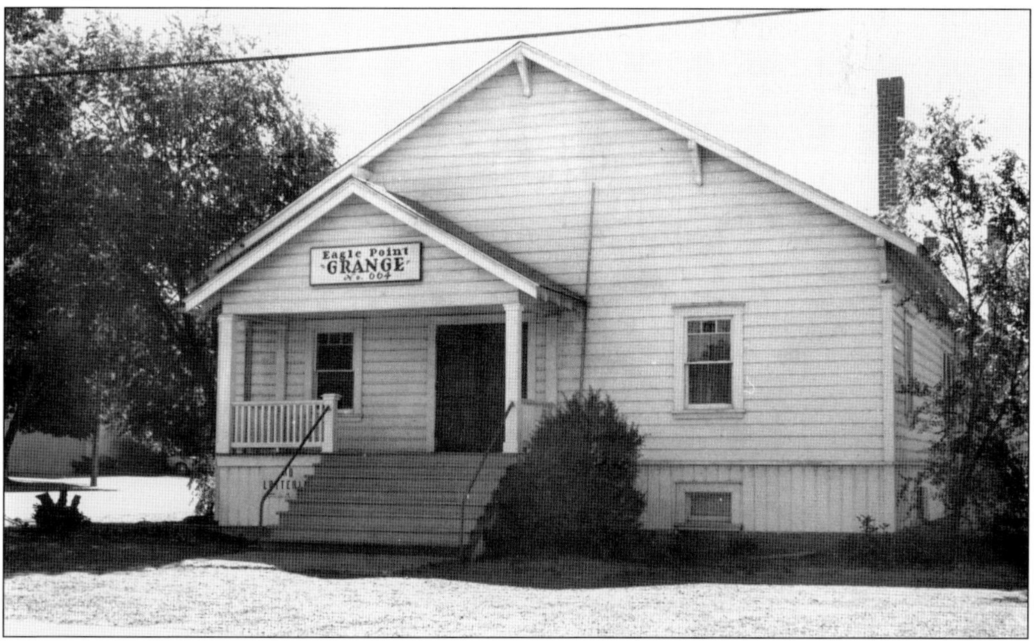

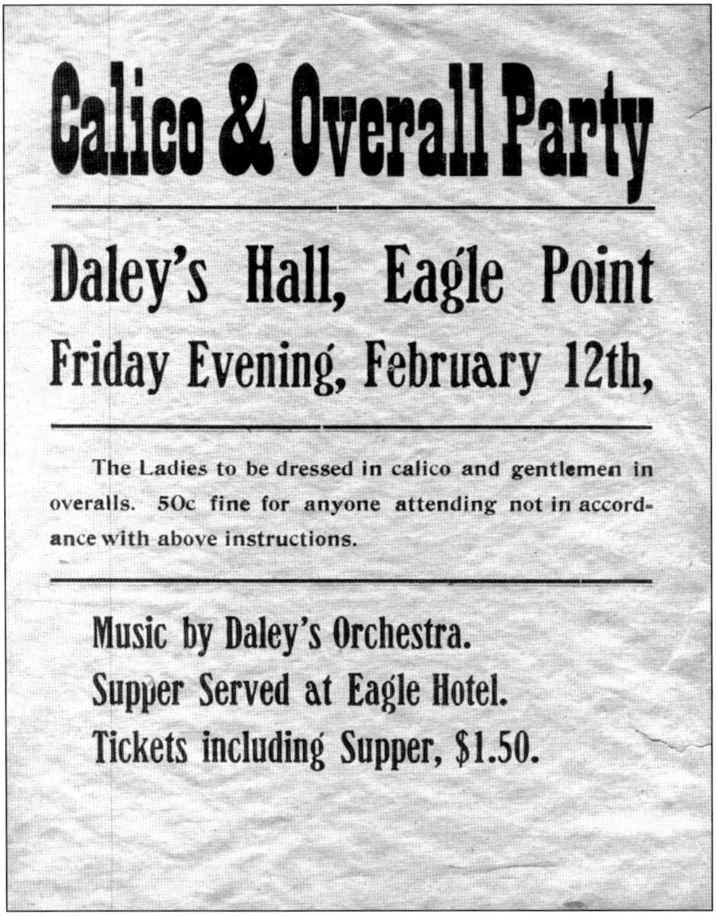

Calico & Overall Party

Daley's Hall, Eagle Point

Friday Evening, February 12th,

The Ladies to be dressed in calico and gentlemen in overalls. 50c fine for anyone attending not in accordance with above instructions.

Music by Daley's Orchestra.
Supper Served at Eagle Hotel.
Tickets including Supper, $1.50.

The townsfolk worked hard all week, but enjoyed socializing on the weekends. This poster announces a "calico and overall party" on Friday, February 9, 1909, at Daley's Hall. The announcement goes on to say that ladies not dressed in calico and men not dressed in overalls will be fined 50¢. The cost to attend the party was $1.50, which included supper at the Eagle Hotel. The 1907 Valentine's Day Dance at Daley's Hall, pictured below, was well attended.

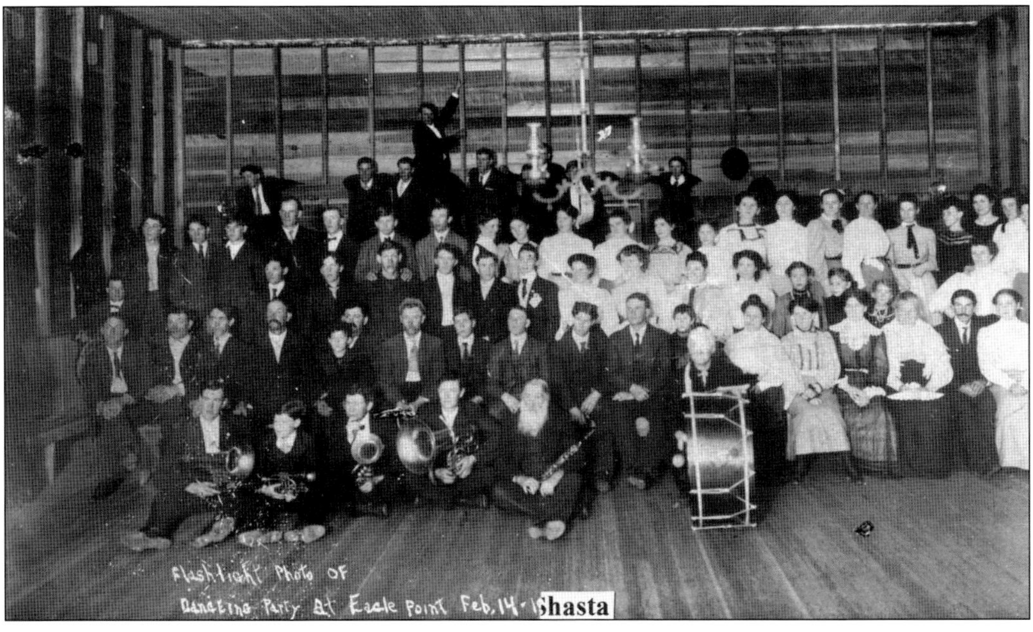

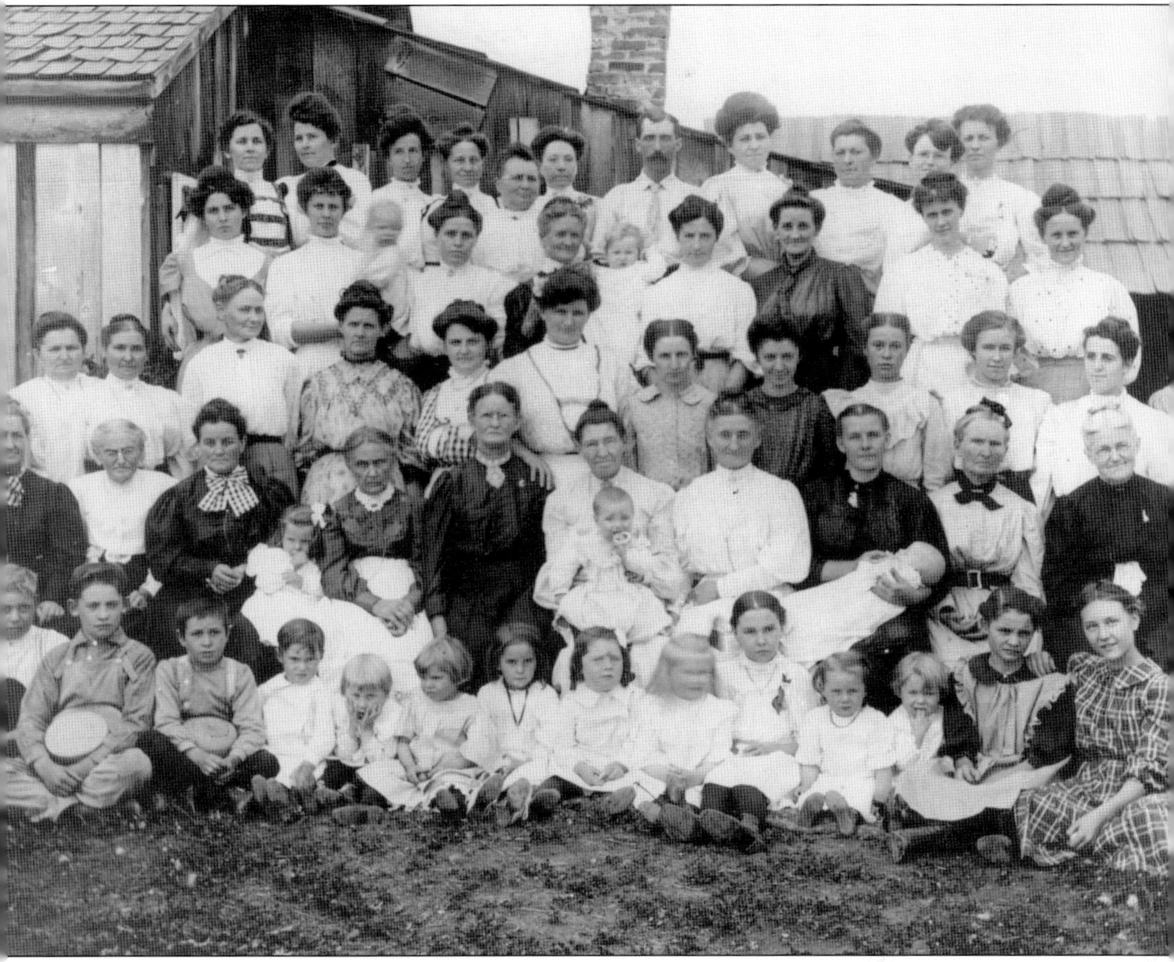

Quilting bees have been a popular form of socialization across America for decades. The women pictured here are at Susan "Ma" Howlett's hotel. Women would get together to work on quilts or to make a special quilt to give to someone as a wedding, graduation, or baby present. Before the pioneer woman crossed the plains, they would make a few extra quilts to trade for necessities, such as food or shoes, at trading posts along the Oregon Trail. The Log Cabin Quilt pattern was popular with the pioneers and it remains a favorite today. Before women had the right to vote, they sometimes expressed their political views through their quilt patterns. Many early quilts showed stars, stripes, and eagles. There were quilts for Whig supporters, Abraham Lincoln supporters, and those who honored George Washington. During the Temperance Movement, many quilting groups created quilts such as the Drunkard's Path pattern, then raffled them off to raise money for their cause.

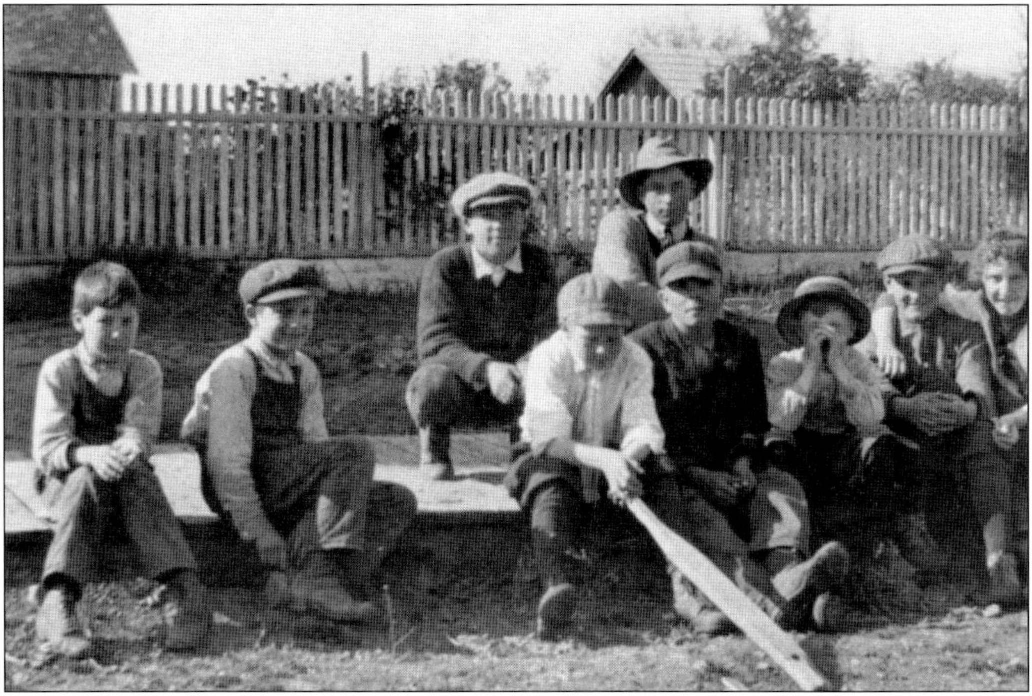

Some of these young boys include Jud Florey, Harold Vanscoy, Bob Harnish, Lyle Natwick, Adin Hazelton, Lyle Vanscoy, Winston Vance, and Hazel Brown.

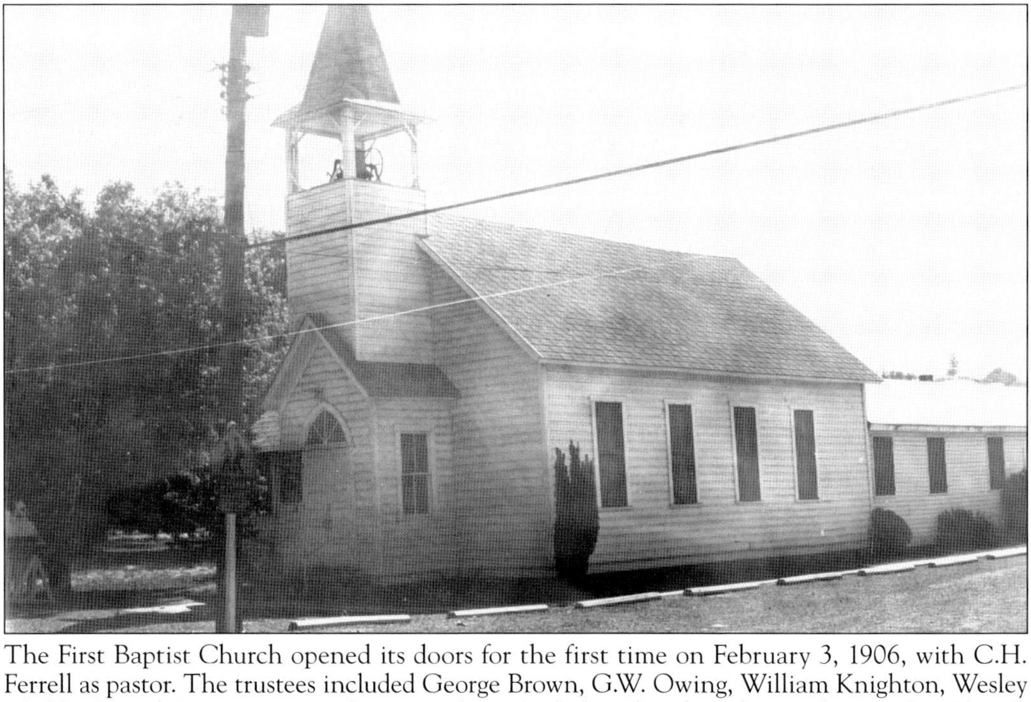

The First Baptist Church opened its doors for the first time on February 3, 1906, with C.H. Ferrell as pastor. The trustees included George Brown, G.W. Owing, William Knighton, Wesley Childreth, and G.P. Moomaw. There was also a Catholic Church and a Fundamentalist Church in town by the beginning of the 20th century. As the years passed, the First Baptist Church became a Presbyterian Church, then a Community Bible Church.

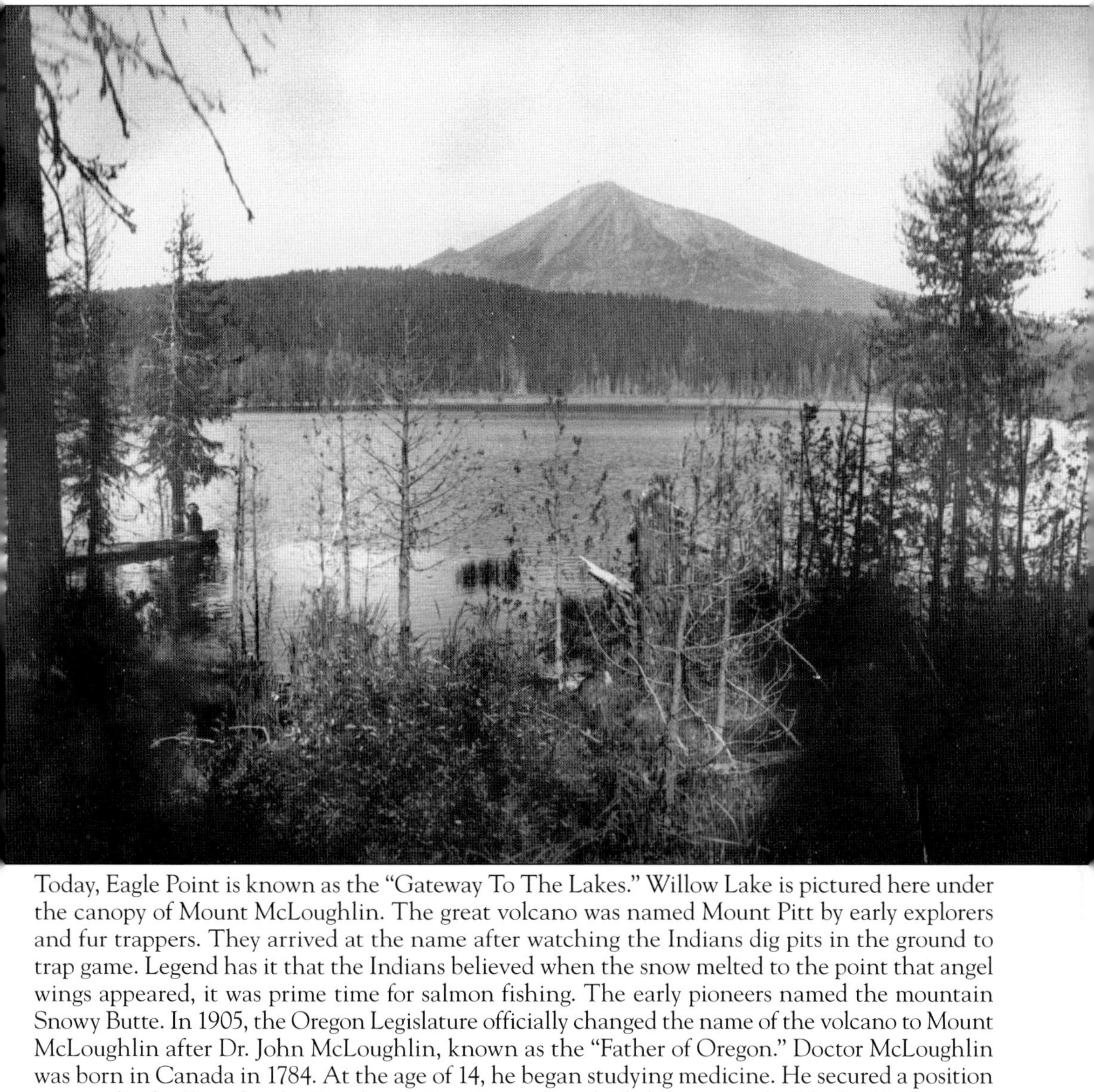

Today, Eagle Point is known as the "Gateway To The Lakes." Willow Lake is pictured here under the canopy of Mount McLoughlin. The great volcano was named Mount Pitt by early explorers and fur trappers. They arrived at the name after watching the Indians dig pits in the ground to trap game. Legend has it that the Indians believed when the snow melted to the point that angel wings appeared, it was prime time for salmon fishing. The early pioneers named the mountain Snowy Butte. In 1905, the Oregon Legislature officially changed the name of the volcano to Mount McLoughlin after Dr. John McLoughlin, known as the "Father of Oregon." Doctor McLoughlin was born in Canada in 1784. At the age of 14, he began studying medicine. He secured a position as a medical officer for the Northwest Fur Company, which later merged with the Hudson Bay Company. In the early 1820s, Doctor McLoughlin arrived in Oregon and built Fort Vancouver. He is credited with helping both the Indians and the white settlers.

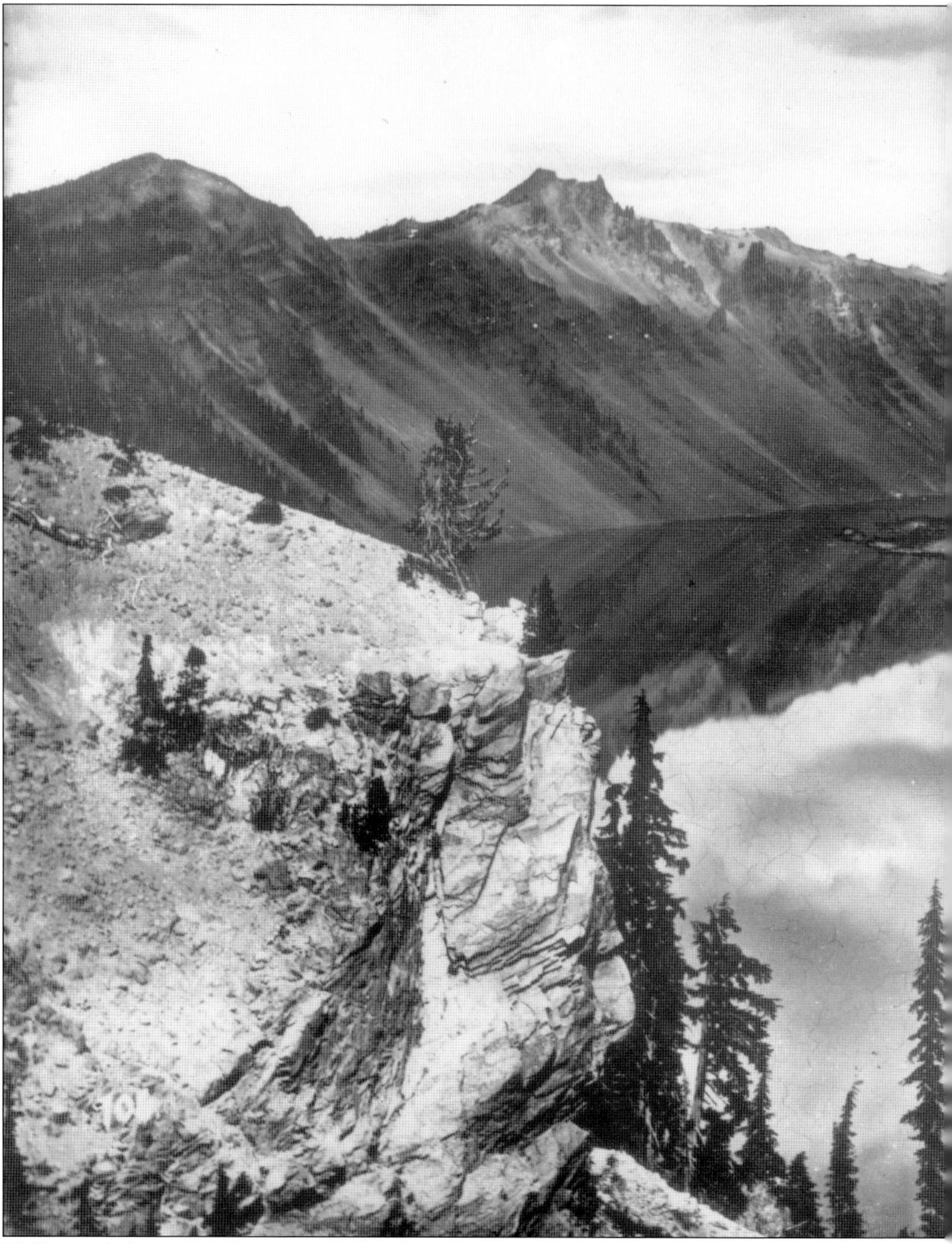

William Gladstone Steel was just a schoolboy in Kansas in the 1860s when he first read about a beautiful lake in Oregon, and he vowed that one day he would visit the lake. William was 31 years old before he was able to fulfill his childhood dream. Upon seeing the lake for the first time, he wrote, "An overmastering conviction came to me that this wonderful spot must be saved, wild and beautiful, just as it was, for all future generations, and that it was up to me to do something. I

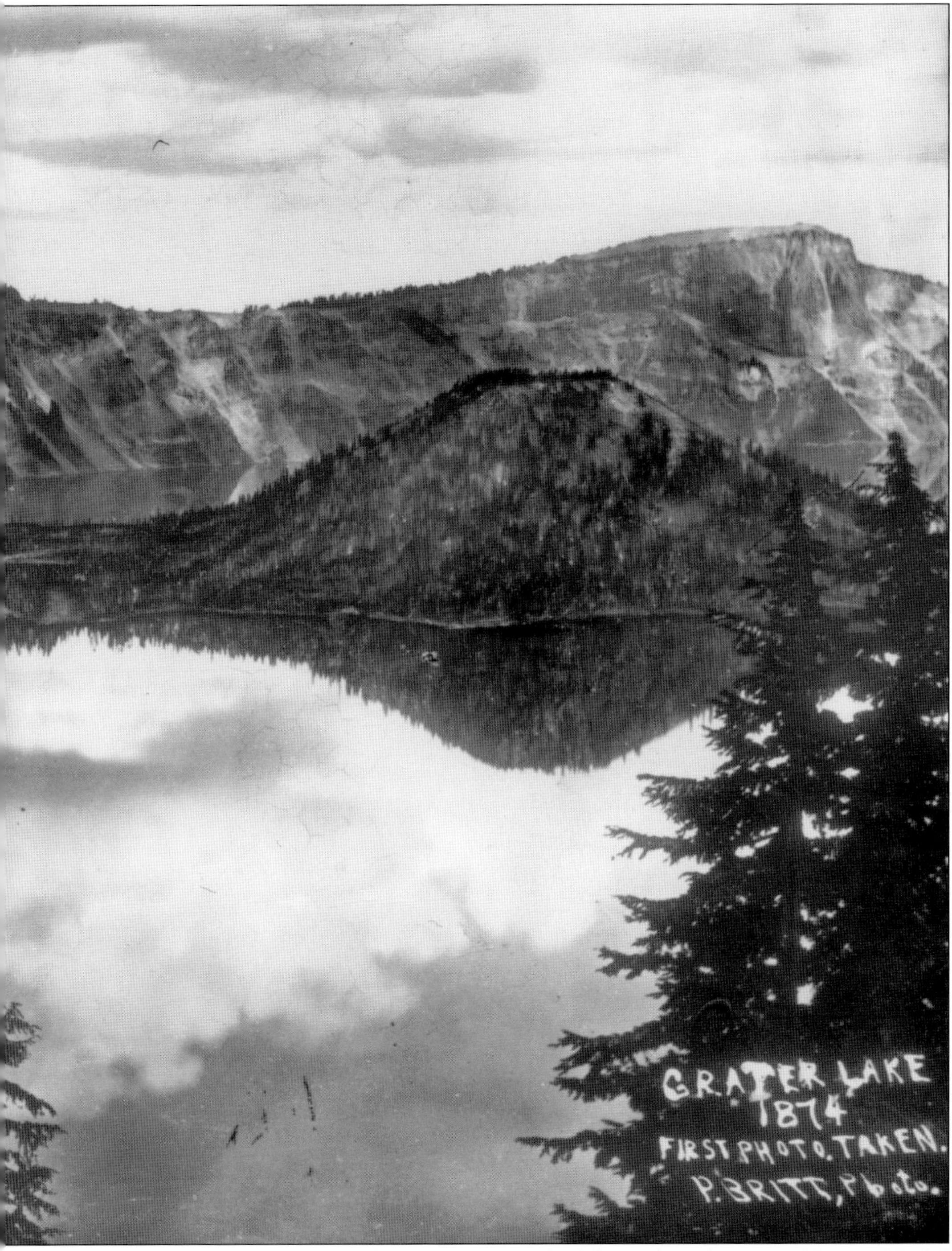

then and there had the impression that in some way, the lake ought to become a National Park." At the time, the only National Park was Yosemite. Undaunted, he began working on his project. It took 17 years, but finally, in 1902, William was able to convince Pres. Theodore Roosevelt to sign a law making Crater Lake a National Park.

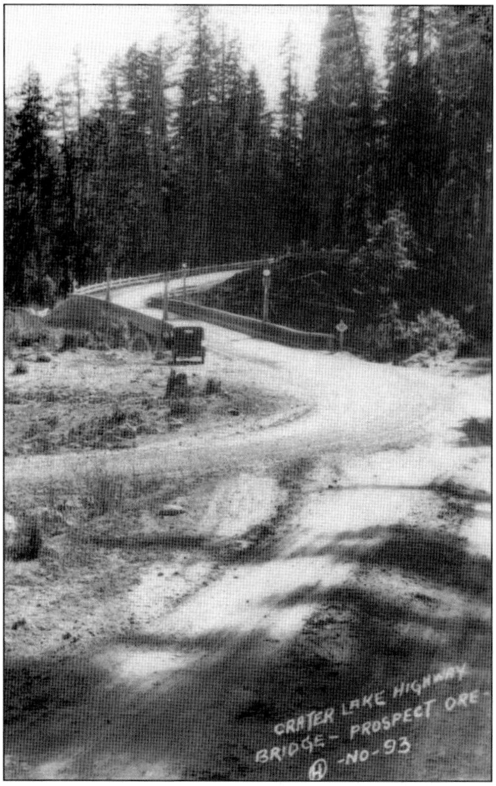

Even with the advent of the automobile, a trip to Crater Lake could take two to three days. Many attempts were made to build a railroad spur from Medford to Crater Lake, but it never came to fruition.

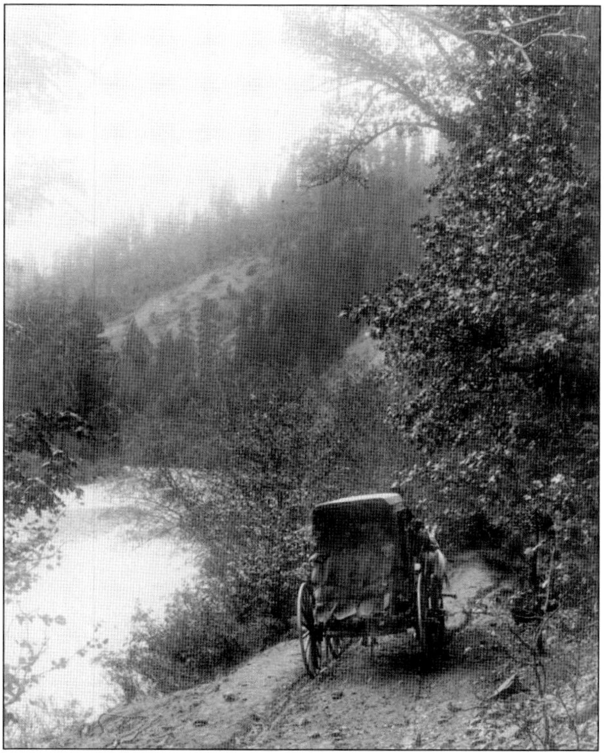

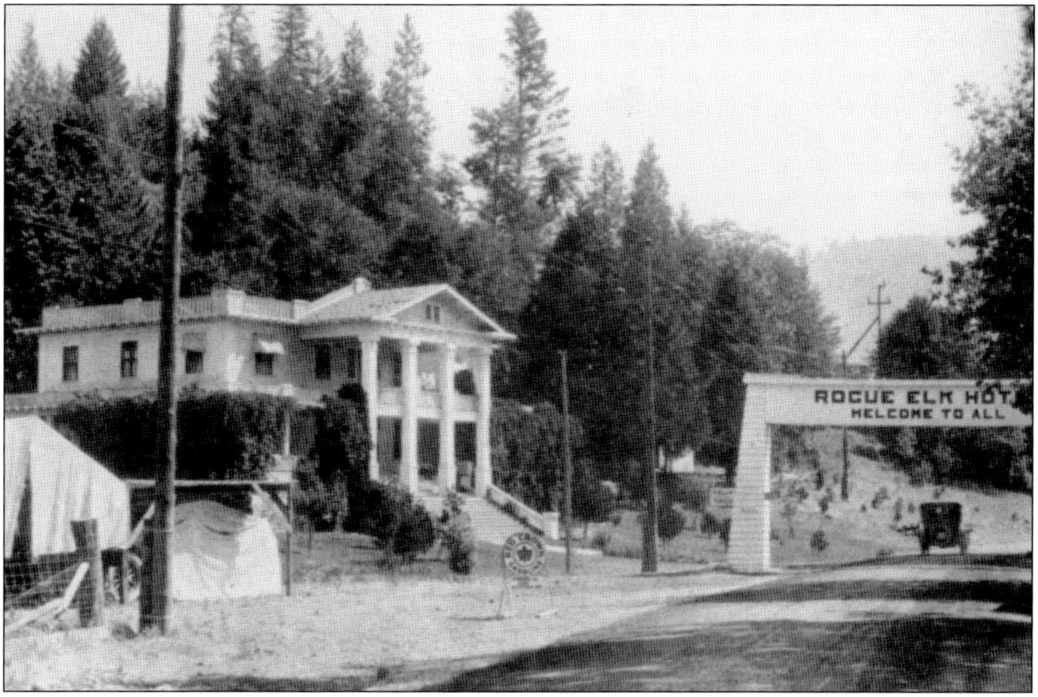

The Rogue Elk Hotel, in the Upper Rogue Valley near Trail, opened in 1916 and provided respite for those traveling the difficult road to Crater Lake. The hotel boasted 5,300 square feet, with electricity, running water, eight bedrooms, and 10 bathrooms. It took 90 tons of native rock to create two massive fireplaces in the hotel. Among the many guests were Pres. Herbert Hoover, actor Clark Gable, and writer Zane Grey. For the more adventurous, Casey's Auto Camp opened in the early 1920s. The automobile camp, pictured below, was operated by James Allen Casey, who provided a small cabin in an idyllic setting. James acted as a fishing guide and his wife, Ethyl, ran a restaurant at the camp. Many locals still remember "Jerry the Bear," which the Caseys kept as a pet to entertain the visitors.

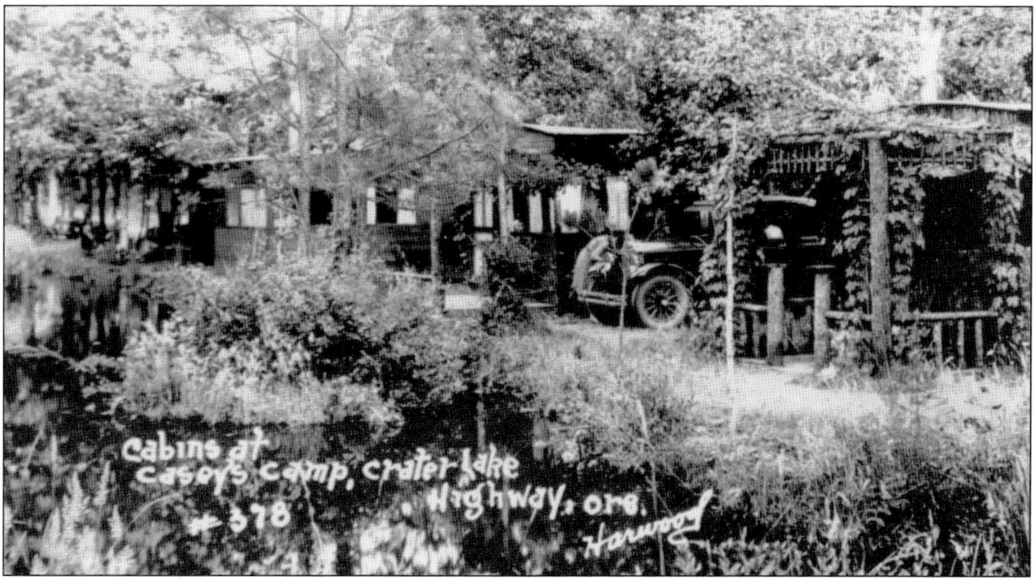

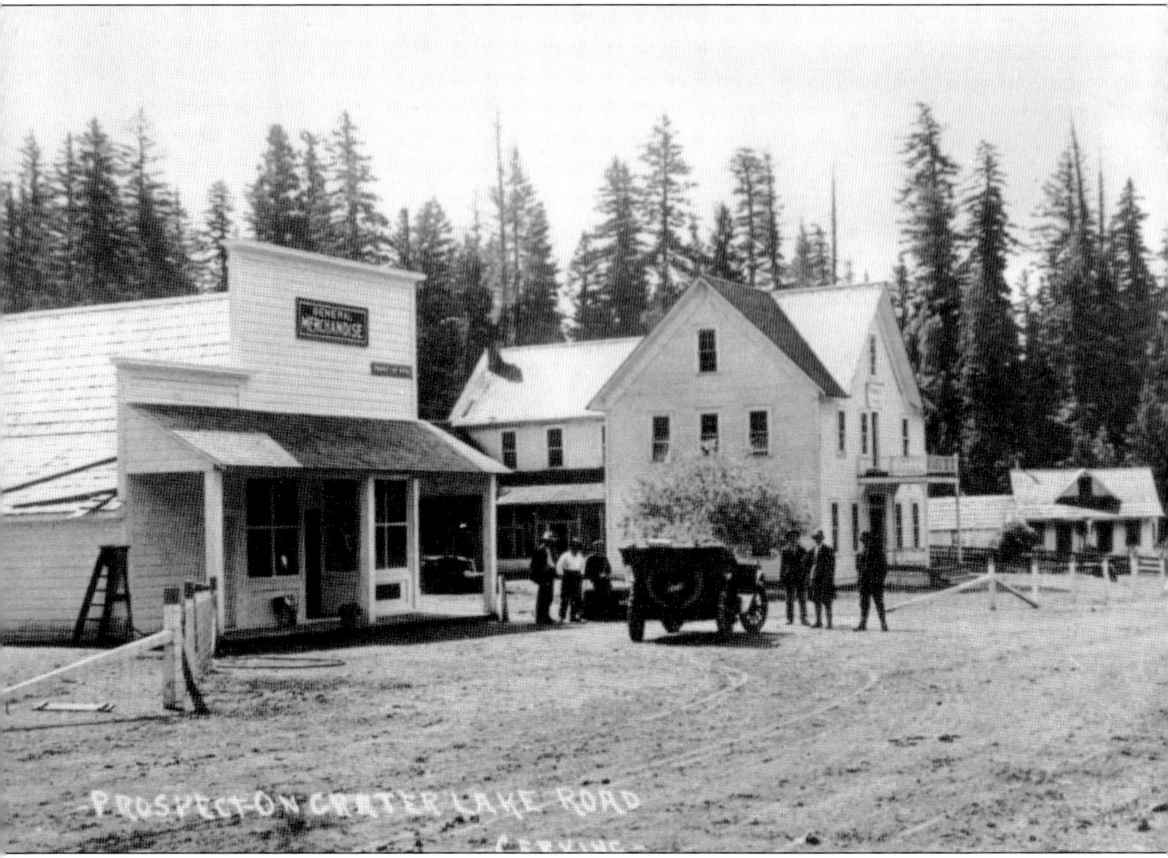

Further up the road was the Prospect Hotel. Prior to the hotel being built, travelers stopped at the Boothby's house in hopes that they could spend the night. The Boothby's owned a large house that looked very inviting to weary travelers. In 1892, they built a hotel, which allowed them to rent out 10 rooms. In 1910, John Grieve moved his family to Prospect. John was employed as a road supervisor and immediately saw the need for a better road to Crater Lake. John contracted with the state prison in Salem to have prison inmates come to the area and build a new road. John bought the Boothby House in 1912 and renamed it the Prospect Hotel. Over the years the guests included Zane Grey, Jack London, William Jennings Bryan, and John Muir.

Six

The Railroad and the Logging Industry

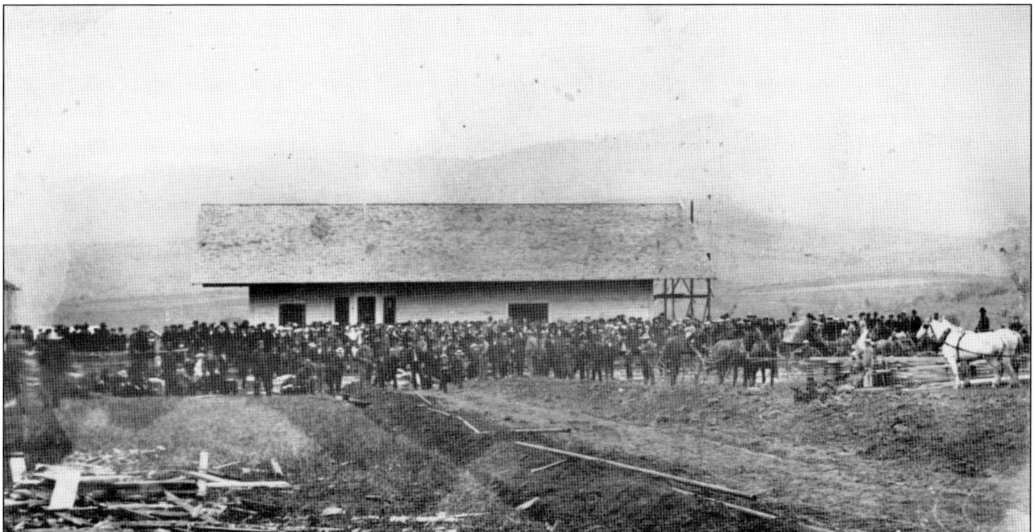

On December 17, 1884, the golden spike was laid just 30 miles from Eagle Point. This was a monumental day for the entire country, because for the first time, the east and west coasts were linked. Just 30 years prior, thousands had walked across the plains to get to the west. Now with the advent of the railroad, people could travel across the country while viewing the landscape of America from the luxury of a train.

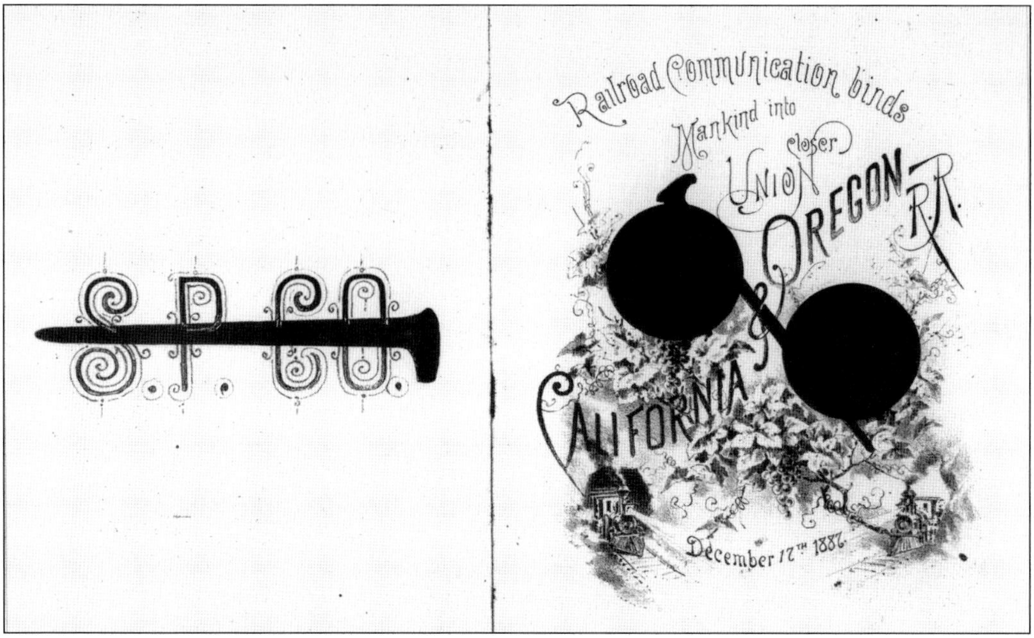

This is a copy of the invitation for the Golden Spike Ceremony. The invitation states, "You are respectfully invited to join an excursion to Portland, Oregon, in celebration of the completion of the California and Oregon and the Oregon and California railroad lines and to participate in the ceremonies of Driving the Last Spike in the construction of railroad communication between the cities of San Francisco and Sacramento in California, and the cities of Portland and Salem in Oregon. The train will leave San Francisco at 4:00 p.m. December 16 and the ceremonies of Driving the Last Spike will take place at Ashland, Oregon 2:00 p.m. Saturday, December 17, 1887."

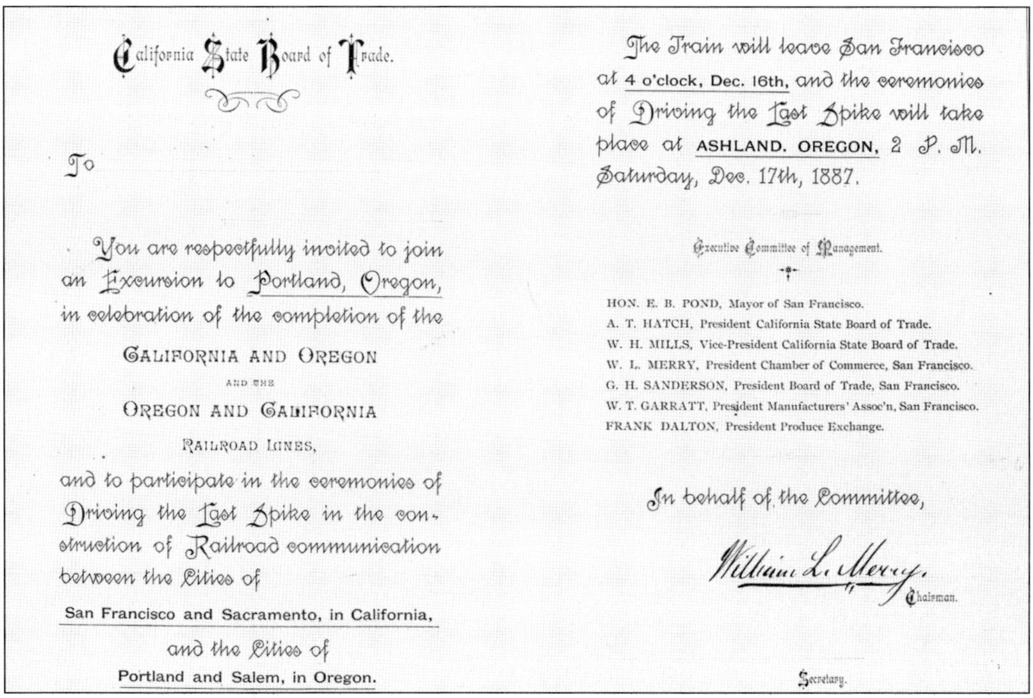

California State Board of Trade.

To

You are respectfully invited to join an Excursion to Portland, Oregon, in celebration of the completion of the

CALIFORNIA AND OREGON

AND THE

OREGON AND CALIFORNIA

RAILROAD LINES,

and to participate in the ceremonies of Driving the Last Spike in the construction of Railroad communication between the Cities of

San Francisco and Sacramento, in California,

and the Cities of

Portland and Salem, in Oregon.

The Train will leave San Francisco at 4 o'clock, Dec. 16th, and the ceremonies of Driving the Last Spike will take place at ASHLAND. OREGON, 2 P. M. Saturday, Dec. 17th, 1887.

Executive Committee of Management.

HON. E. B. POND, Mayor of San Francisco.
A. T. HATCH, President California State Board of Trade.
W. H. MILLS, Vice-President California State Board of Trade.
W. L. MERRY, President Chamber of Commerce, San Francisco.
G. H. SANDERSON, President Board of Trade, San Francisco.
W. T. GARRATT, President Manufacturers' Assoc'n, San Francisco.
FRANK DALTON, President Produce Exchange.

In behalf of the Committee,

William L. Merry,
Chairman.

Secretary.

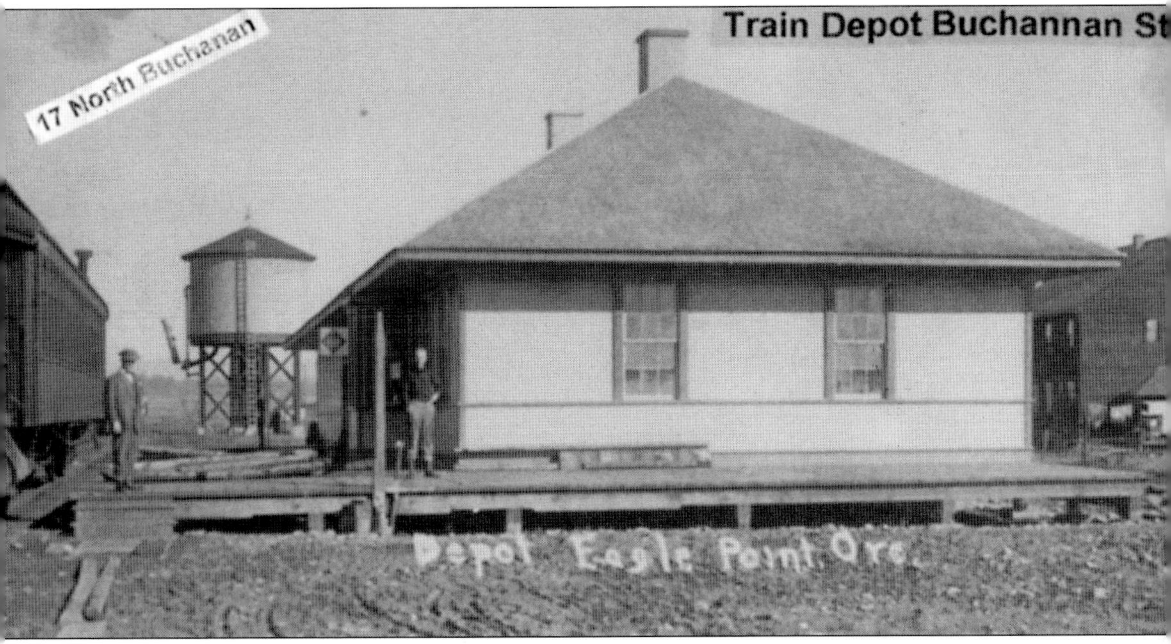

In 1904, the locals learned that the railroad was coming to town. The *Medford Mail Tribune* announced, "The time which has been looked forward to for many years by our most progressive citizens has at last arrived. The vast forests of the Cascades are to be reached by a railroad, and the immense timber wealth, which has been going to waste for the past two decades, is to be utilized and become part of the varied resources of Southern Oregon." On December 5, 1905, residents heard a train in their town for the very first time. The excitement was short lived, as winter weather prevented the train from returning for the next six months. On June 27, 1906, the train chugged into town again. James Fryer wrote in his journal, "Up early took flowers and cherries to the train, a big turnout, the band was out and they gave the folks of Eagle Point a free ride to Medford and back. Had a gay time, got home at half past four."

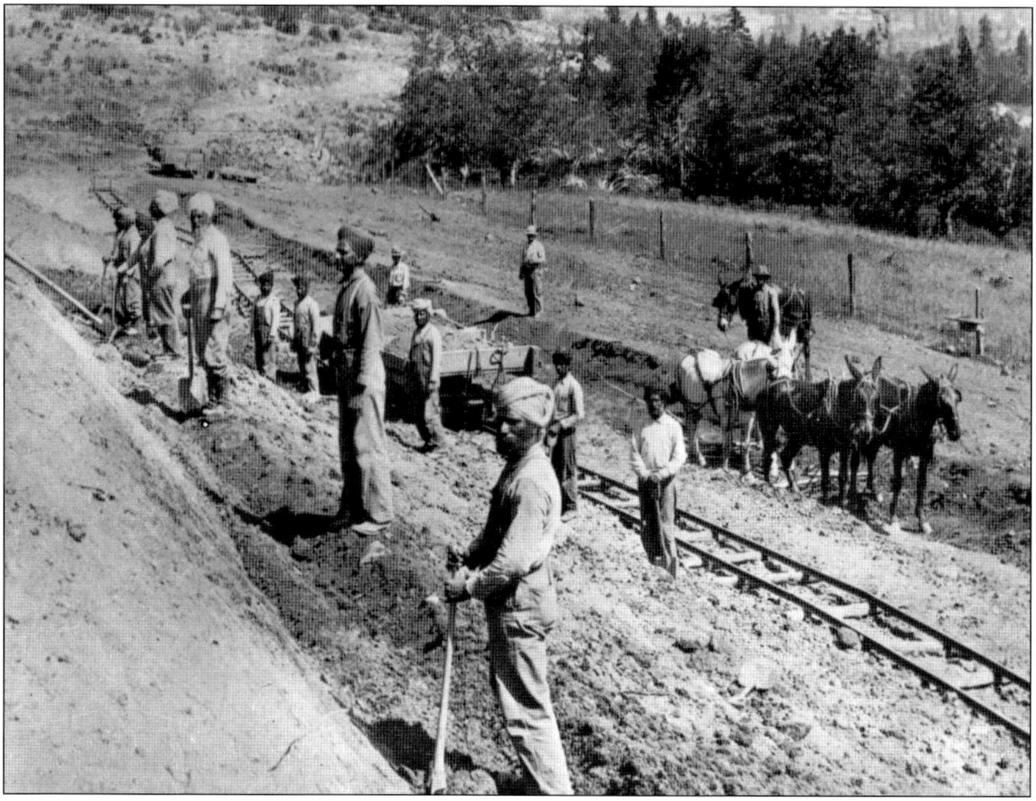

Locals were surprised to see Asian Indians working on the railroad, all of who went by the last name Singh. Nevah Taylor remembered them purchasing eggs, butter, and milk at their family farm. She said they did not speak any English, which made the transaction a bit difficult.

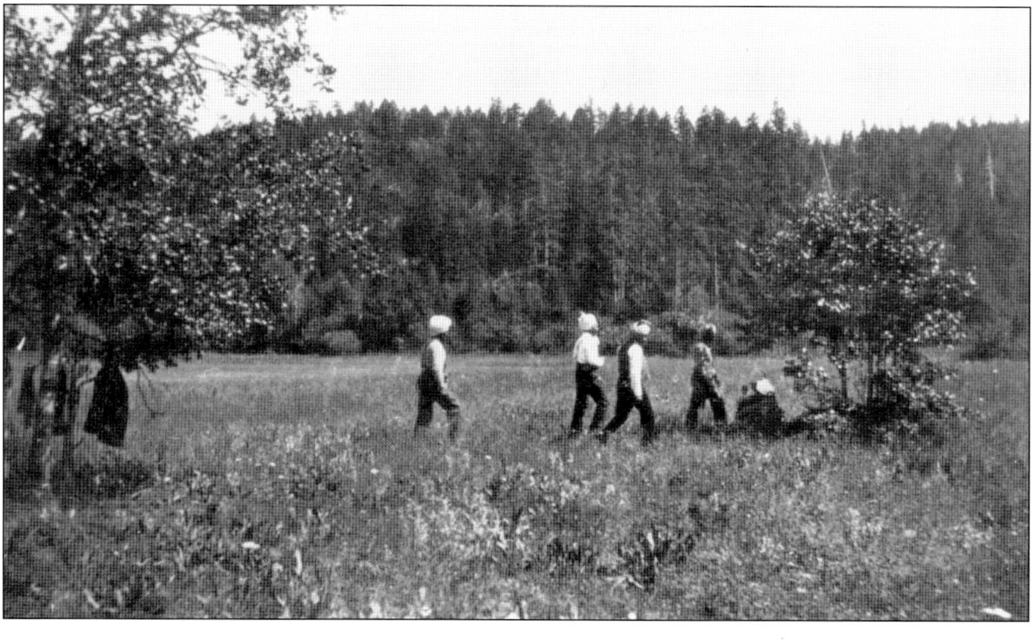

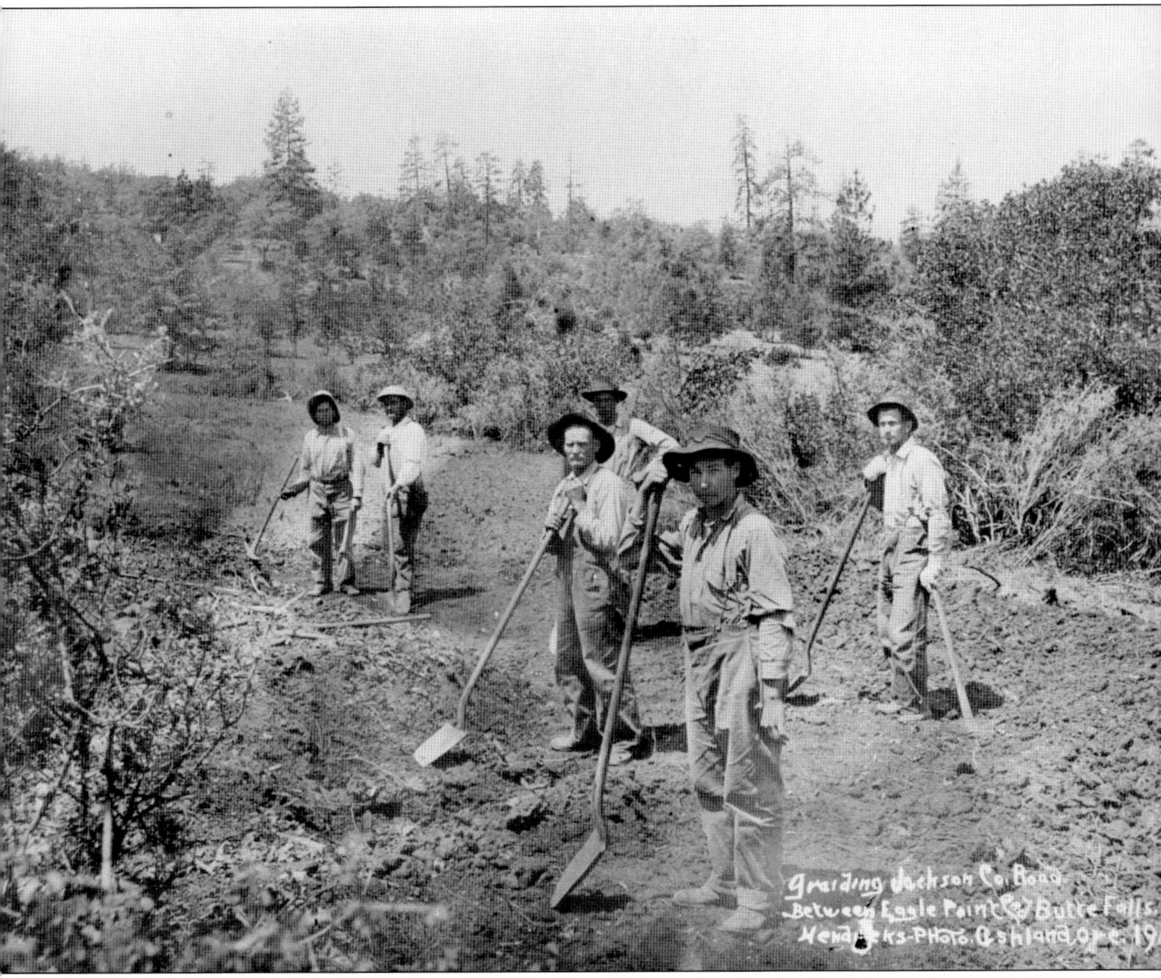

Grading a road was hard work, as these men discovered in 1910. They are working on a road that will connect Eagle Point and Butte Falls.

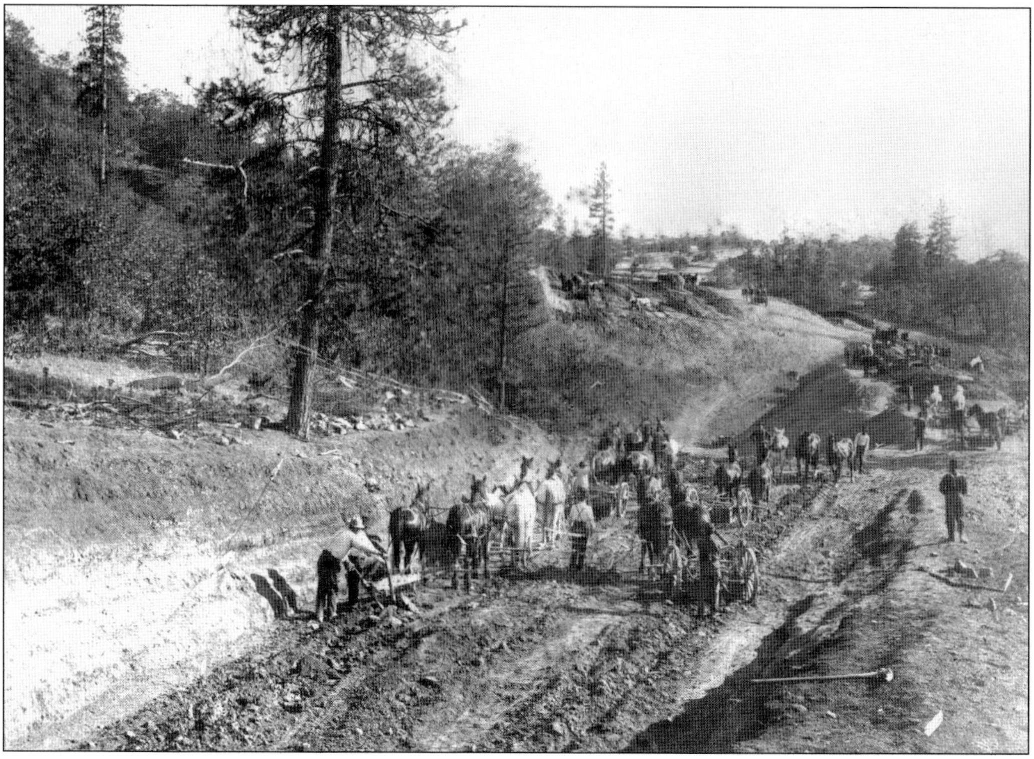

The horses are putting in a hard day's work as they grade the road prior to the railroad tracks being laid outside of Eagle Point. Local men with their own horse teams were paid $4 per day to prepare the ground for the rails. The original plan was for the train to run from Medford to Crater Lake, stopping in towns along the way. Financial problems along with the sheer magnitude of the work involved kept the project from completion.

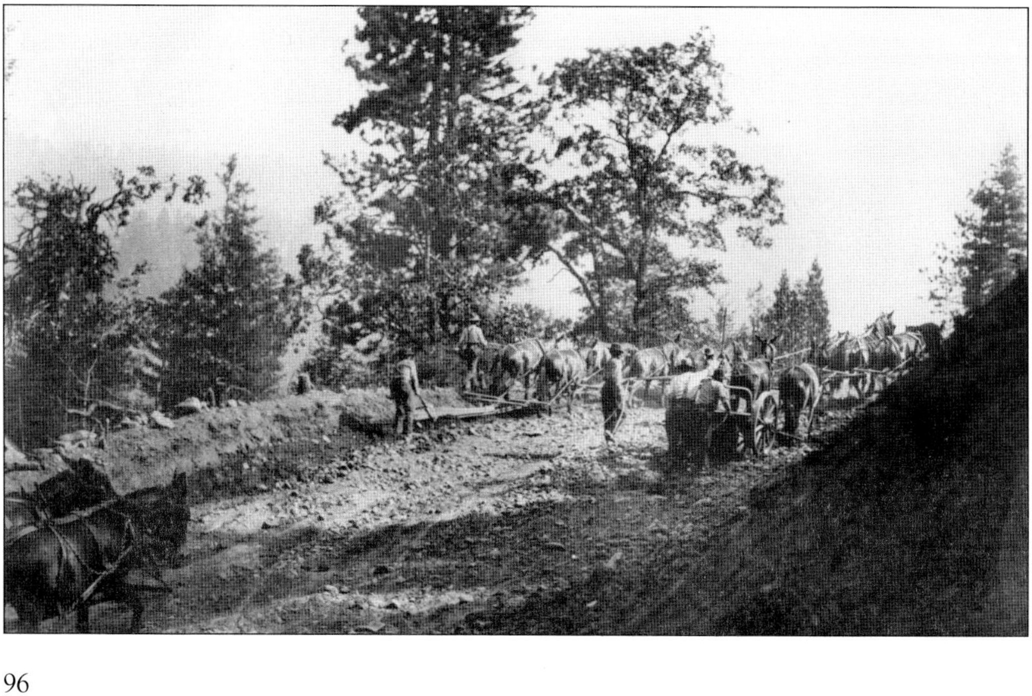

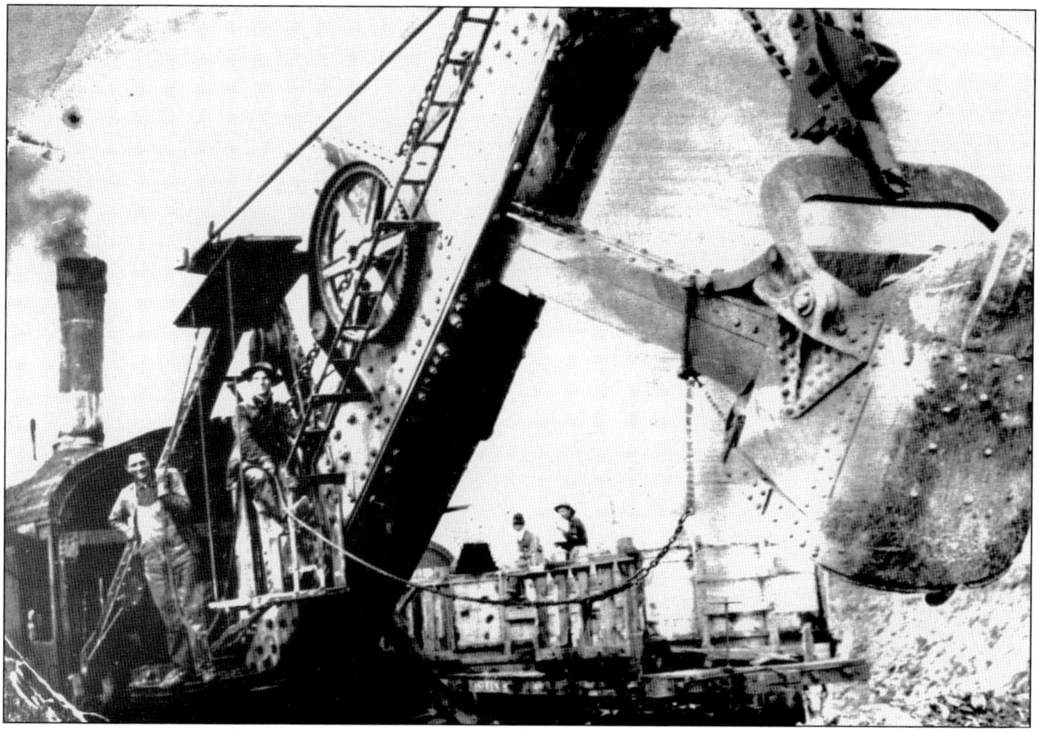

These giant steam shovels could be heard throughout town as it dug a path for the tracks to be laid from Eagle Point to Butte Falls.

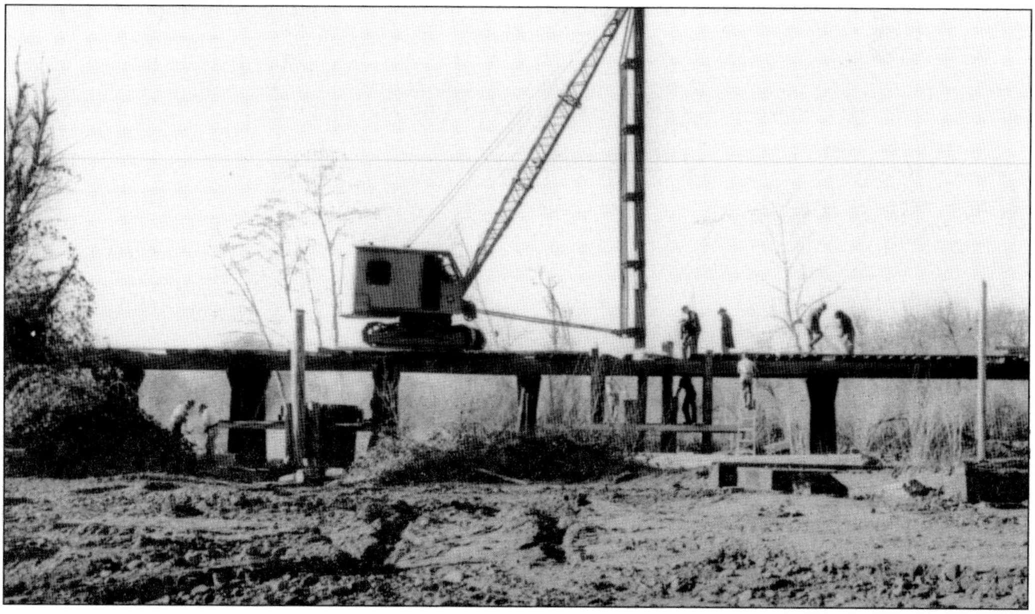

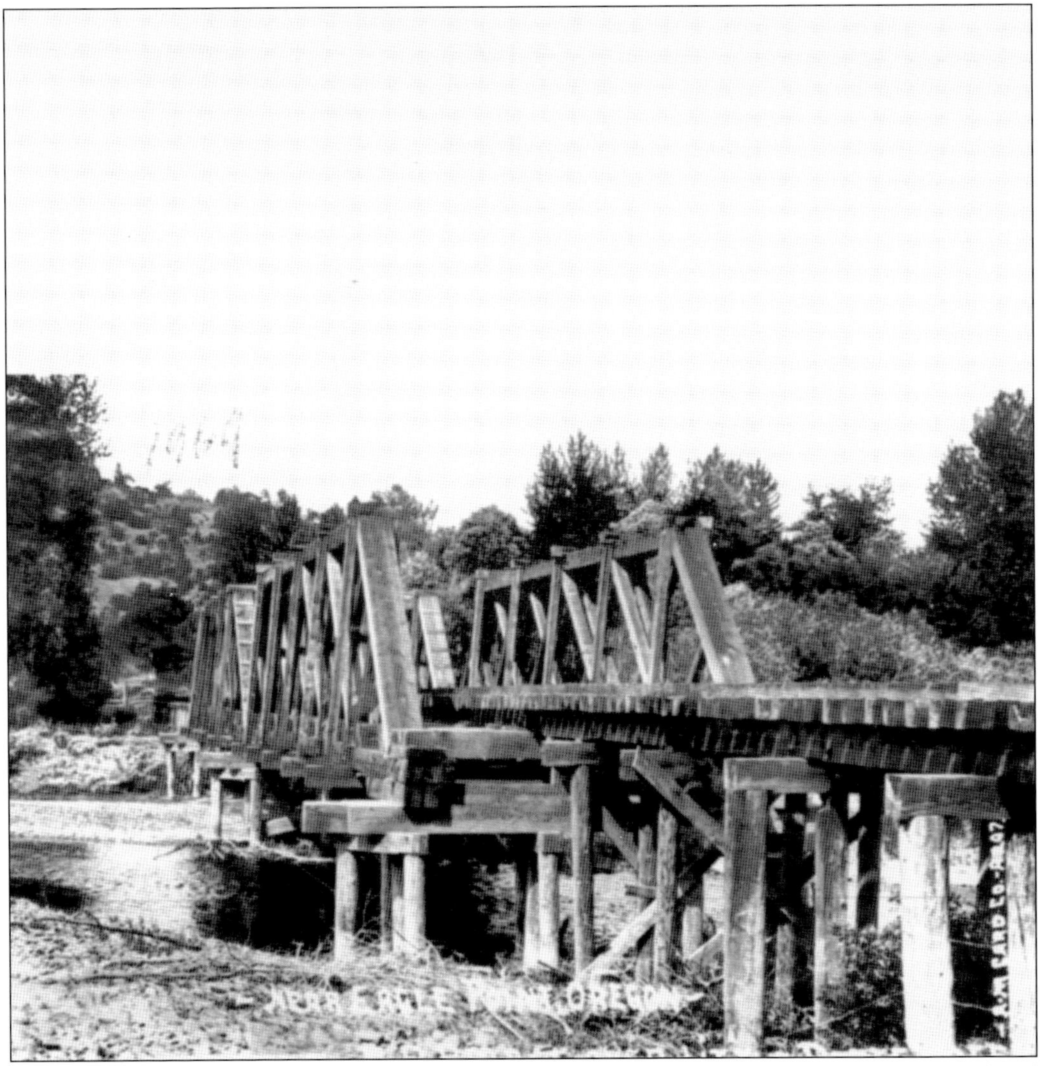

In 1905, this railroad bridge was constructed on Nicholas Young's property. Bringing the railroad to Eagle Point was a tremendous boom for the orchardists who now had a quick method of transporting their fruits to outside markets.

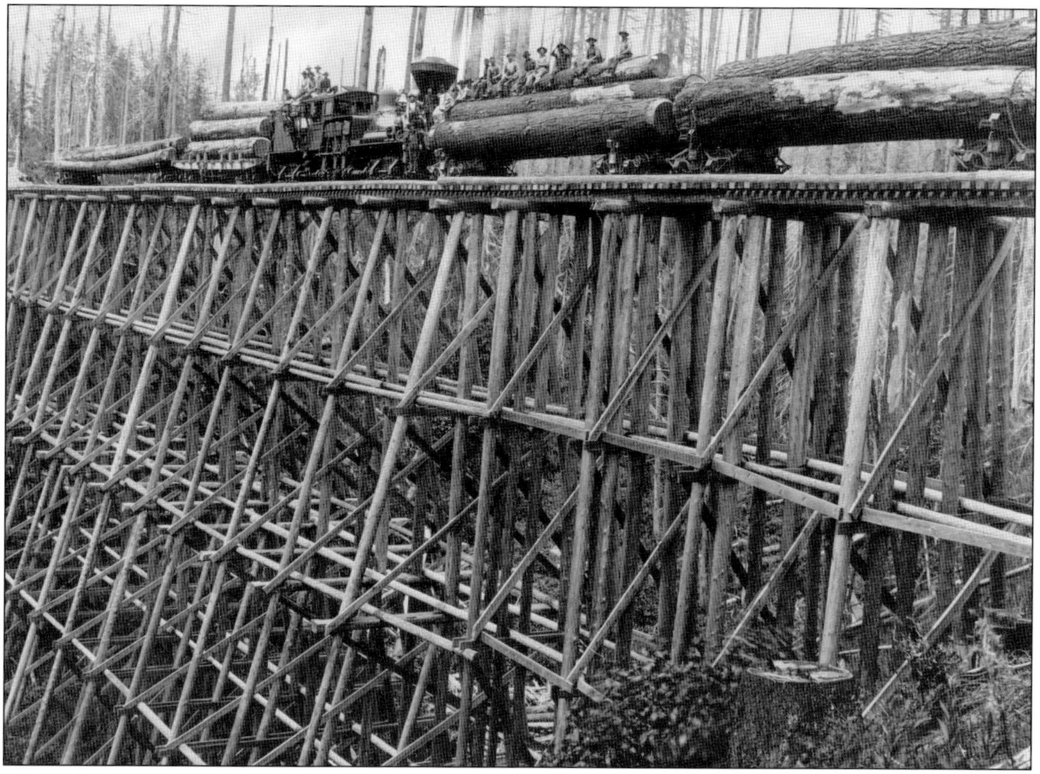

The railroad brought many opportunities to Eagle Point. Many men found work on the railroads. Also, the railroad construction workers from out of the area rented rooms in hotels and boarding houses. This in turn brought business to the restaurants and bars in town. Building trestles proved to be a challenge throughout Southern Oregon and Northern California due to the mountainous terrain and the unforgiving weather. The trestles built in the canyons near Butte Falls were no different. A total of nine gigantic trestles were built and six smaller ones.

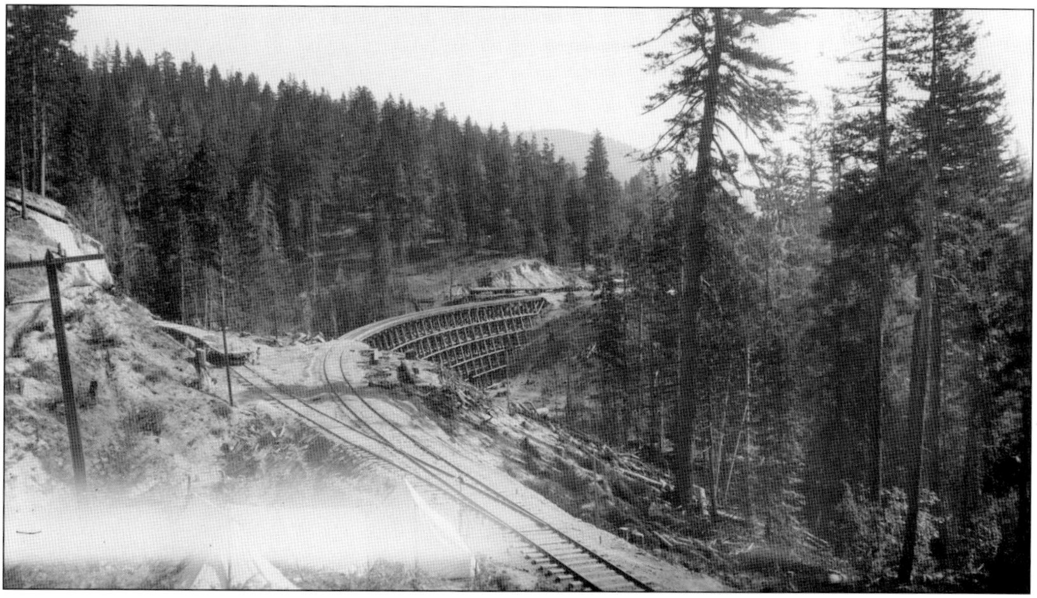

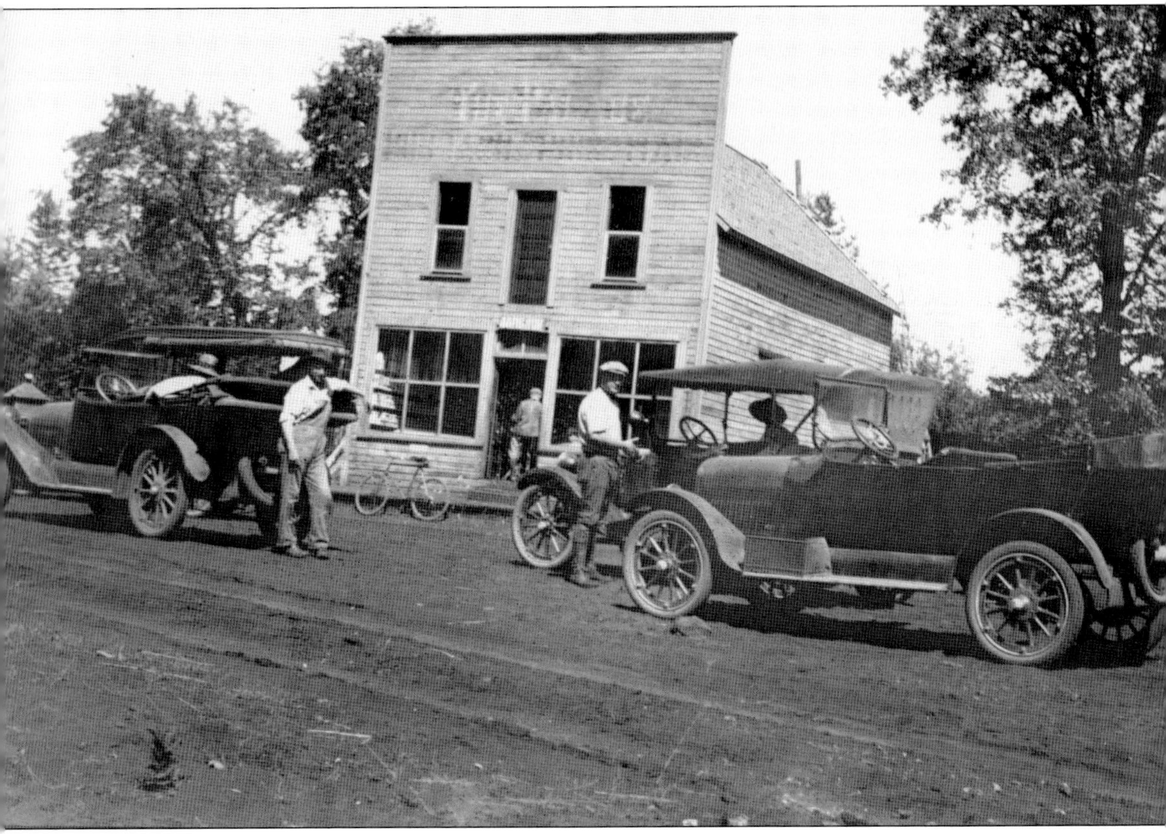

Not far from Eagle Point is the town of Butte Falls. When Bert Harris arrived in the area, he set up a sawmill on the banks of Big Butte Creek and plotted out a town he called Big Butte. The roaring falls fell 15 feet, which was more than enough to power a few large sawmills. In 1904, the name of the town was changed to Butte Falls. The land was rich in sugar pine timber. The town grew slowly, but eventually families arrived and a town began to take shape. The first students were taught in a private home, and years later were taught in a log cabin. Above is a photograph of the Butte Falls Post Office.

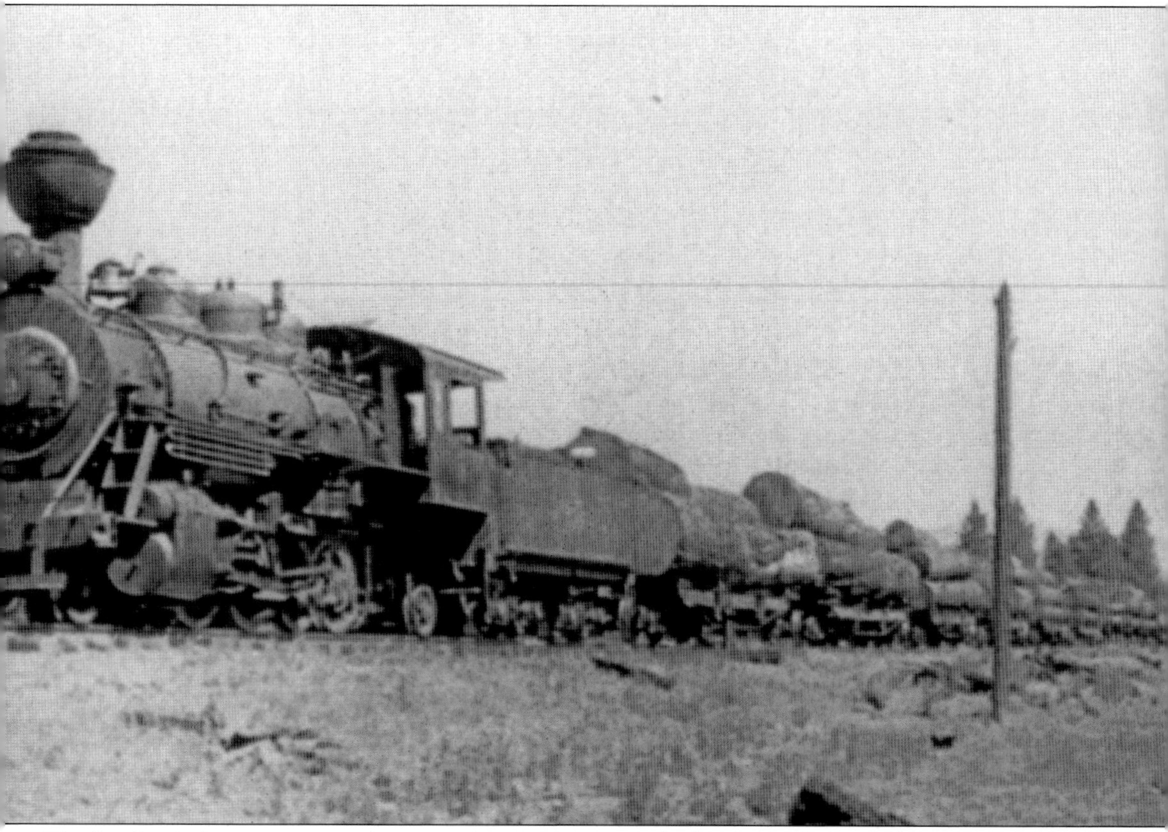

The lumber industry continued to grow, but transporting the logs out of Butte Falls was extremely challenging. In 1910, railroad tracks were laid from Medford to Butte Falls. This presented the lumber industry with opportunities to move their lumber throughout the country. They were no longer dependent on freight wagons, which could only go a limited distance. It also meant those living in Butte Falls could take the train to Medford. Prior to the railroad, the townsfolk had to make the journey by wagon, which could take two days round-trip. Once the railroad came to town, businesses opened and soon the town had a hardware store, a barbershop, two billiard halls, a hotel, restaurants, and an athletic club. The town was incorporated in 1911. Upon incorporation, it was decided that cows should not be allowed in town. Cattle guards were put in place at each end of the Butte Falls, and it is because of this that Butte Falls was once listed in *Ripley's Believe It Or Not* for being the only town in America with cattle guards at each end of the town.

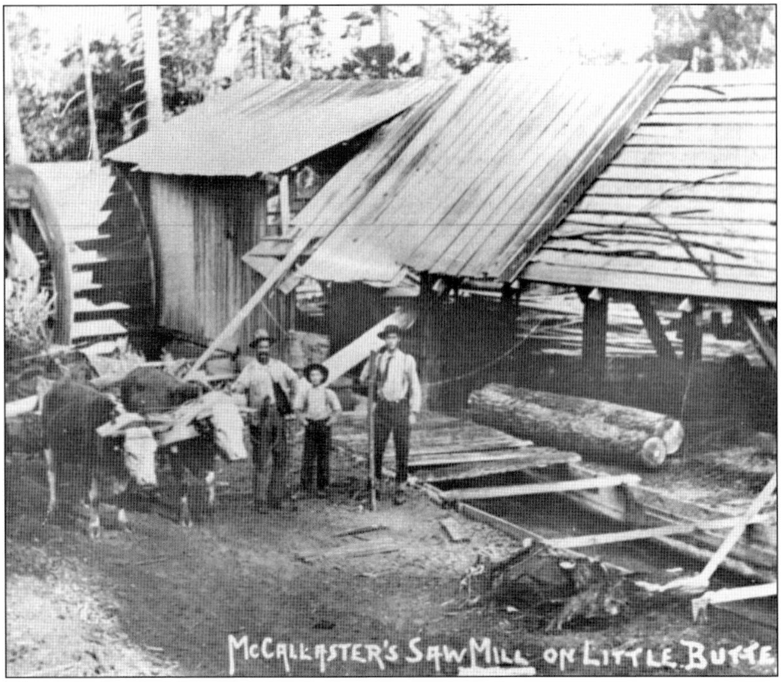

John McCallister operated this sawmill on Little Butte Creek. John grew up in Eagle Point and his father was a schoolteacher before opening a broom-making business. John married Carrie Adelia and they had eight children.

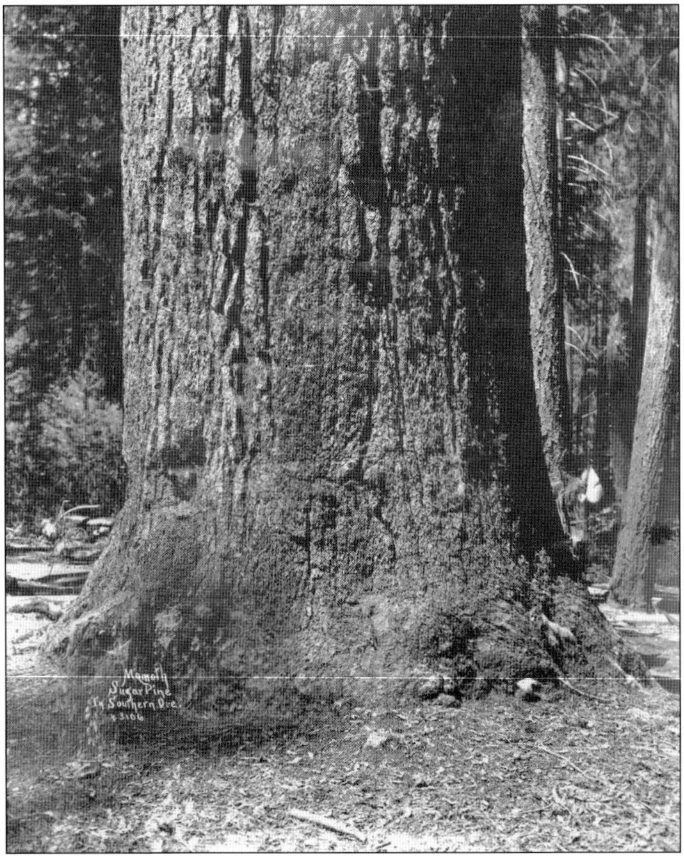

Sugar Pine trees were not only plentiful—they were gigantic. The men who felled the trees only had rudimentary equipment such as saws, axes, and ropes.

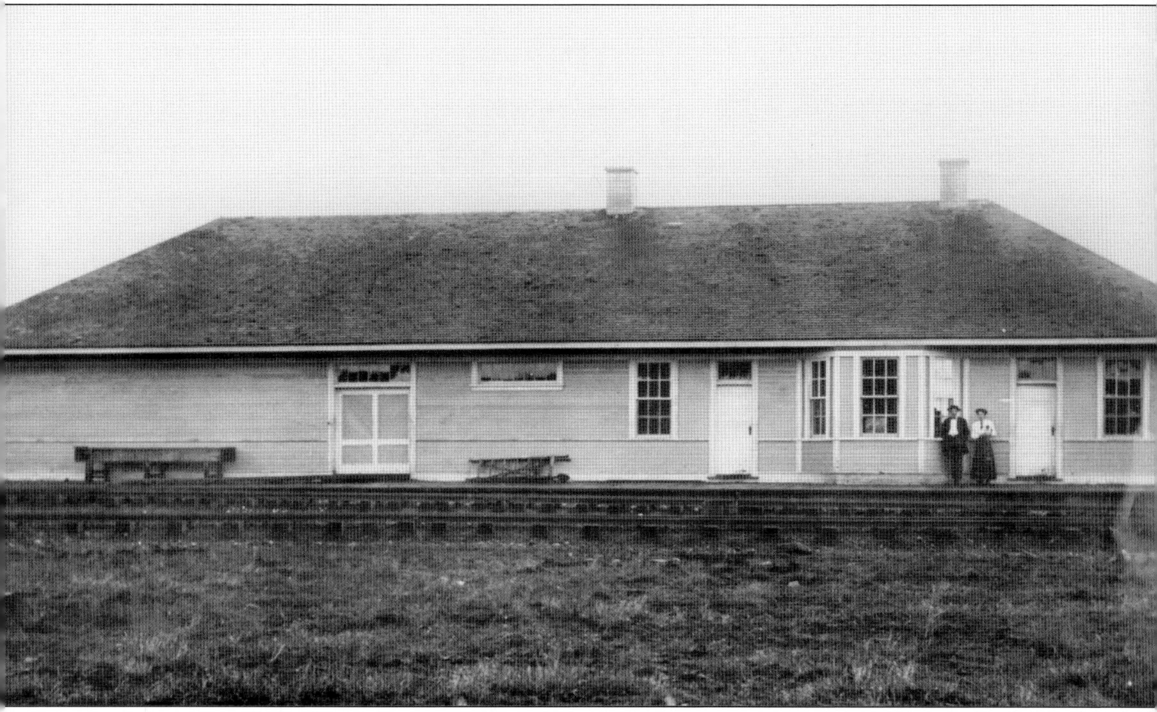

A new train depot measuring 90-feet-by-120-feet was constructed in Eagle Point. The building included quarters for the railroad agent to live, a freight room, and two waiting rooms. The officials explained the need for two rooms by saying, "One for the ladies and one for the men, so that the men who want to, can smoke and talk without being embarrassed by the ladies. And the ladies will not be annoyed by the smoking etc., of the men."

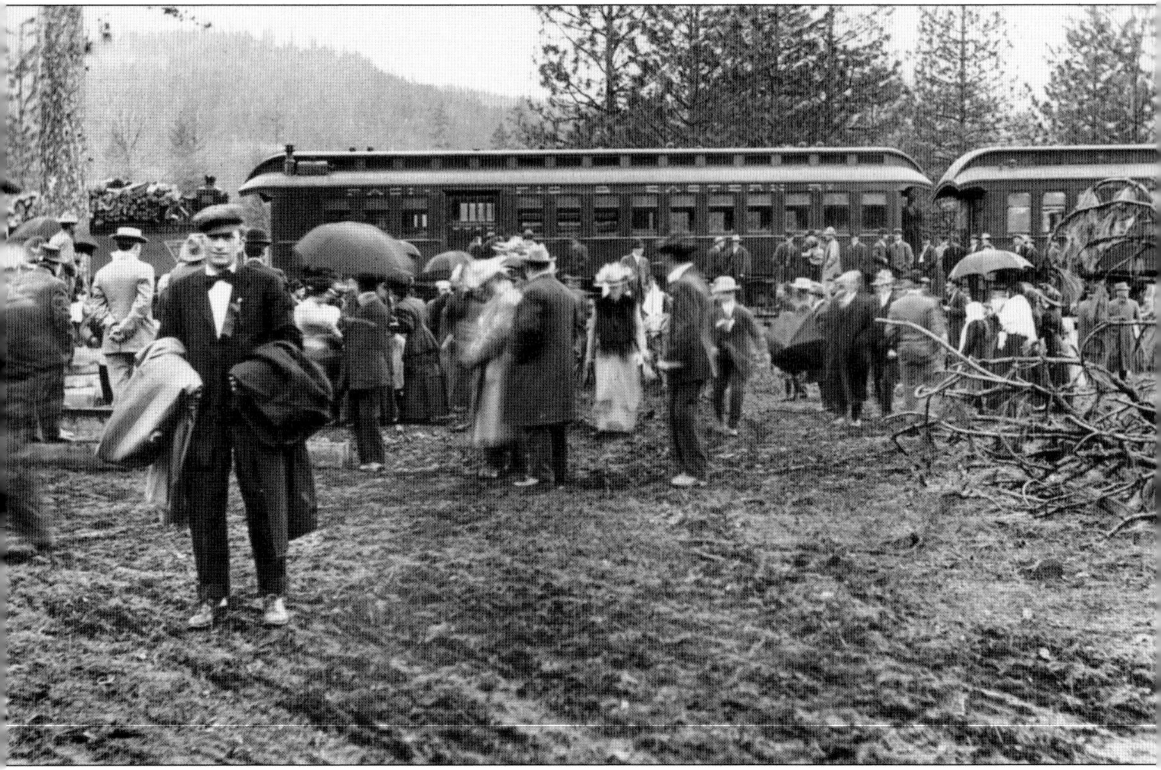

Butte Falls advertised its clean, fresh mountain air and cooler temperatures. A train ticket from Medford to Butte Falls cost $1. The train left Medford at 8:14 a.m. and arrived in Butte Falls at 11:00 a.m. after making six stops. In 1912, the *Medford Mail Tribune* reported large crowds taking the train to Butte Falls. Once there, they could camp or stay in a hotel and enjoy their time in the mountains. The railroad advertised, "Families can now camp in the woods during the summer and the business man can leave Medford at 3:00 p.m. on Saturday afternoon, spend Sunday with the family and be back in Medford by 10:00 Monday morning."

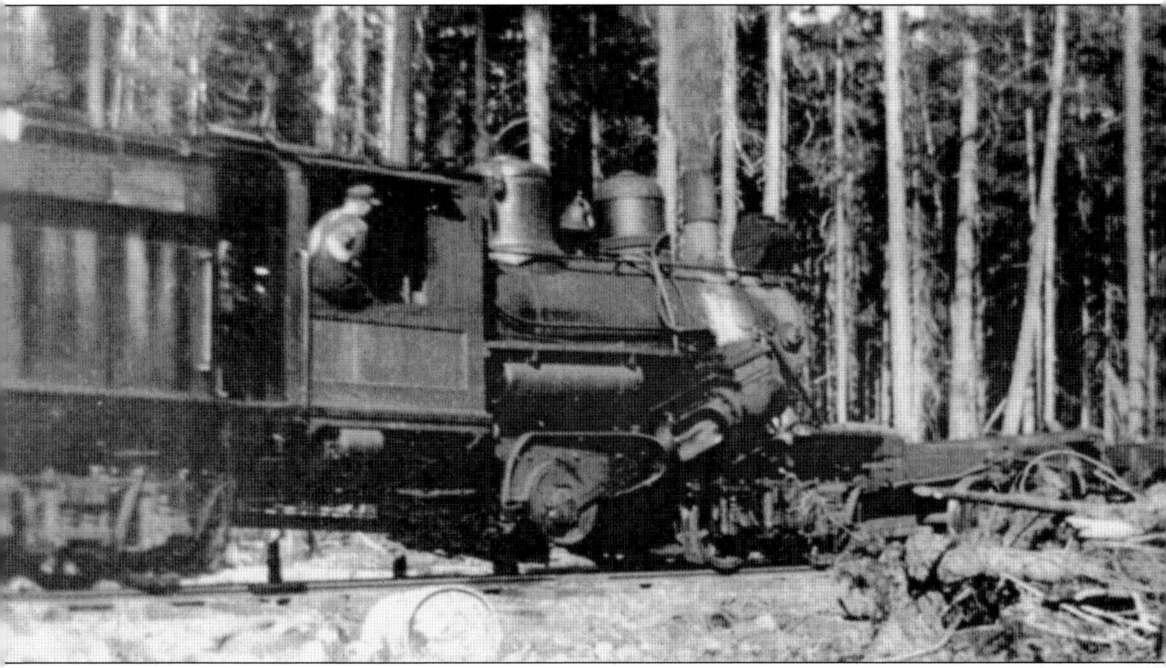

This train is making its way past Eagle Point, heading towards Butte Falls where it will pick up a large load of logs. The logs will be taken to Medford and then transported to all parts of the country.

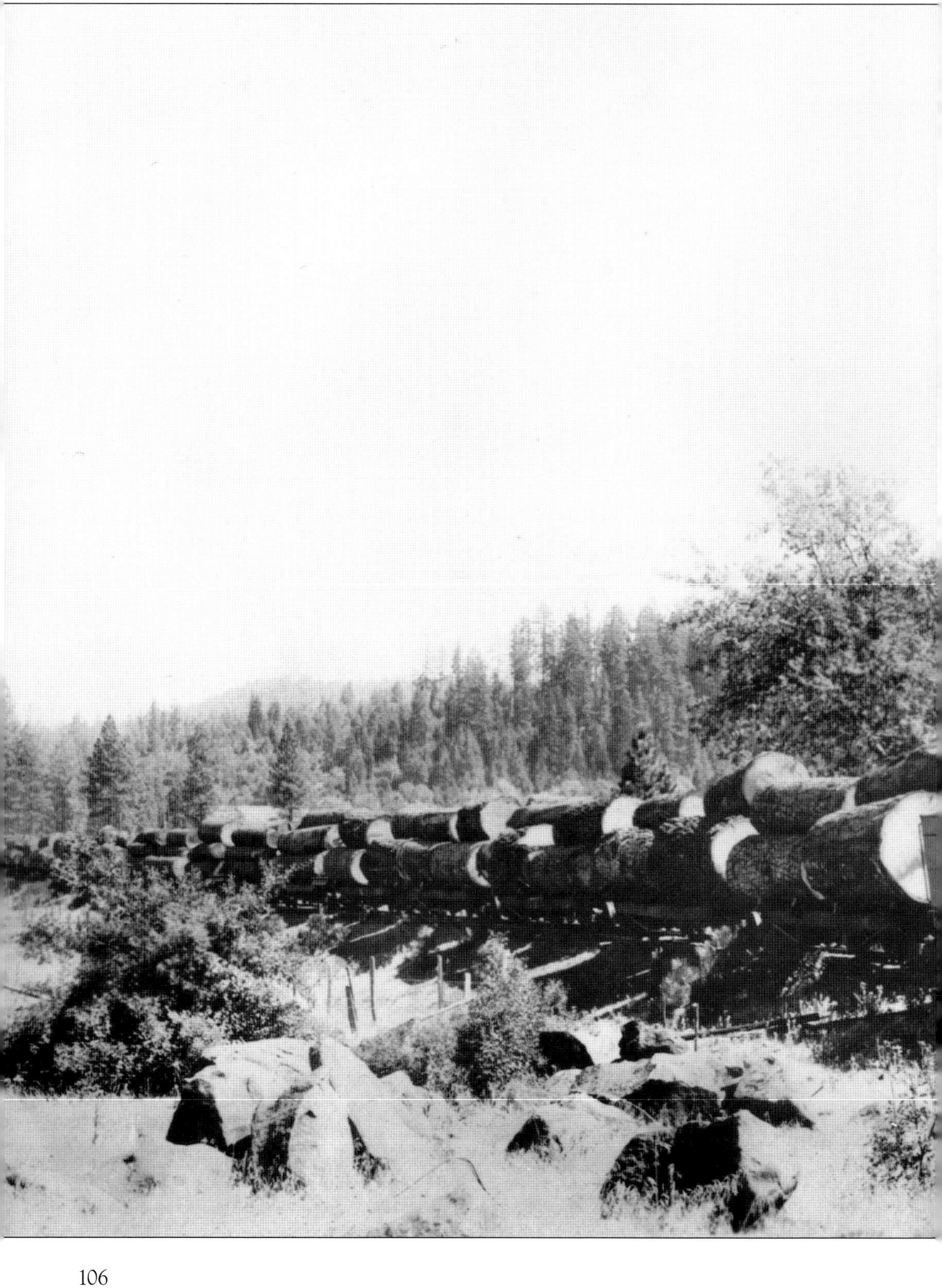

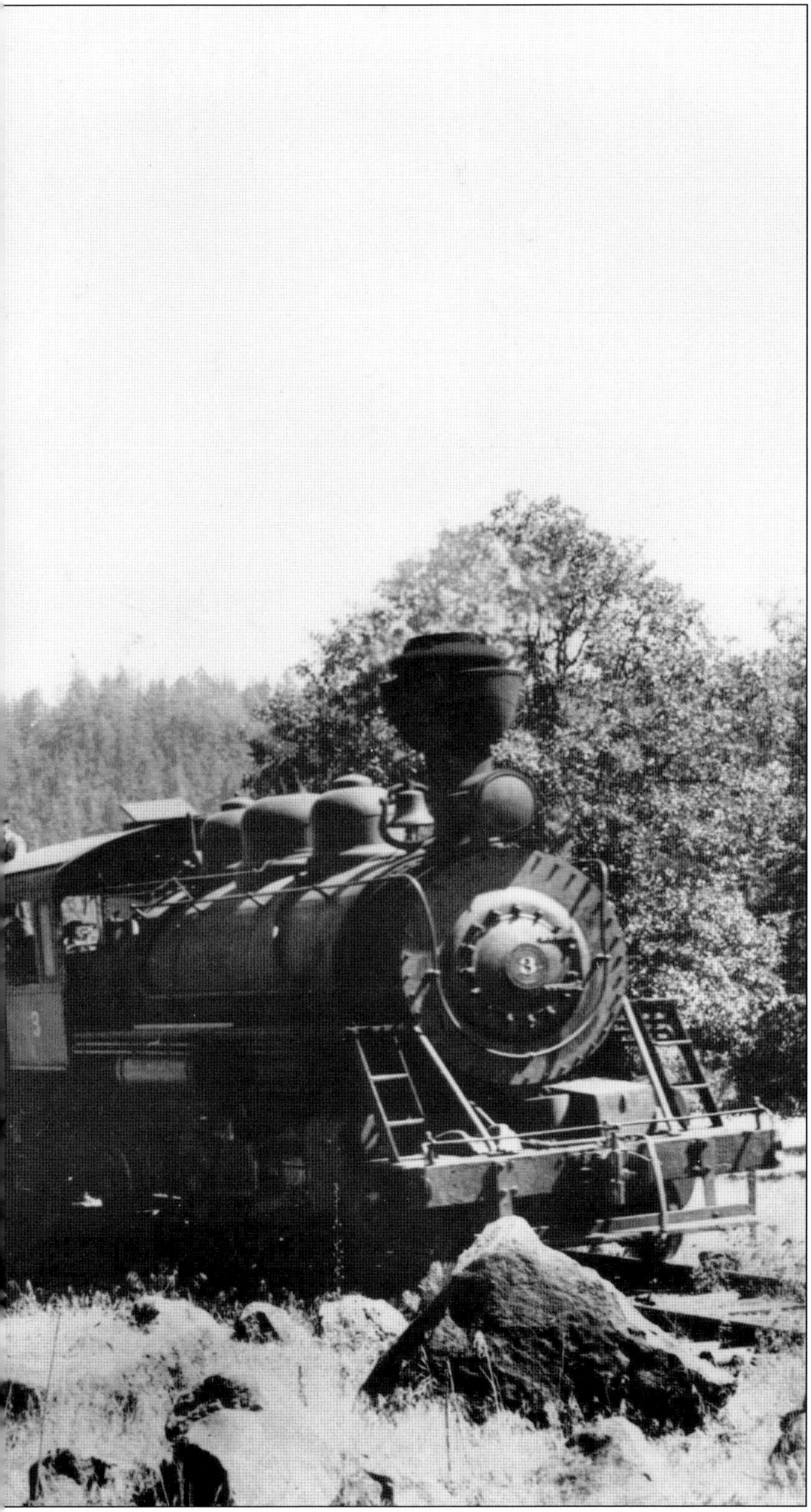

Bringing the train as far as Butte Falls provided the logging industry with a way to transport the mammoth logs out of the dense forests.

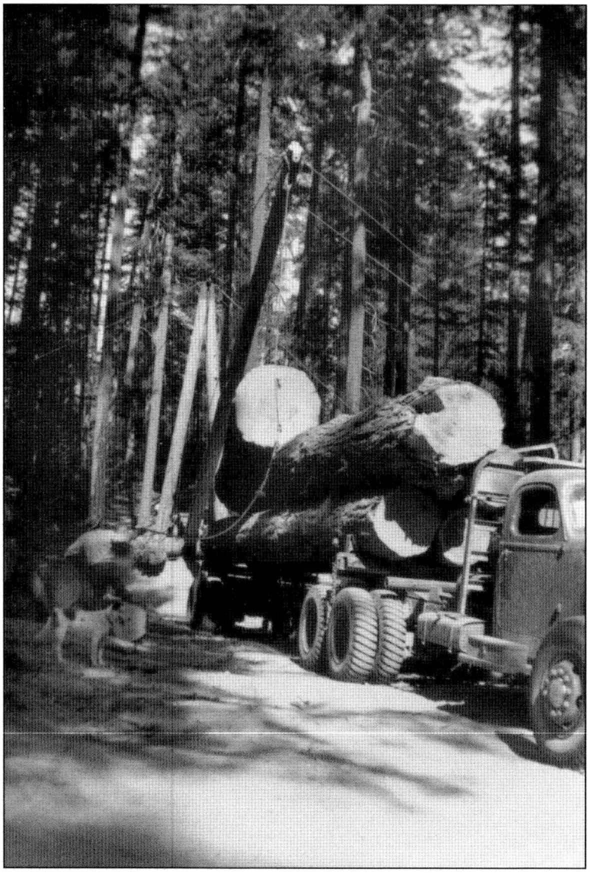

The Medford logging train made two trips a day through Eagle Point. Additionally, there were two passenger trains that went through town daily. One line ran from Medford to Butte Falls and the other ran from Medford to Prospect. Eventually, heavy-duty trucks offered a more economical method of moving the logs. The railroad tracks were removed and the sound of a train leaving the depot became a distant memory.

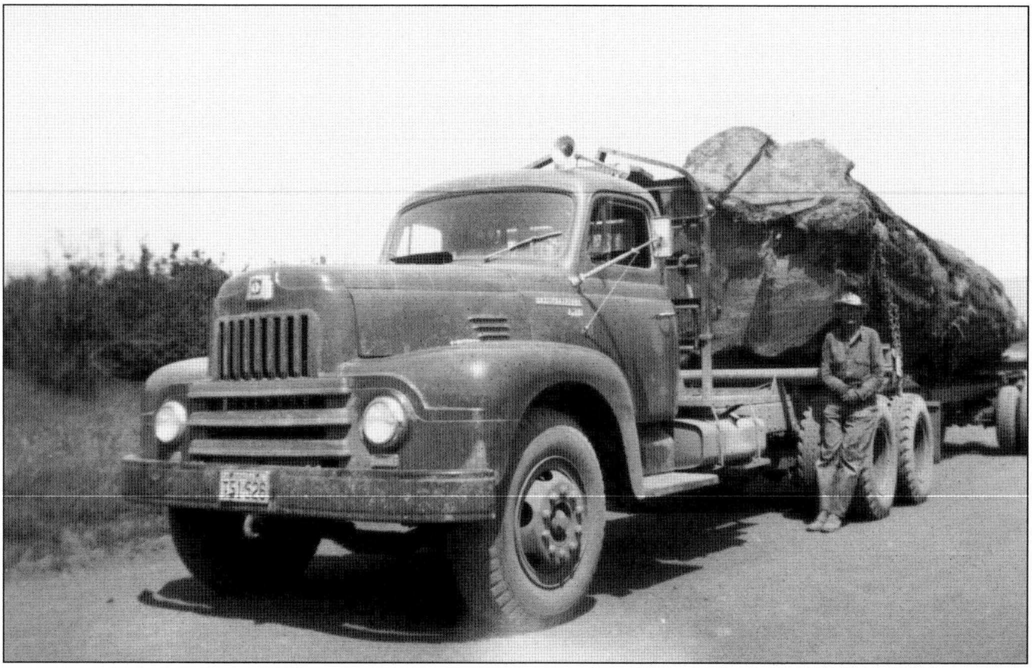

Seven

Camp White's Impact on Eagle Point

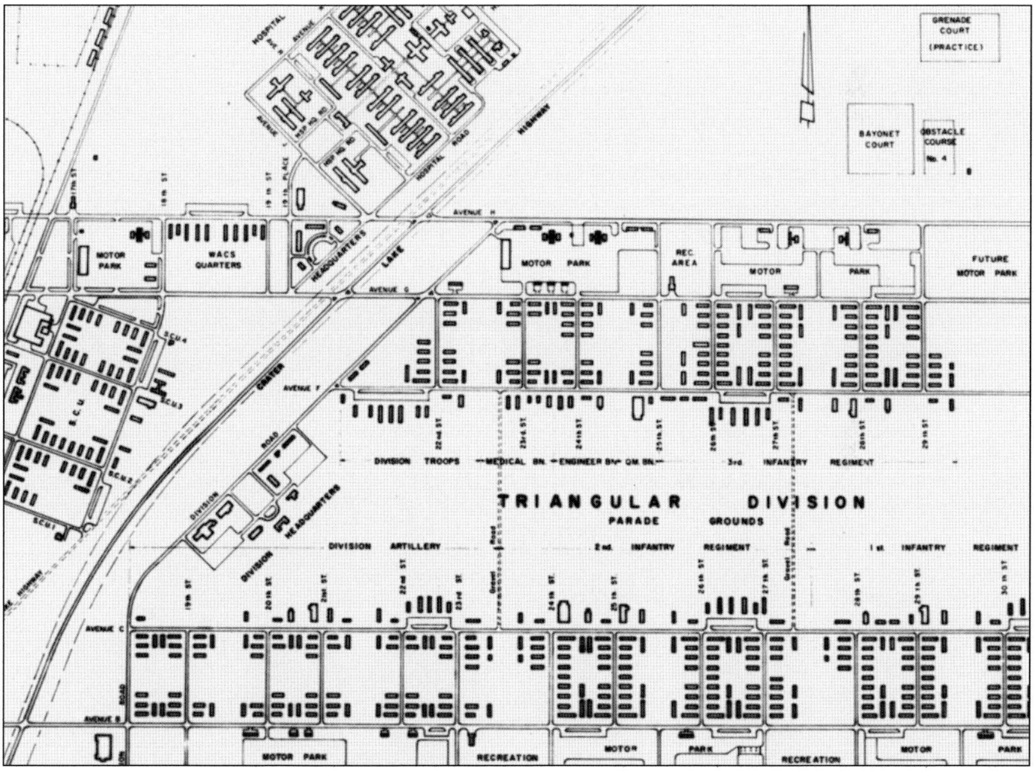

Just one month after the attacks on Pearl Harbor, an announcement was made that a cantonment would be built just outside of Eagle Point in the Agate Desert. The cantonment was named Camp White in honor of Maj. Gen. George Ared White. Major General White began his career in the Army during the Spanish-American War. During World War I, he served as a colonel. In 1907, he joined the Oregon National Guard and is credited with reorganizing the Guard. In 1930, he was promoted to major general as commander of the 41st Infantry Division. Major General White died just one month prior to the start of World War II. The government dedicated $27 million for the construction of the 77-square-mile camp.

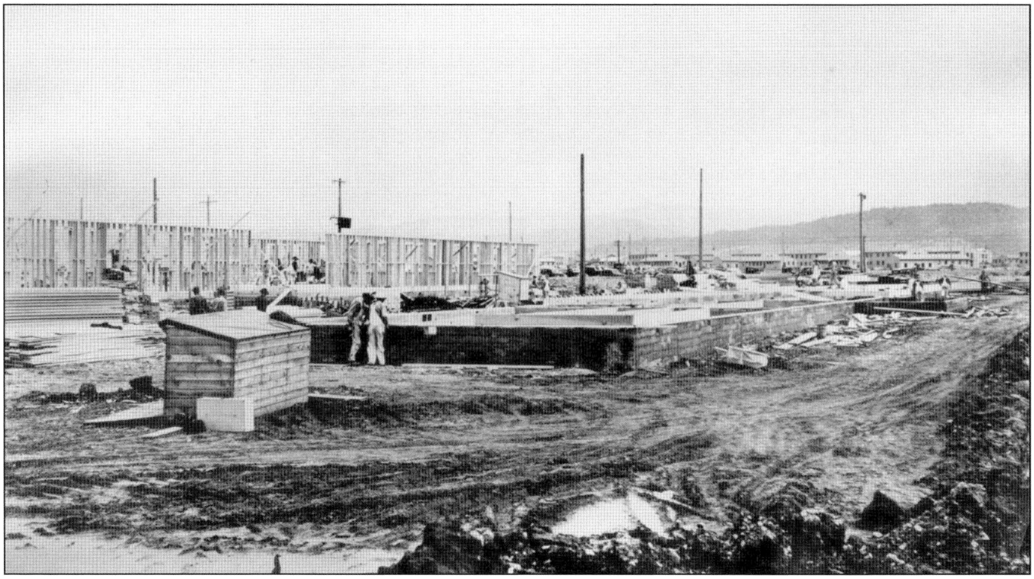

Work on the Camp White project began in earnest on February 25, 1942. The work was done at a feverish pace, with crews working around the clock. Many men from Eagle Point secured jobs in the construction industry. In all, 10,000 construction workers built 1,300 buildings. Most of the workers lived in tents in what became known as "Tent City." Many of the workers headed into Eagle Point for some relaxation when they had free time. Camp White was officially dedicated on September 15, 1942; however, it was not entirely completed until December 14, 1942. At the time that Camp White was under construction, eight other military training bases were being built in the United States.

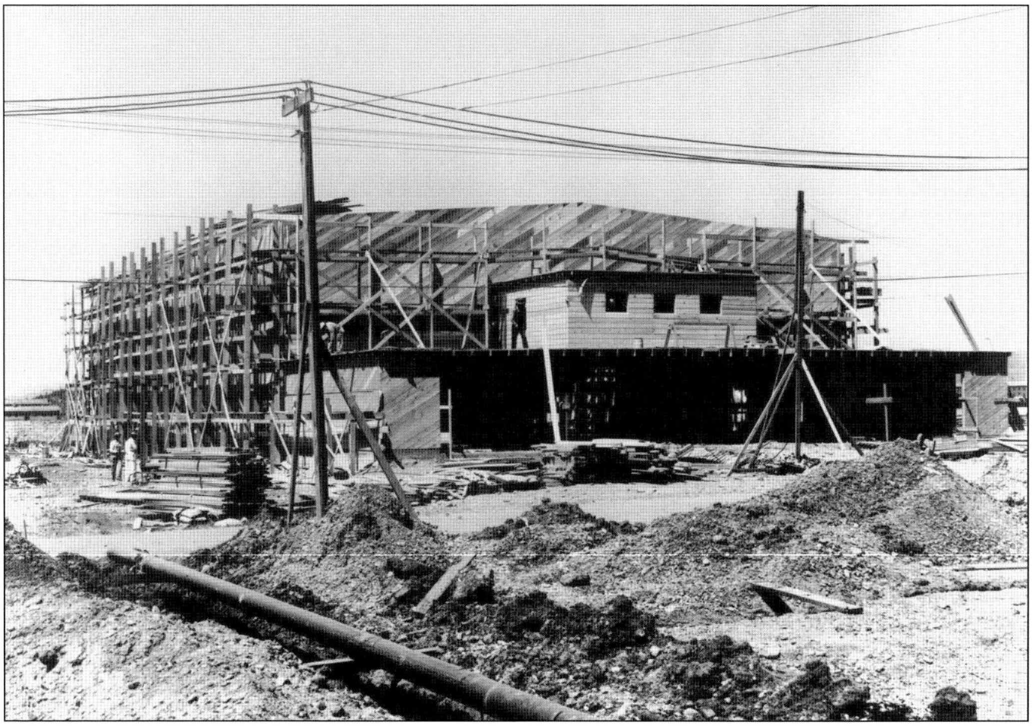

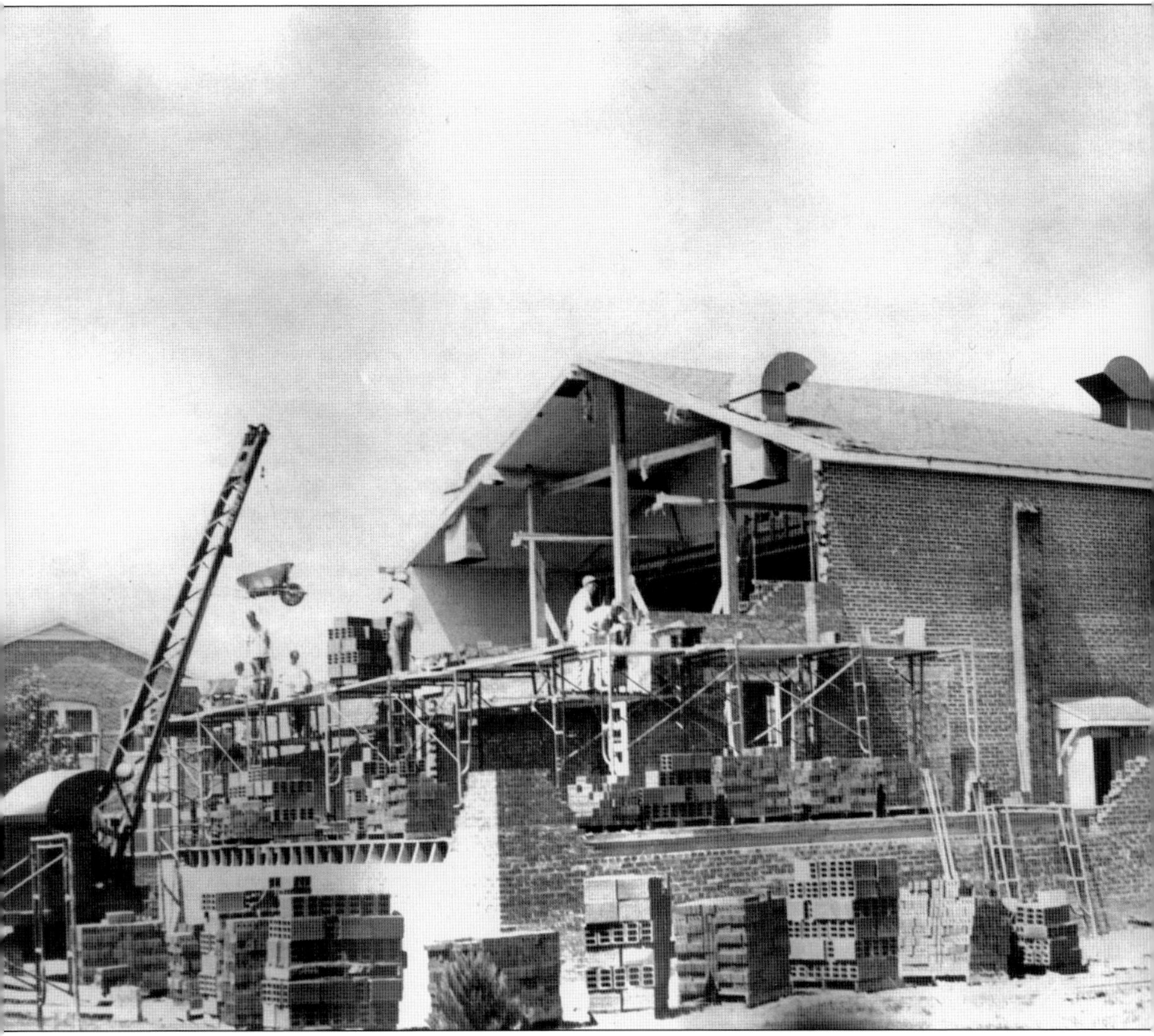

The headlines of the *Medford Mail Tribune* screamed, "HOUSING SHORTAGE." Suddenly, thousands of soldiers were arriving in this otherwise quiet area only to discover that there was no place to stay while they waited for their barracks to be built. One enterprising young soldier ran an advertisement in the Medford newspaper with the following offer: "Reward: Three-month-old Sally will reward someone with a pair of her Mommy's precious nylons for a furnished apartment or house. She really needs a home. Call Lt. Kimball, Holland Hotel." At the time, women's nylons were in short supply due to rationing. The newspaper ran articles pleading with the locals to open their homes, barns, and even chicken coops to the soldiers. The term "hot beds" was used to describe how people in Medford rented out a bed in their home for eight hours at a time. When the soldier's eight hours was up, he left and the next soldier came in for an eight-hour shift. Many Eagle Point residents opened their hearts, homes, and barns to the soldiers in need.

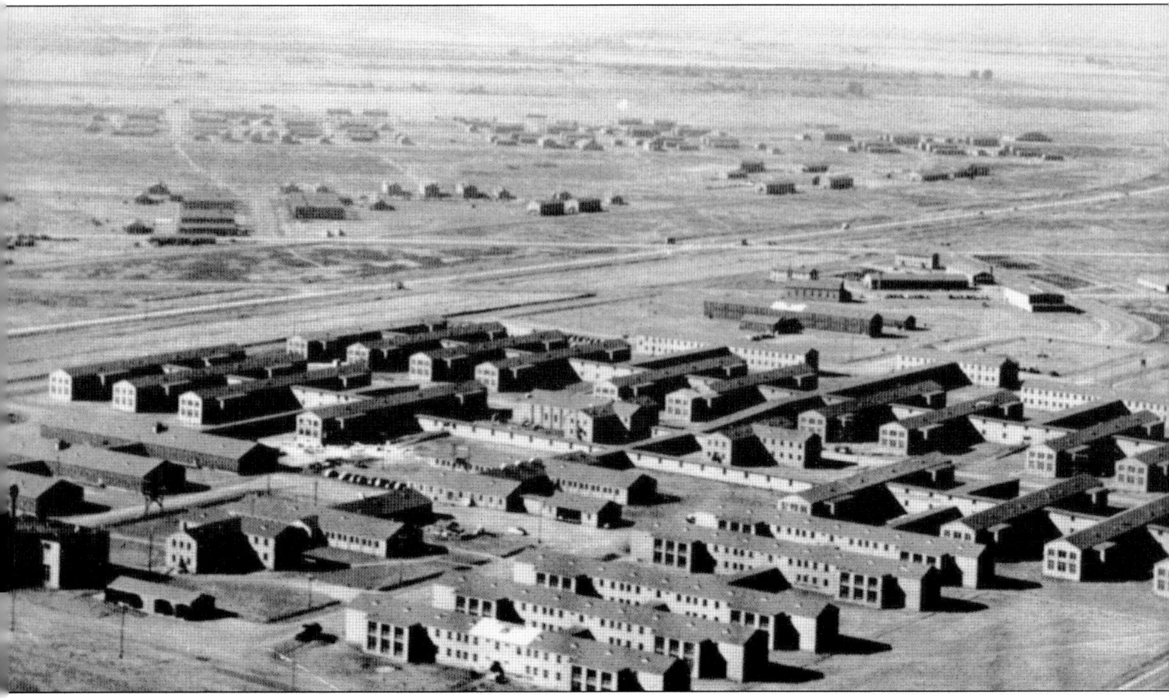

Before the cantonment was built, the land that would become Camp White was known as the Agate Desert. The Rogue River National Forest donated 1,000 trees to beautify the grounds. A 60-foot Oregon fir was planted in honor of the 91st Division's emblem. The Medford Garden Club donated 100 lilac bushes, and other garden and civic clubs donated plants and materials to make Camp White beautiful for those who were stationed there.

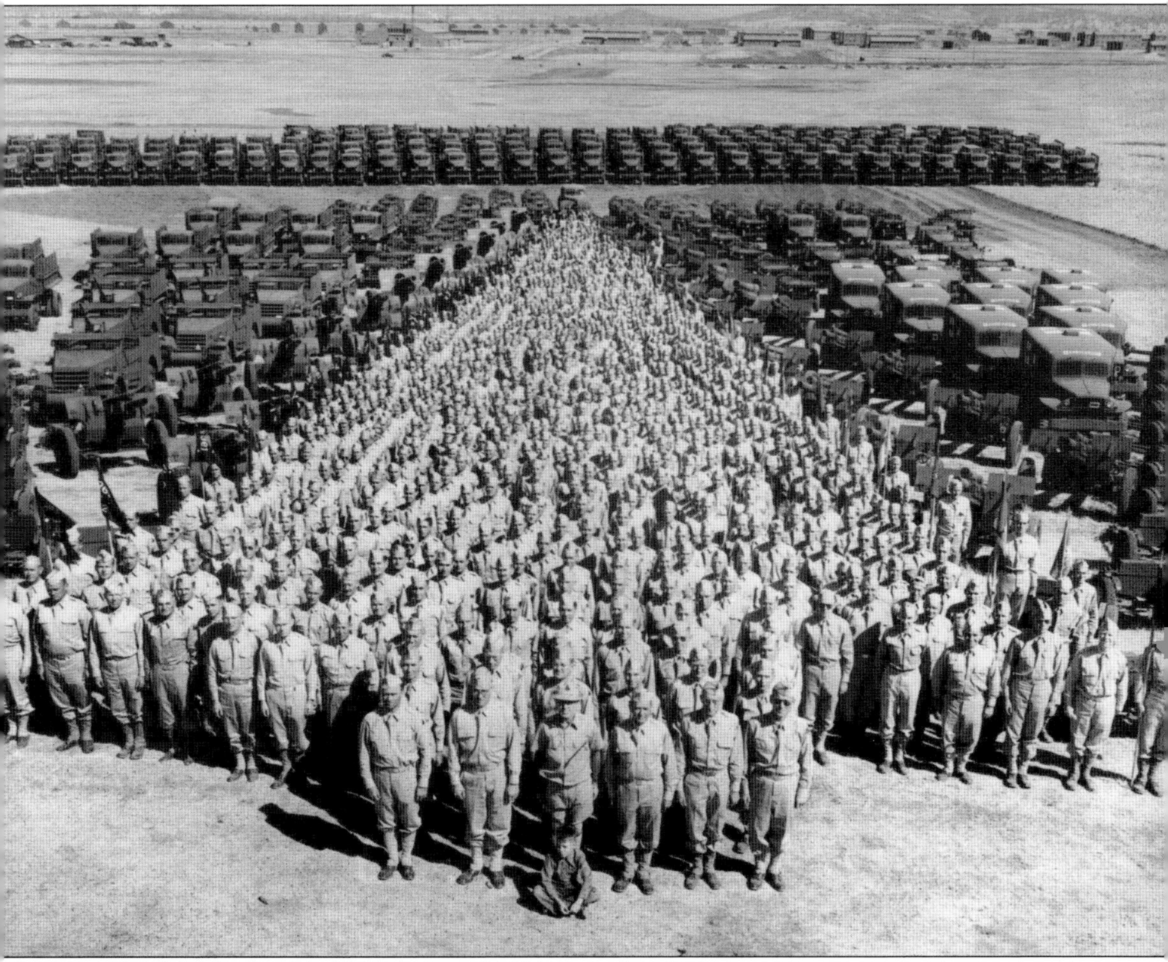

Members of the 91st Division are shown here in formation. The 91st Division was designated as a triangular division meaning that the infantry, artillery, medical staff, and engineers were all under one commander.

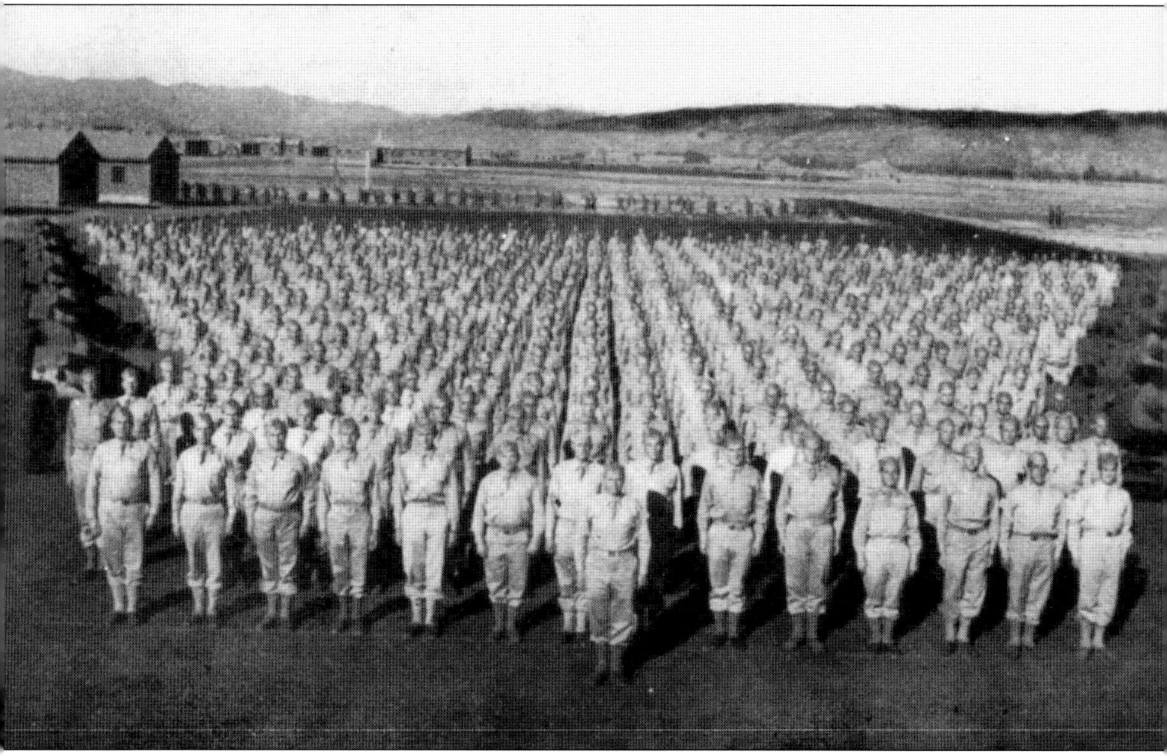

The 91st Division was originally activated in 1917 at Fort Lewis, Washington, just prior to World War I. Its slogan was "Powder River, Let'er Buck," and its emblem was a Western fir tree.

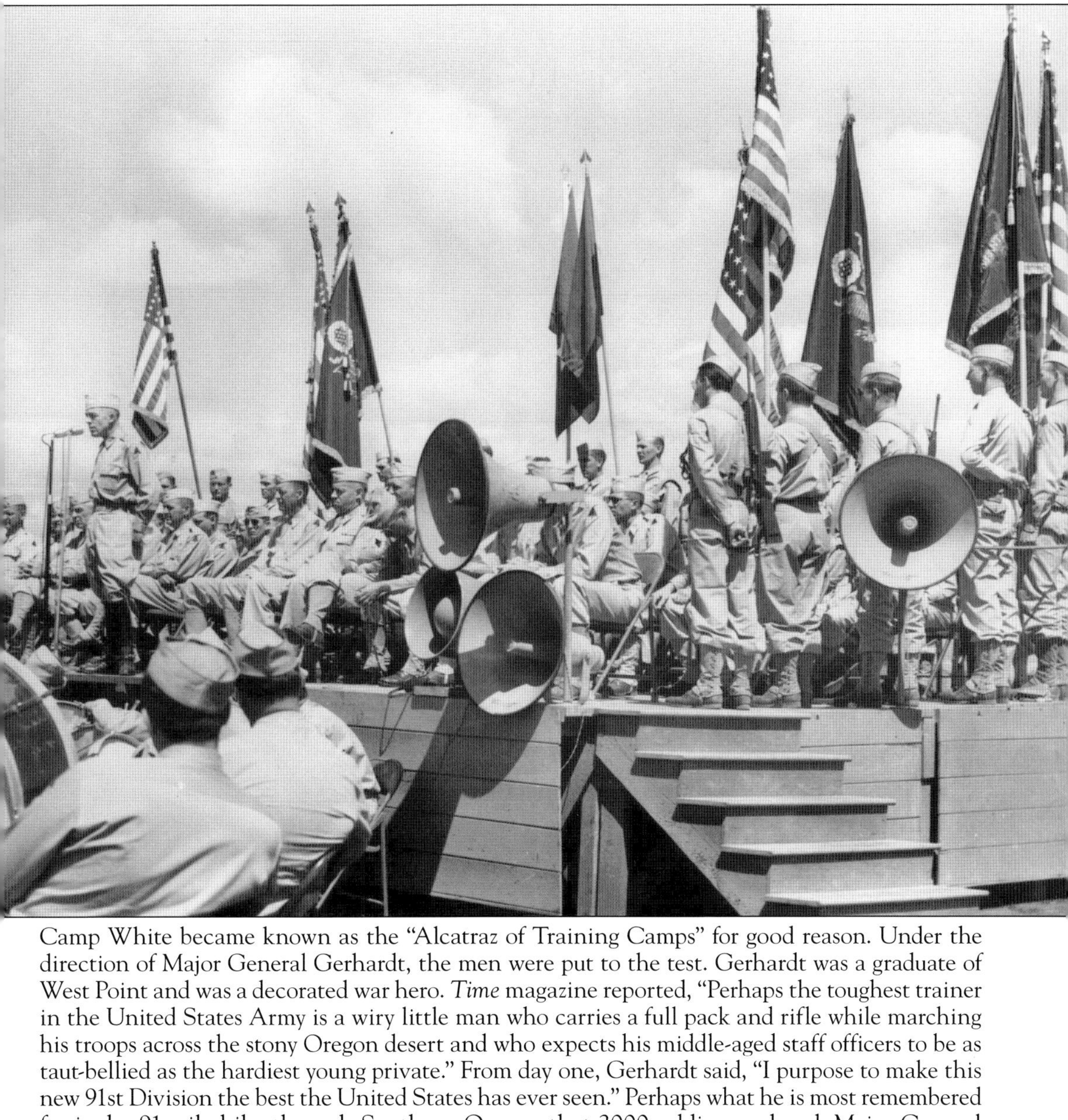

Camp White became known as the "Alcatraz of Training Camps" for good reason. Under the direction of Major General Gerhardt, the men were put to the test. Gerhardt was a graduate of West Point and was a decorated war hero. *Time* magazine reported, "Perhaps the toughest trainer in the United States Army is a wiry little man who carries a full pack and rifle while marching his troops across the stony Oregon desert and who expects his middle-aged staff officers to be as taut-bellied as the hardiest young private." From day one, Gerhardt said, "I purpose to make this new 91st Division the best the United States has ever seen." Perhaps what he is most remembered for is the 91-mile hike through Southern Oregon that 2000 soldiers endured. Major General Gerhardt is pictured here giving a speech.

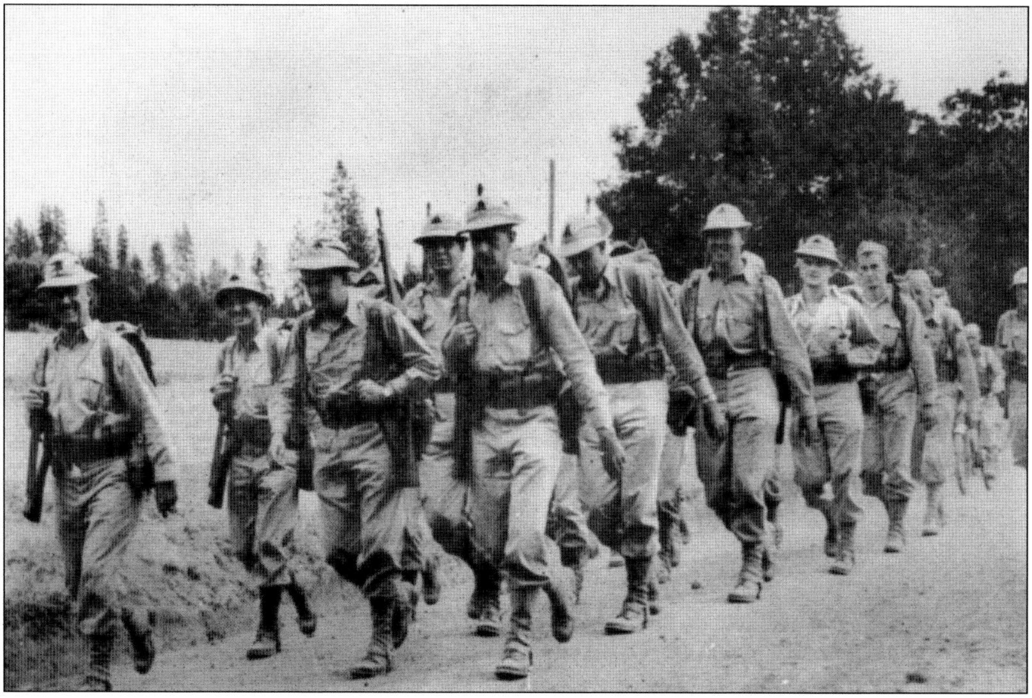

At first, the locals were surprised to see the soldiers marching and practicing maneuvers in Eagle Point. Many families got to know the soldiers and enjoyed having them over for dinner. Restaurants and taverns benefitted from the soldiers who came into town for a bit of rest and relaxation. The Nichols building, located at 111–113 West Main Street, was used as the headquarters to watch for enemy aircraft. Men were positioned at the front and the back of the building with spyglasses to keep watch. There were never any reported sightings of anything out of the ordinary. Downstairs in that same building was a laundry and dry-cleaning business, which received the contract to do the dry-cleaning for Camp White.

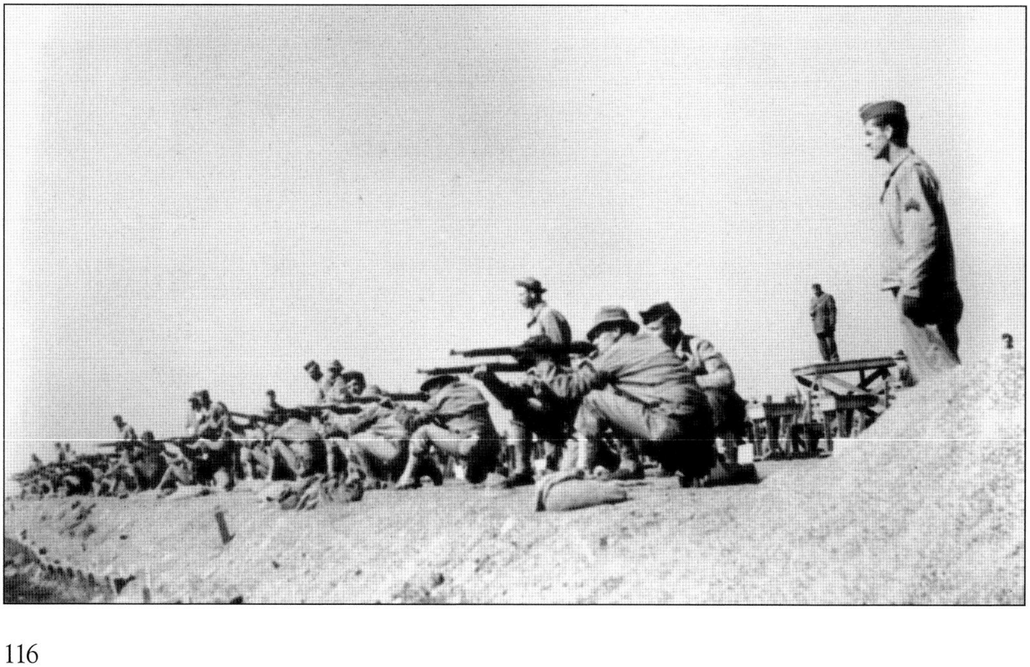

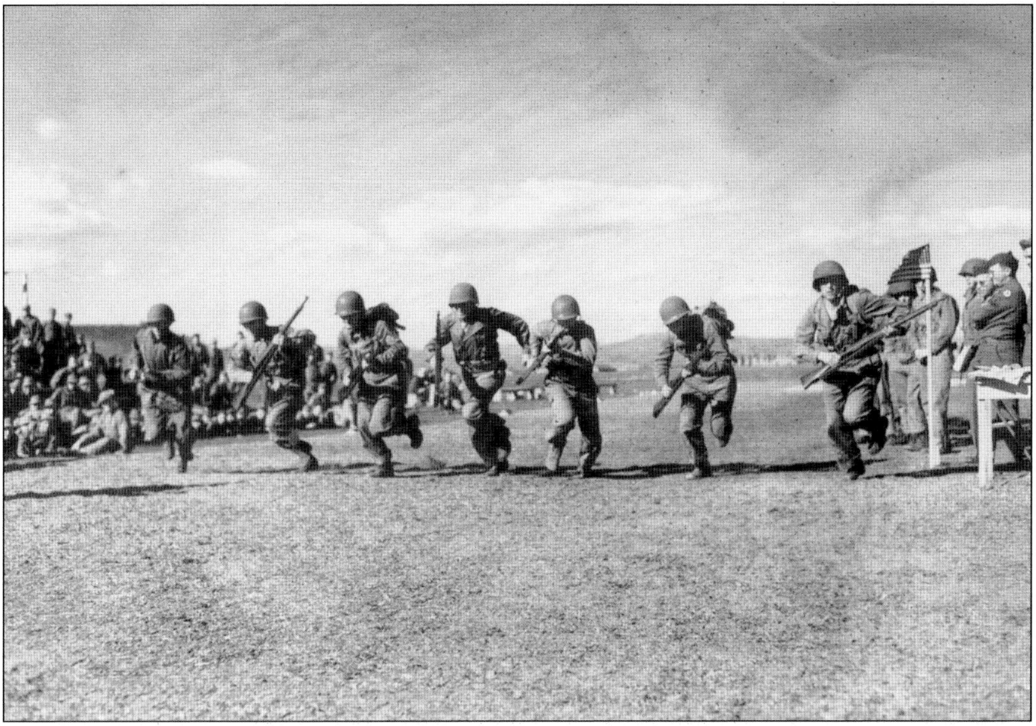

Training in the Agate Desert was grueling, whether on land or in water. A former soldier, Randy Hanes, recalled a training exercise wherein the soldiers had to build a bridge across the Rogue River. He said, "One of our mishap experiences was our attempted crossing of the angry Rogue River in Oregon; assembling a floating foot bridge one section at a time. One of the assault boats upriver got out of control overturning and spilling troops into the swift current and then crashed into our partially assembled cork foot bridge midway from the far point and the river bank. Tommy Renfro and myself were stranded in midstream. Luckily, the rope handles did not break and we pulled ourselves to shore—wet but safe."

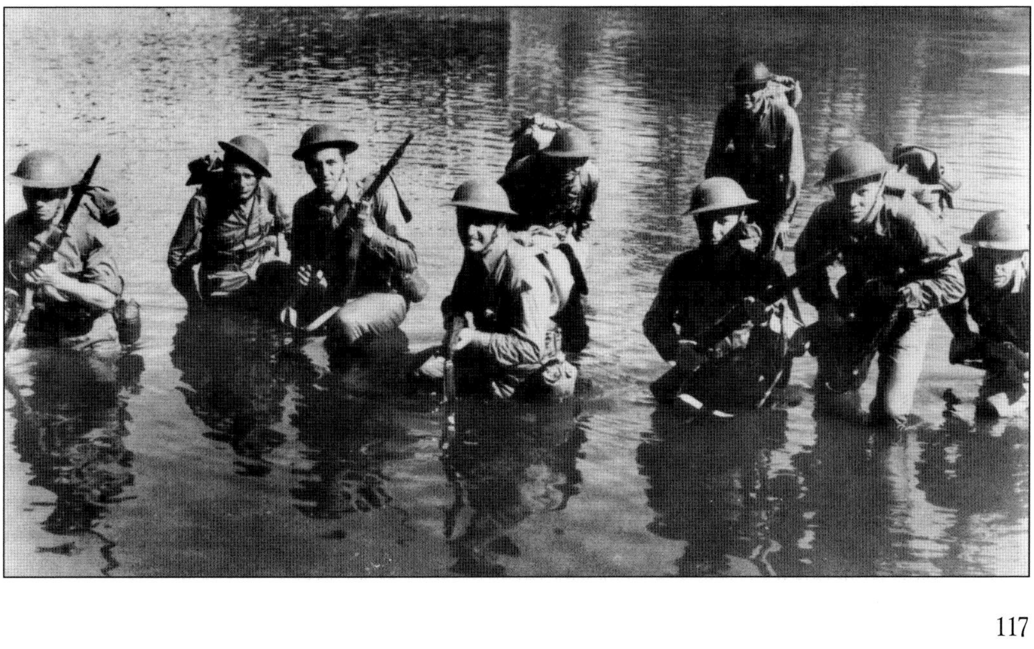

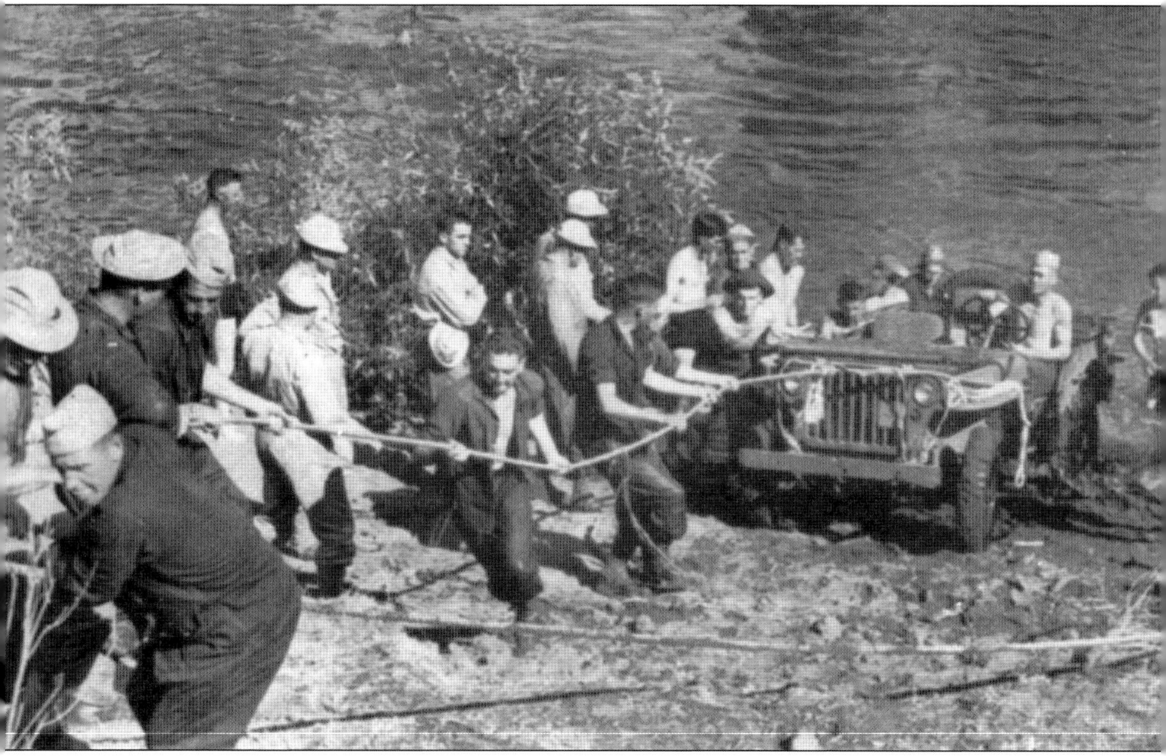

Despite the treacherous training the soldiers endured at Camp White, many had fond memories of their time in the Rogue Valley. Even the prisoners of war who were incarcerated at Camp White during the war spoke highly of the treatment they received in the Rogue Valley. The POWs worked in the agricultural industry due to the shortage of workers available during the war.

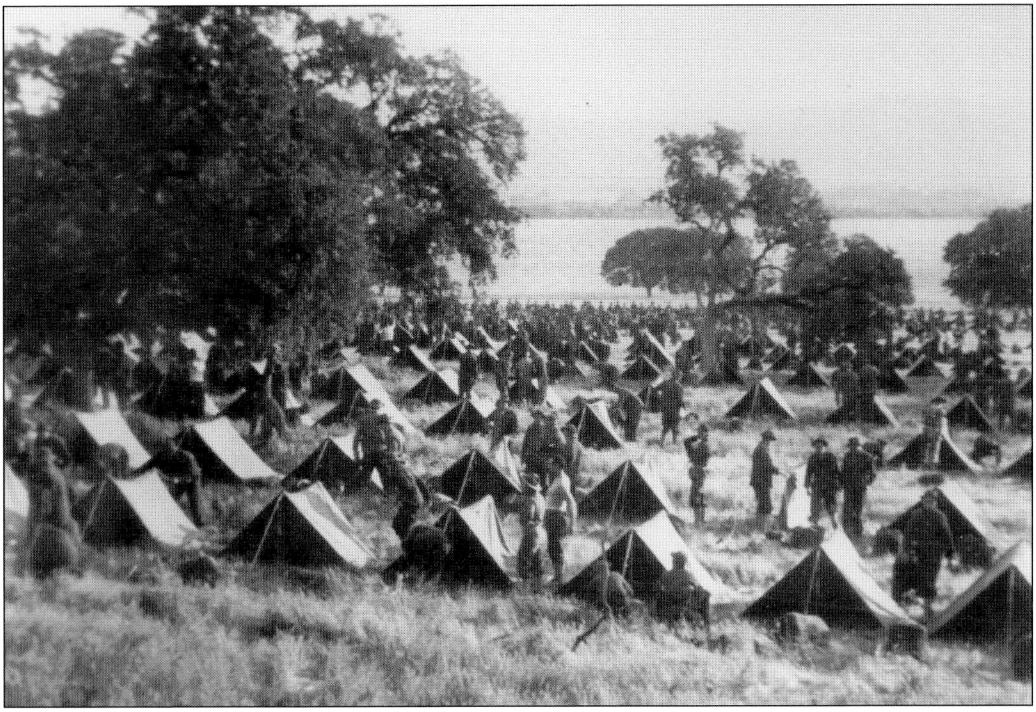

The photograph above was taken during the 91-mile hike as the soldiers prepared to set up camp for the night. Below, the troops are pictured marching through Medford near the end of their hike. Included in the photograph is Major General Gerhardt's 11-year-old son, Sergeant Charlie, who served as a mascot.

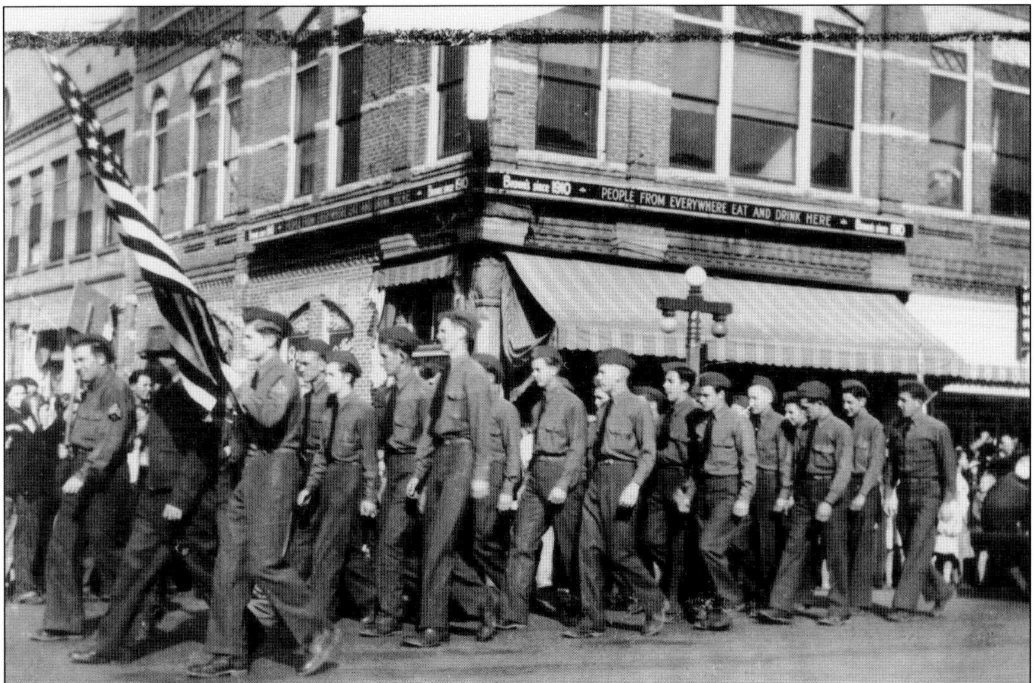

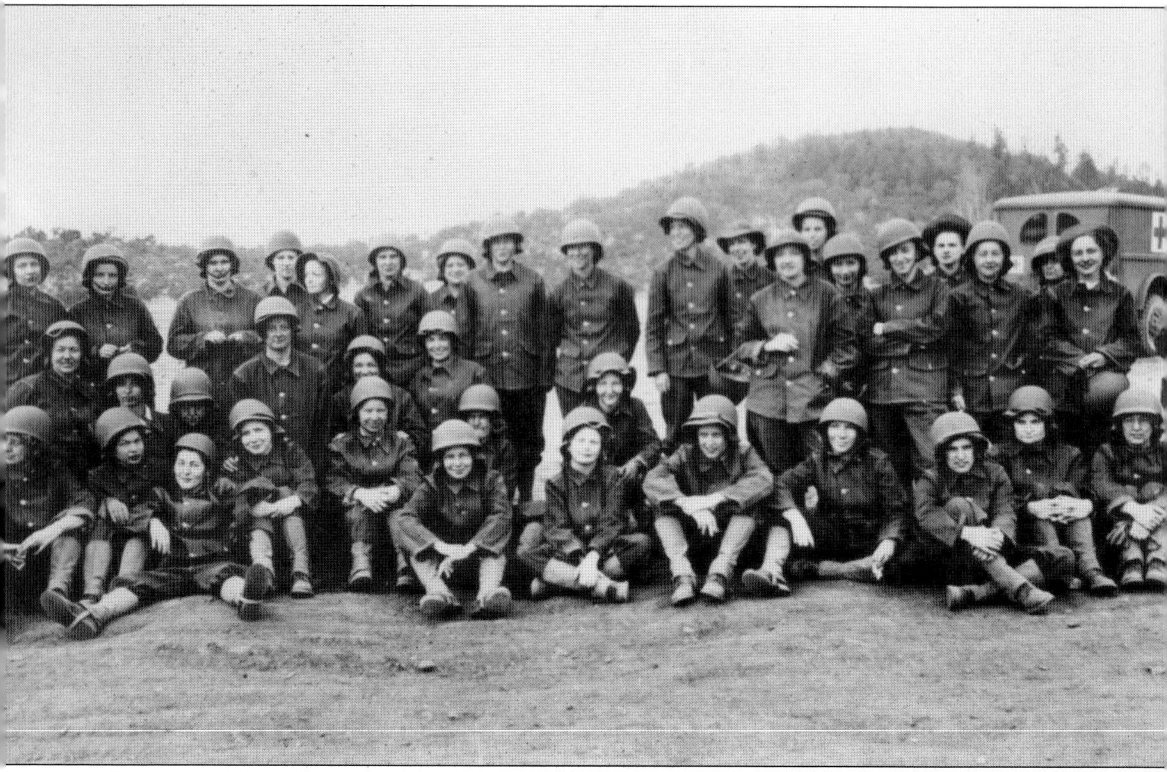

In August 1942, the first women began arriving at Camp White, most of them were assigned to work as nurses. A bulletin went out stating, "Incoming officers of the Women's Army Auxiliary Corps will be shown the same courtesies and greeted as all other officers of the Army, it was emphasized today by headquarter; a tendency upon the part of the public to regard the WAACS too lightly and to underestimate their potential usefulness to the victory effort is unwise."

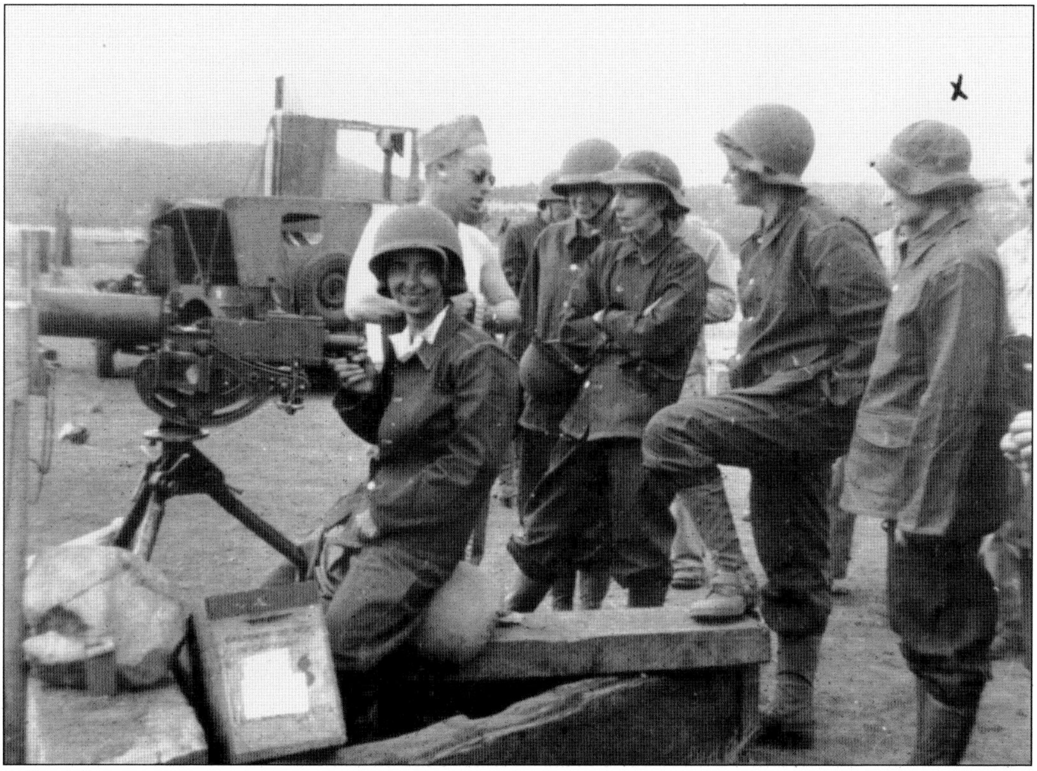

All of the nurses assigned to Camp White were required to undergo the same stringent training regimen as the men. They practiced artillery skills, the use of gas masks, the infiltration course, and they marched to and from Eagle Point. The women were expected to adhere to strict rules. The two-page "Rules for Nurses" document stated, "The status of an Army nurse is that of an officer. She will, therefore, have no social relations with enlisted men. Each nurse will provide bed linen, towels, etc., and pay for laundering of same. Nurses will wear the prescribed uniform at all times. The wearing of colored slips with the white uniform is prohibited. Colored jewelry, earrings, or flowers are not a part of a military uniform and will not be worn."

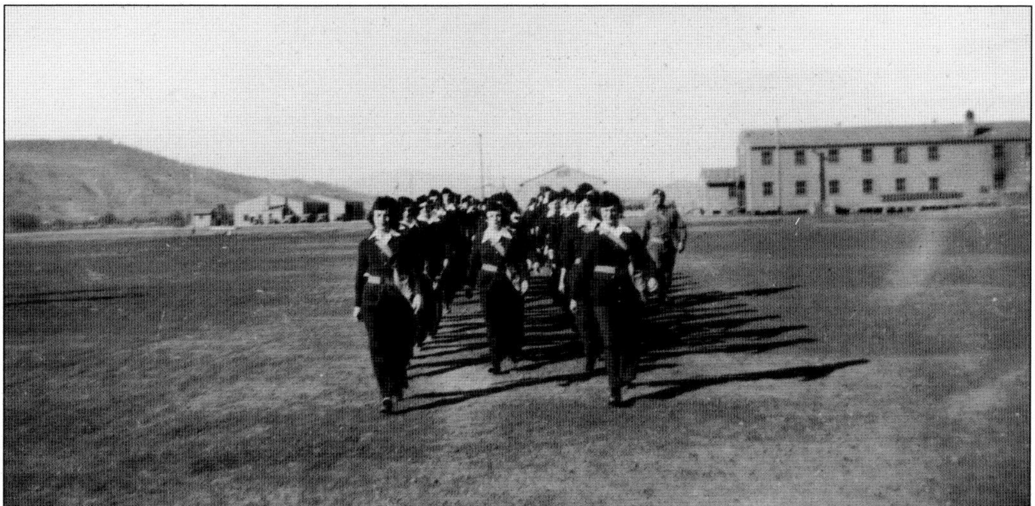

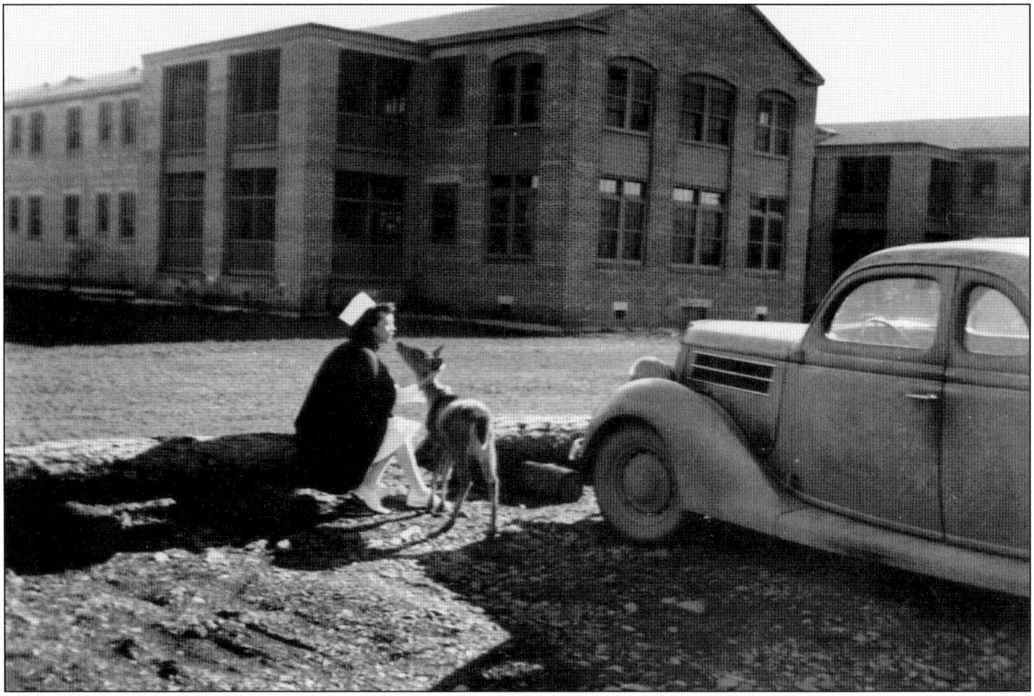

Above, 2nd Lt. Suzy White of the 79th General Hospital shares a quiet moment with Suzie, a deer who was the Camp White mascot. Below, soldiers take quite a liking to Suzie.

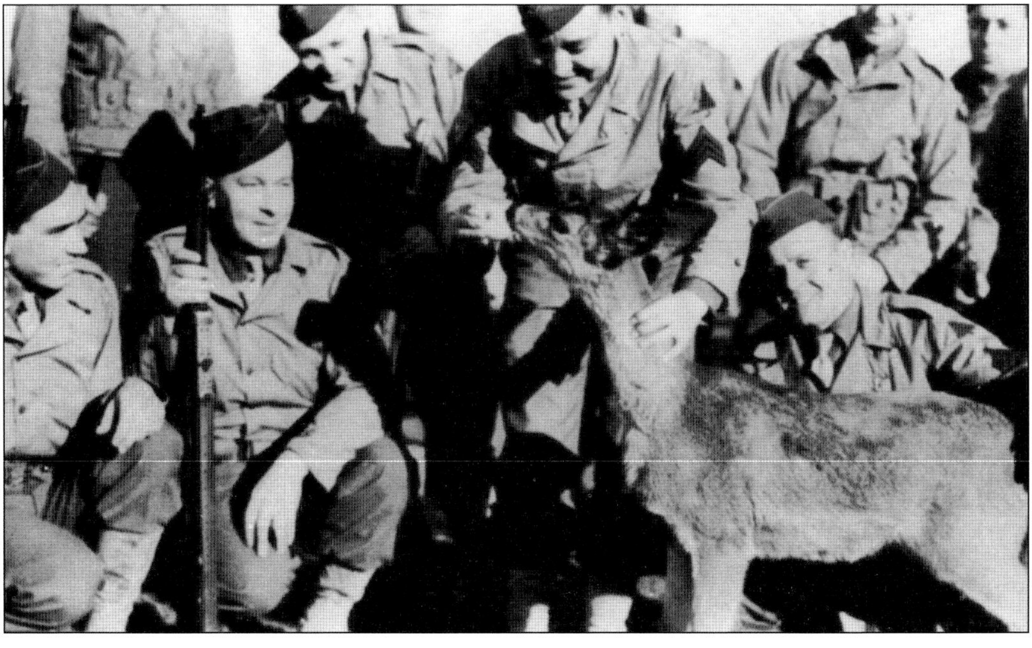

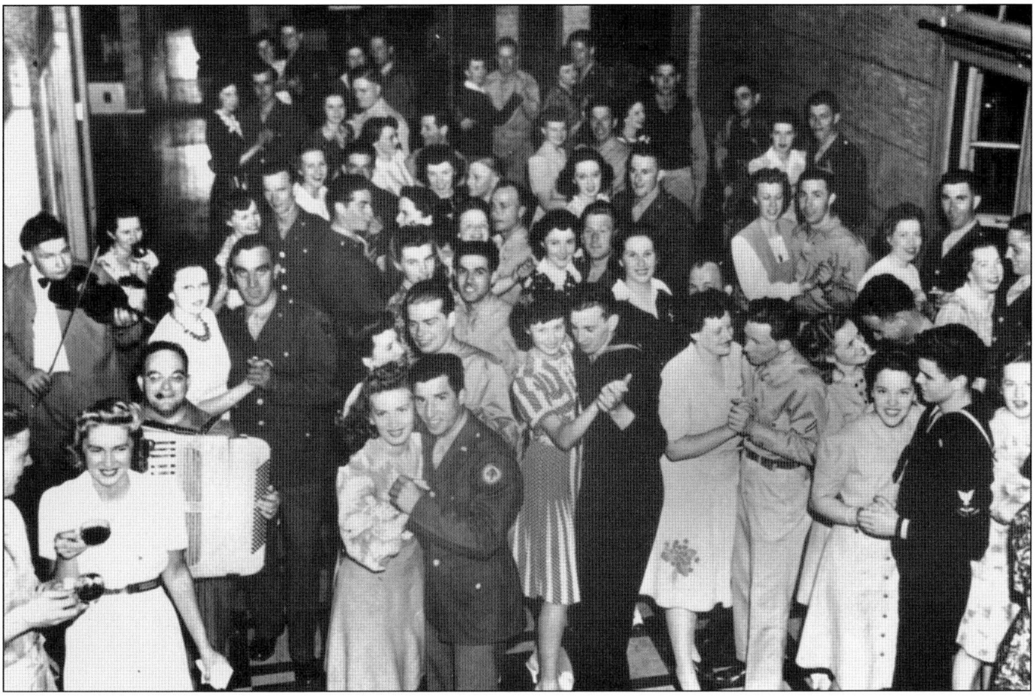

A large US Organization (USO) club opened in Medford. It was said to be the "Largest and one of the best equipped USO centers on the Pacific Coast." It wasn't long after the grand opening that the club could no longer accommodate the crowds. In all, four USO clubs opened in Medford. The neighboring communities all pitched in to help operate the clubs, and local businesses donated materials to decorate them. A group of 800 women, who called themselves "the Cookie Club," voluntarily baked cookies to serve at the USOs. In just over one year, they baked nearly 225,000 cookies.

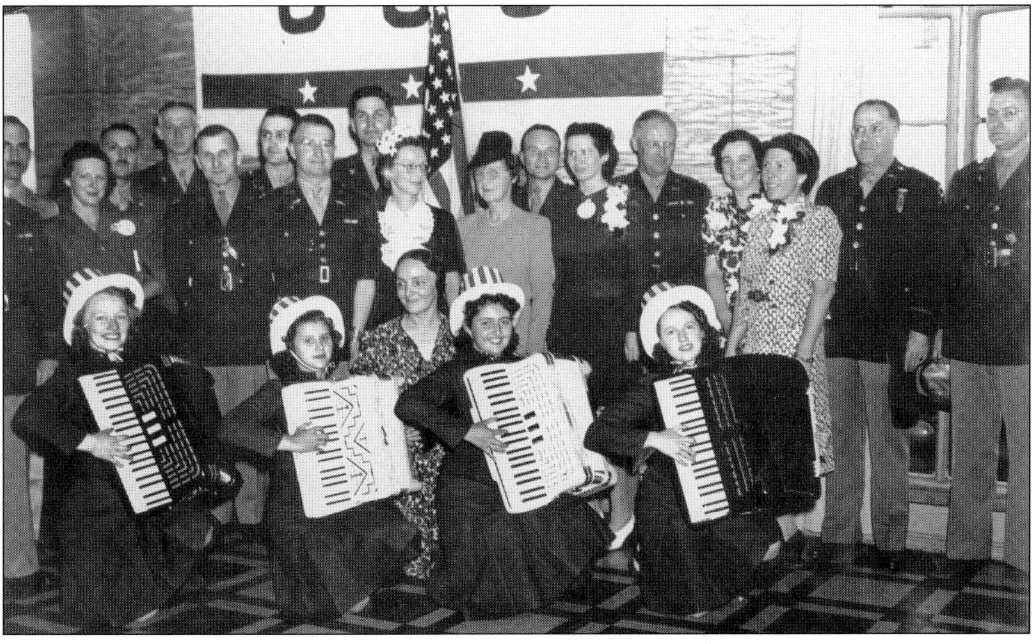

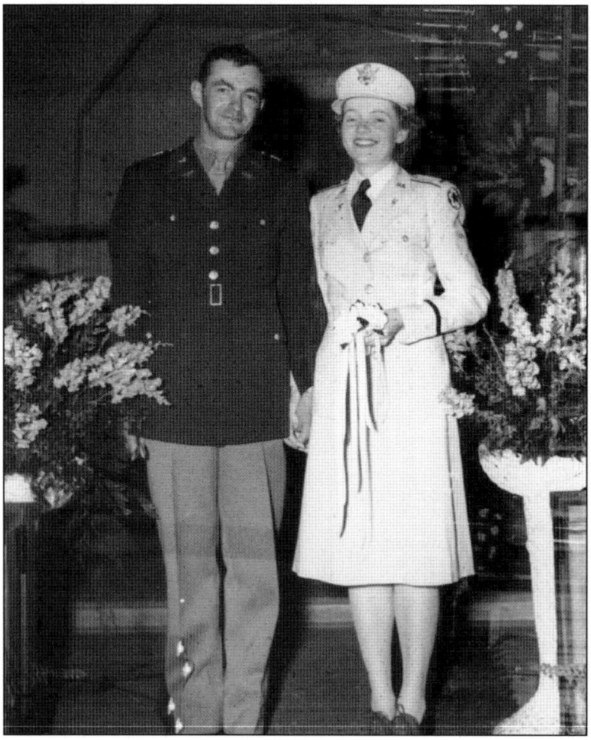

On May 7, 1943, Lt. Raymond H. Stewart (Company K, 363rd Infantry, 91st Division) wed Second Lt. Grace Evory (ANC 79th, General Hospital) at Camp White.

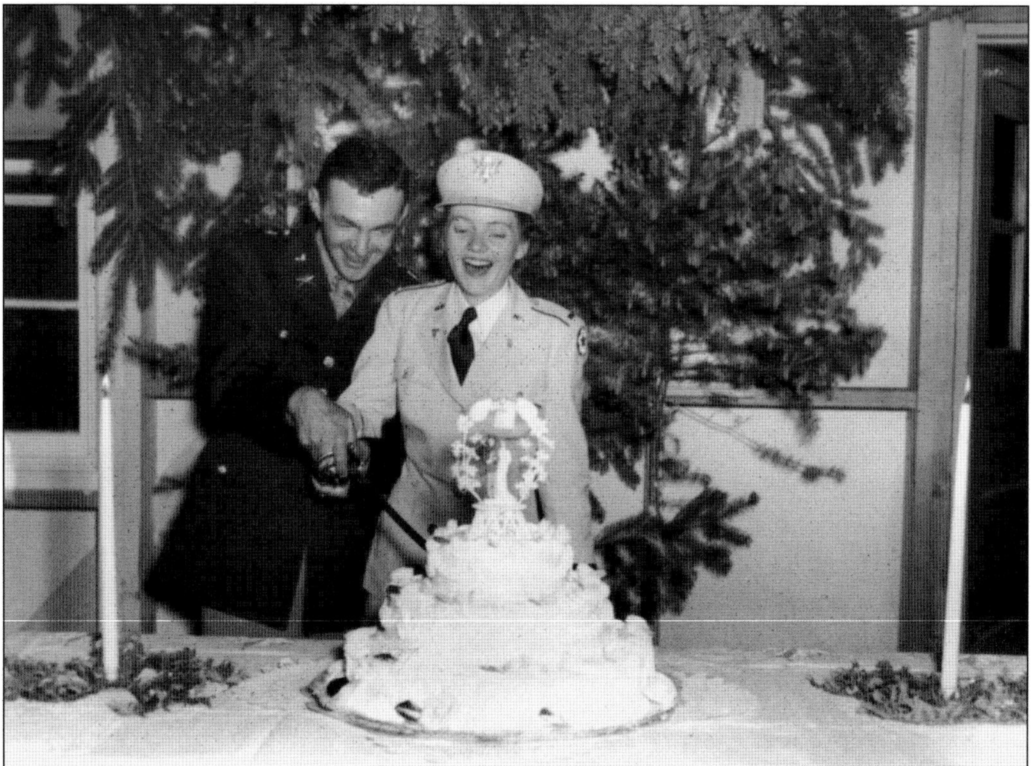

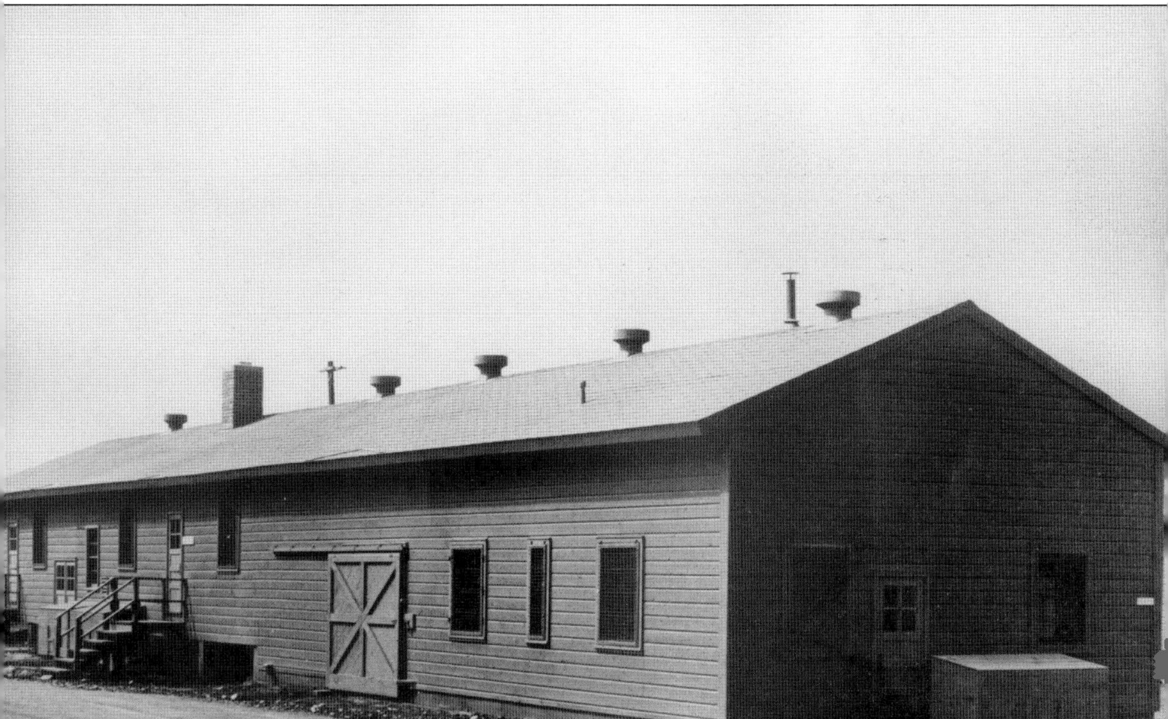

In 1946, the federal government declared Camp White "surplus," meaning that many of the buildings were no longer needed. Many residents and businesses in the Rogue Valley took advantage of the well-built structures that were available at bargain prices. It has been said that the valley took on a "green hue" as many of the buildings with their original Army-green color found new locations around the valley. Some buildings were torn down and the lumber, plumbing, and electrical components were sold. The City of Eagle Point benefitted by purchasing sewer pipe, electrical wire, tools, and supplies that had been difficult to purchase during the war.

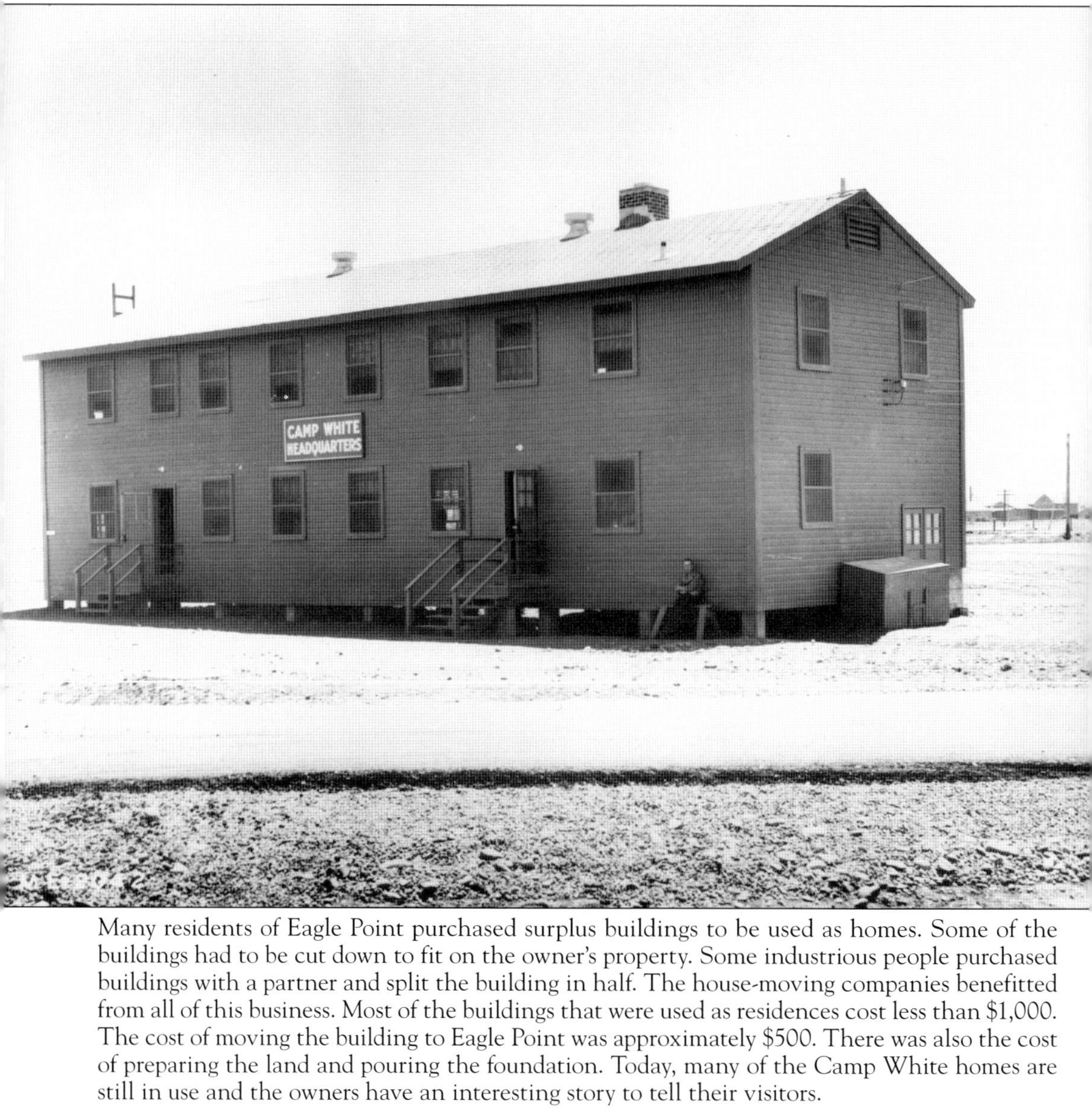

Many residents of Eagle Point purchased surplus buildings to be used as homes. Some of the buildings had to be cut down to fit on the owner's property. Some industrious people purchased buildings with a partner and split the building in half. The house-moving companies benefitted from all of this business. Most of the buildings that were used as residences cost less than $1,000. The cost of moving the building to Eagle Point was approximately $500. There was also the cost of preparing the land and pouring the foundation. Today, many of the Camp White homes are still in use and the owners have an interesting story to tell their visitors.

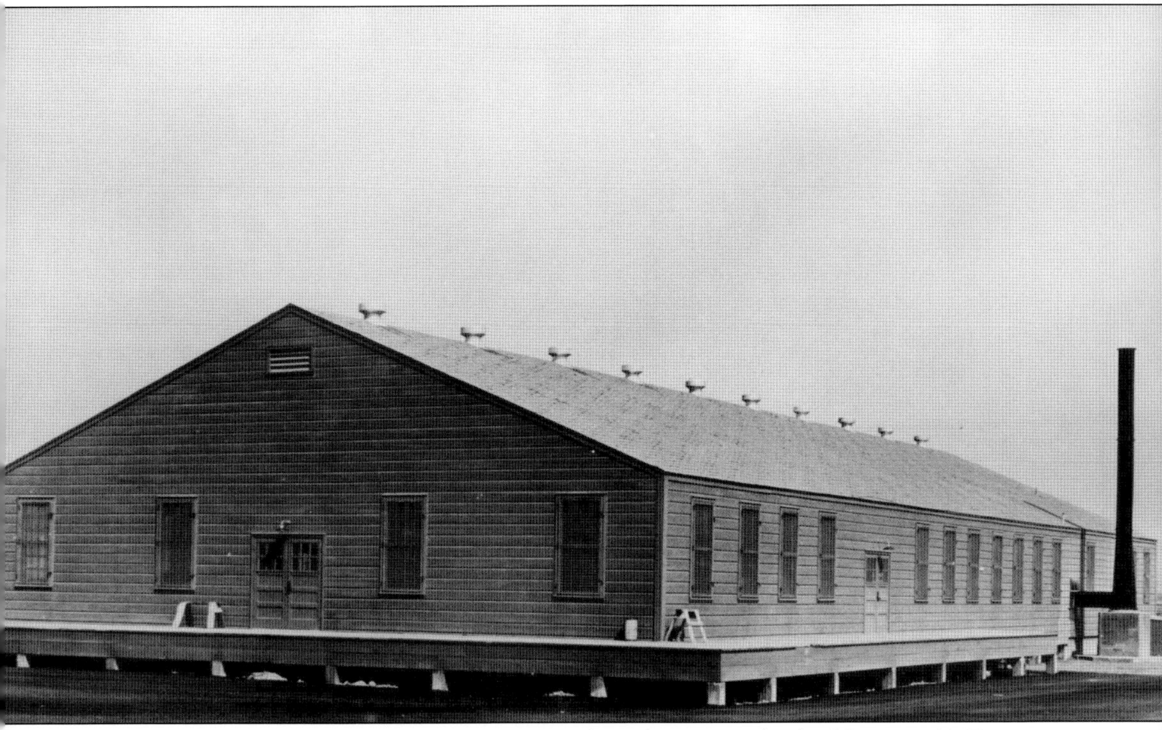

The City of Eagle Point School District No. 9 purchased nine surplus buildings in 1947, paying $1,126.75 for the buildings. The buildings had been used for recreation, administration, a repair shop, and an athletic pavilion. The pavilion was the most expensive at $607, the repair shop cost $405, and the other buildings cost less than $15 each. These prices represented a 95-percent discount of their value. The pavilion was put to use as a school gymnasium, the repair shop became a bus barn, and the other buildings were used for classrooms. Today, the remaining Camp White buildings that were not deemed surplus are home to the Veteran's Administration Southern Oregon Rehabilitation Center and Clinics in White City.